ENGINEERING CHEMISTRY

As per SGBAU NEP 2020 syllabus

Dr. Ashish V. Kadu,

Dr. Nilesh S. Ghotkar,

Ms. Preeti G. Rajas

Copyright © Dr. Ashish V. Kadu, Dr. Nilesh S. Ghotkar,
Ms. Preeti G. Rajas 2024
All Rights Reserved.

This book has been published with all efforts taken to make the material error-free after the consent of the author. However, the author and the publisher do not assume and hereby disclaim any liability to any party for any loss, damage, or disruption caused by errors or omissions, whether such errors or omissions result from negligence, accident, or any other cause.

While every effort has been made to avoid any mistake or omission, this publication is being sold on the condition and understanding that neither the author nor the publishers or printers would be liable in any manner to any person by reason of any mistake or omission in this publication or for any action taken or omitted to be taken or advice rendered or accepted on the basis of this work. For any defect in printing or binding the publishers will be liable only to replace the defective copy by another copy of this work then available.

CONTENTS

PREFACE

Engineering Chemistry is a cornerstone of the First-Year Engineering curriculum, providing the essential chemical principles that underpin various engineering disciplines. This book, specifically designed for first-year engineering students at Sant Gadge Baba Amravati University (SGBAU), Amravati, adheres to the NEP 2020 syllabus and scheme, reflecting the university's dedication to a comprehensive and integrated educational approach.

The aim of this book is to offer a thorough understanding of fundamental concepts in chemistry while relating them to practical applications in engineering. We have designed the content to meet the specific needs of SGBAU students, ensuring it is both relevant and accessible.

The book is divided into 11 chapters which cover all topics of SGBAU Amravati NEP based curriculum as well as other universities in India. Topics include Water technology, Nanotechnology, Energy sciences, Energy storage system, Corrosion, corrosion controls, Bioinformatics, etc. Each chapter begins with clear learning objectives and includes numerous examples, illustrations, and practice problems to reinforce the material.

We believe that this book will serve as a valuable resource for first-year engineering students, helping them build a solid foundation in chemistry that will support their academic and professional growth. By aligning with the NEP 2020 guidelines, we aim to provide a holistic education that integrates scientific knowledge with practical skills, preparing students for the challenges and opportunities of the engineering profession.

We extend our sincere gratitude to the faculty members and experts who have contributed to the development of this book. Their insights and feedback have been invaluable in ensuring the content is accurate, up-to-date, and pedagogically sound.

We hope that students will find this book engaging and informative and that it will inspire a lifelong interest in the fascinating field of chemistry.

Dr. Ashish V. Kadu
Dr. Nilesh S. Ghotkar
Ms. Preeti G. Rajas

About the Authors

Dr. Ashish V Kadu is working as an Associate Professor and Head of the First Year Engineering Department at Prof Ram Meghe College of Engineering and Management, a prestigious NAAC A+ institute located in Badnera- Amravati, Maharashtra, India. He is member of Board of studies- Humanities , Applied Sciences and General Engineering at Sant Gadge Baba Amravati University, Amravati. He has 20 years of teaching experience of Chemistry subject at undergraduate level. With 15 years of research experience, his expertise lies in synthesizing semiconductor nanomaterials and their application in Metal oxides based gas sensors and supercapcitors application. He has published more than 30 research papers at reputed international journals and presented more than 40 research articles at National and International Conferences. He specializes in chemical growth techniques for textured and epitaxial thick films, coupled with thorough characterization methods. Dr. Kadu possesses a profound understanding of both chemistry and materials science, particularly in the realm of nanostructured materials and their characterization. His current focus involves researching nanomaterials and their characterization for gas sensor and electrochemical application.

Dr. Nilesh S. Ghotkar serves as the Associate Professor and Head of the First Year Engineering Department at Takshashila Institute of Engineering and Technology (formerly known as Dr. Sau. Kamaltai Gawai Institute of Engineering and Technology), a distinguished NAAC B++ accredited institution in Darapur, Tq. Darayapur, Amravati, Maharashtra, India. He is also a member of the Board of Studies for Humanities, Applied Sciences,  and General Engineering at Sant Gadge Baba Amravati University, Amravati.

With 20 years of experience in teaching Chemistry at the undergraduate level and 13 years of research experience, Dr. Ghotkar is a recognized expert in Green Chemistry, eco-friendly catalyst synthesis, and multicomponent reactions. He has authored more than 14 research papers in reputed international journals and presented over 20 research articles at national and international conferences. Additionally, he has been granted 3 Indian patents and has filed 8 more patents in the field of Chemistry. He has also received 5 copyrights. His specialization includes antibacterial drug synthesis and microwave-assisted synthesis. Dr. Ghotkar possesses a deep understanding of both chemistry and environmental science, with his current research focusing on developing eco-friendly and nonhazardous methods for chemical preparations.

Prof. Preeti G. Rajas serves as an Assistant Professor at Sipna College of Engineering and Technology, a distinguished NAAC A+ and NBA accredited institution in Amravati, Maharashtra, India. With 12 years of experience in teaching Chemistry at the undergraduate and diploma levels and 9 years of research experience, Prof. Rajas is a recognized expert in semiconductor  materials. She has authored more than 6 research papers in reputed international journals and has presented over 5 research articles at national and international conferences. Additionally, she has been granted 3 Indian patents and has filed 8 more patents in the field of Chemistry. She has also received 2 copyrights. Her specialization includes the characterization and synthesis of doped polypyrrole using various dopants and oxidants.

Prof. Rajas possesses a deep understanding of Engineering Chemistry, Organic Chemistry, and Inorganic Chemistry, with her current research focusing on developing new semiconductor materials optimized for use in advanced sensors and materials.

CHAPTER 1

WATER TREATMENT & ANALYSIS

1.1 INTRODUCTION

Water is an essential component for the existence of life on earth, and it plays a vital role in both human life and industries. Here are some details on the importance of water for human life and industries:

The Importance of Water for Human Life

- **Hydration:** Water is necessary for the human body to function correctly, and it plays a crucial role in maintaining body temperature, transporting nutrients, and removing waste. It also helps to regulate blood pressure and lubricate joints.
- **Digestion:** Water helps to break down food and aids in digestion. It helps to move food through the digestive system and prevent constipation.
- **Brain function:** The brain is composed of about 73% water, and staying hydrated is important for cognitive function. Dehydration can lead to fatigue, headaches, and impaired memory and concentration.
- **Kidney Function:** Water is essential for the kidneys to function properly. It helps to filter waste and maintain electrolyte balance.
- **Disease Prevention:** Drinking water can help prevent diseases such as kidney stones, urinary tract infections, and constipation.

The Importance of Water for Industries

- **Manufacturing:** Water is used in manufacturing processes, such as cooling, cleaning, and lubricating. For example, in the production of paper and textiles, water is used to clean and remove impurities.
- **Energy Production:** Water is used to generate hydroelectric power and is also used in cooling systems in thermal power plants.
- **Agriculture:** Water is necessary for the production of crops and raising livestock. Irrigation systems use water to supply crops with the necessary amount of moisture to grow.
- **Transportation:** Waterways are used for transporting goods, and ports rely on water for the movement of ships.
- **Waste Treatment:** Water is used in the treatment of wastewater, and it is essential for the proper disposal of waste.

Water is a valuable resource that is essential for human life and industries. It is crucial to manage and conserve water resources to ensure that they are available for future generations.

Types of Impurities

There are several types of impurities that can be found in water, including:

a. **Suspended Solids:** Solid particles that are visible in water, such as silt, clay, and sediment.
b. **Dissolved Solids:** Soluble minerals and organic compounds, including salts, metals, and pesticides.
c. **Biological Impurities:** Microorganisms such as bacteria, viruses, and parasites that can cause disease.
d. **Chemical Impurities:** Industrial chemicals, such as heavy metals, and household chemicals, such as cleaning products.
a. Dissolved inorganic salts: Ca^{2+}, Mg^{2+}, Cl^-, CO_3^{2-}, SO_4^{2-} etc.
b. Dissolved Gases: CO_2, O_2, N_2, NO_x etc.
e. **Radiological Impurities:** Radioactive elements that can be naturally occurring or a result of human activity.

Standards of Drinking Water: As per Indian Standards (IS 10500-1983)

Characteristics	Desirable limit
pH value	6.5 to 8.5
Odour	Unobjectionable
Colour (Hazen unit), maximum	10
Test	Agreeable
Turbidity (NTU) maximum.	5
Total dissolved solids (TDS) in ppm	500
Total hardness (ppm).	300
Calcium (ppm)	75-200
Magnesium (ppm)	30-150
Iron as Fe (ppm)	0.1-1.0
Chloride (as Cl) ppm.	200-600
Nitrate (NO_3) ppm	45
Sulphate (SO_4) ppm	200 – 400
Phosphate (PO_4) ppm	10 – 15
Organic matter (ppm).	0.2-1.0

1.2 HARDNESS OF WATER

Hardness of water is a measure of the concentration of dissolved minerals, primarily calcium and magnesium ions, in water. The degree of hardness depends on the type and amount of impurities present in the water. Hardness also depends on the amount of carbon dioxide in solution. Water hardness can have significant effects on the properties and behaviour of water, including its taste, ability to form lather with soap, and tendency to cause scaling or corrosion in pipes and appliances.

Hardness is the property of water which prevents it from lathering. Water which does not produce lather with soap solution but produces white precipitate (scum) is called hard water, and water which produces lather readily with soap solution is called soft water. When soap is rubbed with water, if no lather is formed, then the water is called hard water.

Soap + Soft water → Lather formed

Soap + Hard water → No Lather formed

This is due to the presence of certain salts like Ca^{+2}, Mg^+, and other heavy metals dissolved in water. Soaps (Sodium or Potassium salts of higher fatty acids) like Stearic acids ($C_{17}H_{35}COONa$).

$$2C_{17}H_{35}COONa + CaCl_2/MgCl_2 \rightarrow (C_{17}H_{35}COO)_2Ca/Mg + 2NaCl$$
soap (soluble) salts (soluble) insoluble scum

The relation between the type of water and degree of hardness is as given below.

Types of Water	Hardness in ppm
Soft	0-75
Moderate hard	75-150
Hard	150-300
Very Hard	Above 300

Types of hardness: There are two main types of water hardness: temporary hardness and permanent hardness.

1. **Temporary Hardness**

    Temporary hardness is caused by the presence of dissolved bicarbonate minerals, primarily calcium bicarbonate and magnesium bicarbonate, in the water. When water containing these minerals is heated, the bicarbonate minerals decompose to form insoluble carbonates, which can result in the formation of scale or buildup in pipes, appliances, and fixtures. The bicarbonates are converted into insoluble carbonates and hydroxides, which can be further removed by a filtering process.

$$Ca(HCO_3)_2 \rightarrow CaCO_3 \downarrow + H_2O + CO_2$$
$$Mg(HCO_3)_2 \rightarrow Mg(OH)_2 \downarrow + 2CO_2$$

Temporary hardness can be easily removed by boiling the water, which causes the bicarbonate minerals to decompose into carbonates, which are insoluble and can be easily removed. Alternatively, temporary hardness can also be removed by treating the water with lime (calcium hydroxide) or soda ash (sodium carbonate), which precipitates out the calcium and magnesium ions as insoluble carbonates. Hence, temporary hardness is also known as Alkaline and carbonate hardness.

2. **Permanent Hardness:**

Permanent hardness, on the other hand, is caused by the presence of dissolved sulphates, chlorides, and nitrates of calcium and magnesium in the water. Unlike temporary hardness, permanent hardness cannot be removed by boiling the water. This type of hardness can cause scaling, staining, and soap scum. Hence, permanent hardness is also known as non-alkaline and non-carbonate hardness.

Permanent hardness can be removed by using a water softener, which replaces the calcium and magnesium ions with sodium ions through a process called ion-exchange. This results in soft water, which has many benefits including better lathering and reduced buildup in pipes, appliances, and fixtures. However, it is important to note that softened water is not recommended for drinking, as the high sodium content can be harmful to people with high blood pressure or other health concerns.

Units of Hardness:

The hardness of water is a measure of the concentration of certain minerals, primarily calcium (Ca^{2+}) and magnesium (Mg^{2+}) ions. It is typically expressed in terms of the equivalent amount of calcium carbonate ($CaCO_3$) and can be measured using different units and scales. Here are the common units used to express the hardness of water:

1. **Parts Per Million (ppm) or Milligrams per Litre (mg/L):** Both units are numerically equivalent, with 1 ppm being equal to 1 mg/L.

2. **Degrees of General Hardness (°GH or dGH):** One degree of general hardness is equivalent to 10 mg/L (ppm) of CaO (calcium oxide) or approximately 17.1 mg/L of $CaCO_3$. It is Commonly used in Europe.

3. **Degrees of French Hardness (°fH or °F):** One degree of French hardness is equivalent to 10 mg/L of $CaCO_3$. it is used in France.
4. **Degrees of Clark (°Clark or °e):** One degree Clark is equivalent to 1 grain per Imperial gallon of $CaCO_3$. It is used in the United Kingdom.
5. **Milliequivalents per Litre (meq/L):** This unit measures the concentration of ions based on their chemical equivalence.
6. **Grains per Gallon (gpg):** One grain per U.S. gallon is equivalent to 17.1 mg/L (ppm) of $CaCO_3$. Commonly used in the United States.

Relation Between Various Units of Hardness:

$$\text{mg/L} = \text{ppm} = 17.848 \times \text{dGH} = 10 \times °F = 14.254 \times °\text{Clark} = 50 \times \text{meq/L} = 17.118 \times \text{gpg}$$

1.3 DETERMINATION OF HARDNESS OF WATER BY EDTA METHOD:

This method involves a complexometric titration where a water sample is titrated with an EDTA solution using Eriochrome Black-T (EBT) as the indicator. Ethylenediaminetetraacetic acid (EDTA), in its disodium salt form, acts as the complexing agent. The titration relies on the rapid, complete, and stoichiometric 1:1 interaction between metal ions and EDTA, resulting in the formation of stable complexes.

Formula of EDTA

Metal complex of EDTA

To determine the total hardness of a water sample, a buffer solution of NH_4OH-NH_4Cl is used to maintain the pH at 10. A few drops of Eriochrome Black-T (EBT) indicator solution are added. EBT forms a weak complex with metal ions, resulting in a wine-red colour.

The procedure involves titrating the water sample with EDTA. Initially, EBT reacts with the free Ca^{2+} and Mg^{2+} ions from the water sample, forming an unstable, wine-red-coloured metal-EBT complex. During titration, unstable complexes are converted to stable metal-EDTA complexes. At the equivalence point, the colour changes from wine-red to blue, indicating that all metal ions have been complexed by EDTA.

Metal + EBT + Buffer solution $\rightarrow$ **[Metal – EBT] + EDTA** $\rightarrow$ **[Metal – EDTA] + EBT**	
Unstable complex	stable complex
(Wine-red)	(blue)

Chemicals: The following chemicals are required for the titration process.

a) Standard hard water (SHW): Dissolve 1 gm of $CaCO_3$ in a minimum quantity of dil. HCl and then evaporate the solution to dryness and make up the volume up to 1 litre with distilled water.

b) EDTA Solution: 4 gm of EDTA crystals and 0.1 gm $MgCl_2$ dissolved in 1 L of distilled water.

c) Buffer solution: 67.5 g NH_4Cl and 570 ml of Conc. NH_4OH solution diluted with distilled water to 1 L.

d) EBT Indicator: 0.5 g of EBT in 100 ml of ethanol.

Procedure:

- **Step 1: Standardisation of EDTA solution:** The burette is filled with EDTA solution after washing and rinsing. Pipette out 10ml of standard hard water into a 100ml conical flask, 3-5mL of buffer solution and 1-2 drops of EBT indicator are added and titrated against EDTA solution until the wine-red colour changes to blue. Let the volume of EDTA solution consumed be V1 ml.

- **Step 2: Determination of total hardness of water:** As per the same procedure (Step 1), 10ml of the unknown water sample is titrated against EDTA. Let the volume of EDTA solution consumed be V2 ml.
- **Step 3: Determination of permanent hardness of water:** 250ml of the hard water sample is taken in a 500mL beaker and boiled until the volume is reduced to about 50ml. [This step causes all the bicarbonates to decompose respectively into insoluble $CaCO_3$ and $Mg(OH)_2$].

Filter and wash the precipitate with distilled water and quantitatively collect the filtrate and washings in a 250ml conical flask and make up the volume to 250mL with distilled water. 10ml of this boiled water sample is titrated against EDTA solution as in Step 1. Let the volume of EDTA solution consumed be V3 ml.

Calculations:

- **Step 1: Standardisation of EDTA Solution:**
  1 ml of EDTA solution = 10 ml of standard hard water.
  = 10 mg of $CaCO_3$ (1ml contains 1mg of $CaCO_3$)
  1 ml of EDTA = 10 / V1 mg of $CaCO_3$ equivalent hardness. —— (1)
- **Step 2: Determination of Total Hardness of Water:**
  10 ml of unknown hard water sample = V2 ml of EDTA.
  = V2 x 10 / V1 mg of $CaCO_3$ (from equation 1)
  1000 ml of given hard water = V2 x 1000/V1 mg of $CaCO_3$ eq.
  Total Hardness = V2 x 1000/V1 mg of $CaCO_3$ eq. ——- (2)
- **Step 3: Determination of Permanent Hardness of Water:**
  10 ml of boiled water = 3 ml of EDTA
  =V3 x 10/V1 mg of $CaCO_3$ eq.
  1000 ml of given boiled water = V3 x 1000/V1 mg of $CaCO_3$ eq.
  Permanent Hardness = V3 x 1000/V1 mg of $CaCO_3$ eq. ——- (3)
- **Step 4: Determination of Temporary Hardness:**
  Total hardness - Permanent Hardness
  = V2 x 1000/V1 mg of $CaCO_3$ eq - = V3 x 1000/V1 mg of $CaCO_3$
  = (V2-V3)/V1 x 1000 mg/l
  = (V2-V3)/V1 x 1000 ppm or mg/L

1.4   SOFTENING OF WATER

Water used for industrial purposes (such as for steam generation) should be sufficiently pure. It should, therefore, be freed from hardness-producing salts before it is put to use. The process of removing hardness-producing salts from water is known as softening of water. These salts are Ca and Mg salts of carbonate, bicarbonate, chloride, sulphate, etc. These are the main methods used for softening of water for industrial and domestic purposes.

a.   Lime-Soda Process

b.   Zeolite Process

c.   Ion-exchange Process

d.   Reverse Osmosis Process

1.5   ZEOLITE PROCESS:

Zeolite process is also known as Permutit process. The Zeolite process is a method for removing hardness from water by exchanging calcium and magnesium ions with sodium ions using a special type of ion-exchange resin called zeolite. The process can be used to determine the hardness of water by measuring the amount of calcium and magnesium ions exchanged with sodium ions, which is proportional to the total hardness of the water. The hardness can be expressed in terms of calcium carbonate ($CaCO_3$) concentration.

A certain class of naturally occurring aluminosilicate minerals called zeolite is in solid phase. The name zeolite is obtained from Greek words, Zein-lithos, which means boiling stone.

The chemical structure of sodium zeolite may be expressed as:

$$Na_2O.Al_2O_3.x.SiO_2. \ y \ H_2O \text{ where } x = 2 \text{ to } 10 \text{ and } y = 2 \text{ to } 6$$

Zeolite is a hydrated salt of sodium aluminosilicates. It finds application in the softening of water for domestic and industrial purposes due to its capacity to exchange reversibly its sodium ions for multivalent ions of alkaline earth metals (e.g. Ca and Mg ions) and also divalent metal ions in water.

Types of Zeolite:

There are various types of zeolites used for water softening, each with unique properties and applications:

i.   **Natural Zeolite:** The natural zeolite is green in color and referred to as green sand.

   Ex. Thomsonite $(Na_2O.Al_2O_3.3.SiO_2. 2 H_2O)$ Natrolite $(Na_2O. Al_2O_3.4.SiO_2. 2H_2O)$

ii. **Synthetic Zeolite:** Synthetic zeolite is manufactured by heating a mixture of sodium silicates, aluminium sulphate, and sodium aluminates. This results in a porous, gel-like structure. Compared to natural zeolite, synthetic zeolite has a higher ion-exchange capacity. The most widely used artificial zeolite is a white substance known as Permutit, which is made from feldspar, kaolin, clay, and soda. Consequently, the process of using this type of zeolite for water softening is called the Permutit process. In this context, zeolite is referred to as Na_2Z.

Process

For softening of water by zeolite process, hard water is percolated at a specified rate through a bed of zeolite, kept in a cylinder shown in the figure. The Ca^{2+} and Mg^{2+} + ions are taken up by the zeolite and simultaneously release the equivalent sodium ions in exchange for them.

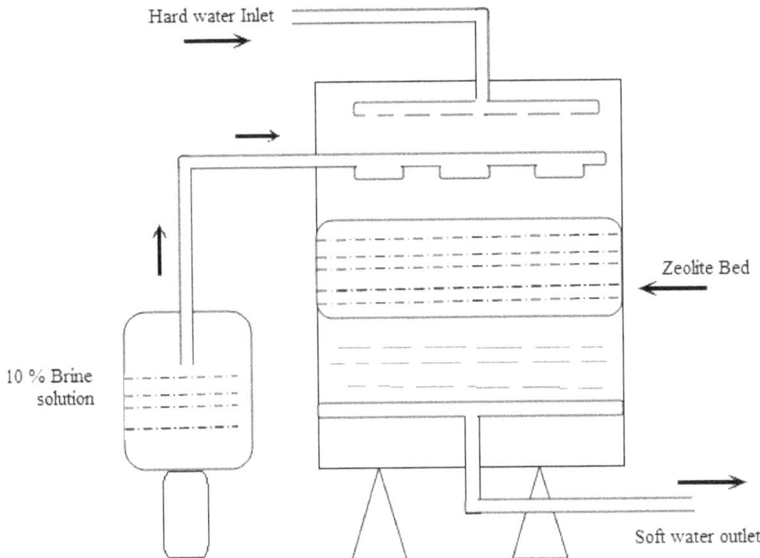

Figure 1.1: *Zeolite Process of Water Softening*

Softening Reactions:

$$Ca(HCO_3)_2 + Na_2Z \rightarrow CaZ + 2NaHCO_3$$
$$Mg(HCO_3)_2 + Na_2Z \rightarrow MgZ + 2NaHCO_3$$
$$CaSO_4 + Na_2Z \rightarrow CaZ + Na_2SO_4$$
$$MgSO_4 + Na_2Z \rightarrow MgZ + Na_2SO_4$$
$$CaCl_2 + Na_2Z \rightarrow CaZ + 2NaCl$$
$$MgCl_2 + Na_2Z \rightarrow MgZ + 2NaCl$$

It is observed in all the above reactions that sodium zeolite is converted to calcium and magnesium zeolite. Relatively small amounts of Fe and Mn may also get removed simultaneously.

Regeneration of Zeolite:

The regeneration of zeolite for water softening involves restoring its ion-exchange capacity by removing the accumulated calcium (Ca^{2+}) and magnesium (Mg^{2+}) ions and replacing them with sodium (Na^+) ions. This process ensures that the zeolite can continue to soften water effectively. A concentrated solution of sodium chloride (brine) is introduced into the zeolite bed. The high concentration of sodium ions in the brine displaces the calcium and magnesium ions on the zeolite.

$$CaZ + 2NaCl \rightarrow CaCl_2 + Na_2Z$$
$$MgZ + 2NaCl \rightarrow MgCl_2 + Na_2Z$$

Here, CaZ and MgZ represent the zeolite with calcium and magnesium ions, respectively.

Advantages of Zeolite Process:

The zeolite process for water softening offers several advantages:

1. Effectively removes calcium and magnesium ions, which cause water hardness.
2. Zeolites can be easily regenerated using a sodium chloride solution, allowing for repeated use.
3. Lower operational and maintenance costs compared to other water softening methods.
4. High ion-exchange capacity ensures efficient and continuous softening.
5. Non-toxic and environmentally safe materials are used.
6. Provides a reliable supply of consistently soft water.
7. Suitable for both residential and industrial applications.

Disadvantages of Zeolite Process:

The zeolite process for water softening has a few disadvantages:

1. Adds sodium to the water, which can be a concern for people on low-sodium diets.
2. Disposal of spent brine from the regeneration process can be environmentally challenging.
3. Requires regular regeneration, which involves downtime and the use of salt.
4. Not effective for removing other contaminants such as iron, manganese, and organic compounds.

5. Higher initial setup cost compared to some other water softening methods.
6. Efficiency can decrease with very hard water or high water usage, requiring more frequent regeneration.
7. The regeneration process can use a significant amount of water.

1.6   ION EXCHANGE PROCESS

This method is also referred to as de-ionisation and de-mineralisation. It involves an ion-exchange process where ions are exchanged between a stationary phase and a mobile liquid phase. In water softening using this technique, ion-exchange resins are employed to eliminate calcium (Ca) and magnesium (Mg) ions, which contribute to hardness.

Ion-exchange resins are composed of cross-linked, long-chain organic polymers with a microporous structure. The functional groups attached to the polymeric chain facilitate the ion-exchange process. These functional groups can be acidic or basic, leading to the classification of resins into two main types.

a.   Cation Exchange Resins

Cation exchange resins are styrene divinyl benzene copolymers, which on sulphonation (or) carboxylation, contain –COOH, –SO$_3$H functional groups responsible for exchanging their hydrogen ions with cations in water. A number of synthetic resin cation exchangers containing sulphonated phenolic or aromatic hydrocarbons have been prepared. Cation exchanger is represented as RH$^+$. The general formula of a cation exchanger is as shown below.

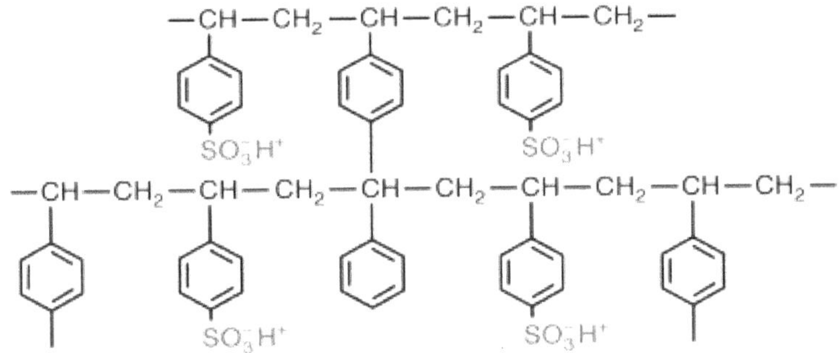

b. **Anion exchange resins:** Anion exchange resins contain basic functional groups like amine, substituted amine, or quaternary ammonium groups as their hydroxide salts are termed as anion exchange resins. They are styrene divinyl benzene copolymers which, because of their basic functional groups, become capable of exchanging their anions with other anions present in water. The resins having–NH_2, $=NH$ groups are weakly basic, whereas those having quaternary ammonium salts are strongly basic. Anion exchange is represented as ROH^-. The general formula of anion exchanger is as shown below.

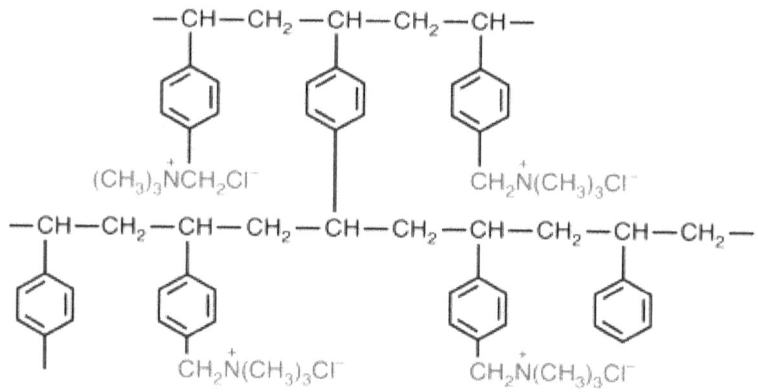

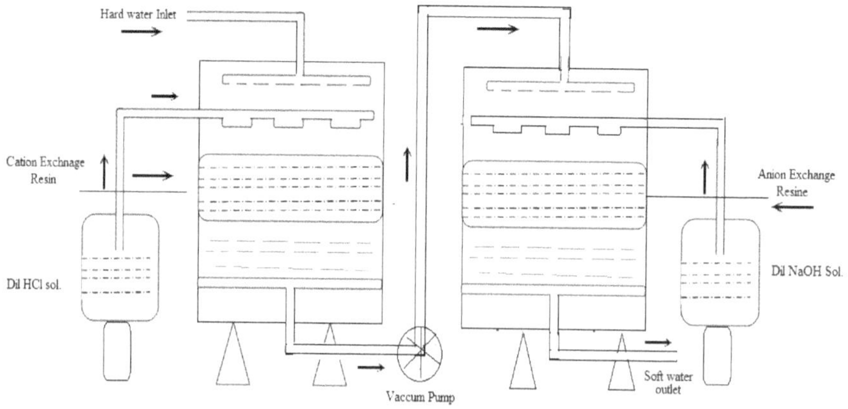

Figure 1.2: *Ion-Exchange process*

Process

The hard water is passed first through the cation exchange column, which removes all the cations like Ca^{2+}, Mg^{2+} etc. present in water, and an equivalent amount of H^+ ions is released from this column into the water.

$$2RH^+ + Ca(HCO_3)_2 \rightarrow R_2Ca + H_2CO_3$$
$$2RH^+ + Mg(HCO_3)_2 \rightarrow R_2Mg + H_2CO_3$$
$$2RH^+ + CaCl_2 \rightarrow R_2Ca + 2HCl$$
$$2RH^+ + MgCl_2 \rightarrow R_2Mg + 2HCl$$
$$2RH^+ + CaSO_4 \rightarrow R_2Ca + H_2SO_4$$
$$2RH^+ + MgSO_4 \rightarrow R_2Mg + H_2SO_4$$

Further, from cation exchange column, the hard water is passed through an anion exchange column with the help of a pump which removes all the anions like SO_4^{2-}, Cl^-, etc. present in the water, and equivalent in the water of OH– ions are released from the column to water.

$$R'OH + HCl \rightarrow R'Cl^- + 2H_2O$$
$$2\,R'OH + H_2SO_4 \rightarrow R'SO_4^{2-} + 2H_2O$$
$$2\,R'OH + H_2CO_3^{2-} \rightarrow R'_2\,CO_3^{2-} + H_2O$$

The water released from anion exchanger is completely free from cations and anions responsible for hardness. This is known as De-ionisation and Demineralisation process. It is pure like distilled water. Thus, by passing hard water through cation hardness is observed by the following reactions. H^+ and OH^- ions, thus released in water from respective cation and anion exchange columns, get combined to produce water molecules.

$$H^+ + OH^- \rightarrow H_2O$$

Regeneration of Resins:

When a cation exchanger loses the capacity of producing H^+ ions and the exchanger loses the capacity of producing OH^- ions, they are said to be exhausted. The exhausted cation exchanger is regenerated by passing it through dilute HCl or dilute H_2SO_4.

$$R_2\,Ca^{2+} + 2HCl \rightarrow 2RH^+ + CaCl_2$$
$$R_2\,Mg^{2+} + 2HCl \rightarrow 2RH^+ + MgCl_2$$

The exhausted anion exchange column is regenerated by passing NaOH solution.

$$R'Cl + NaOH \rightarrow R'OH + NaCl$$
$$R'_2SO_4 + 2\,NaOH \rightarrow 2\,R'OH + Na_2SO_4$$

Advantages of ion-exchange process:

The ion-exchange process for water softening offers several advantages:

1. Effectively removes calcium and magnesium ions, the primary causes of water hardness.
2. The ion-exchange resin can be regenerated using a sodium chloride solution, allowing for repeated use.
3. Lower operational and maintenance costs compared to some other water softening methods.
4. Suitable for both residential and industrial applications.
5. Non-toxic and environmentally safe materials are used.

Disadvantages of ion-exchange process:

The ion-exchange process for water softening has a few disadvantages:

1. Disposal of spent brine from the regeneration process can be environmentally challenging.
2. Requires periodic regeneration, involving downtime and the use of salt.

3. Not effective for removing other contaminants such as iron, manganese, and organic compounds.
4. Higher initial setup cost compared to some other water softening methods.
5. Efficiency may decrease with very hard water, requiring more frequent regeneration.

1.7 REVERSE OSMOSIS (RO) PROCESS:

Reverse osmosis (RO) is a water treatment process that can be used for water softening. The process involves the use of a semi-permeable membrane to remove dissolved minerals and other impurities from water. During the RO process, water is pushed through the semi-permeable membrane at high pressure. The membrane is designed to allow water molecules to pass through while blocking the passage of larger molecules, such as dissolved minerals and salts.

The result of this process is two streams of water: purified water that has had the minerals removed, and a concentrate stream containing the removed minerals and salts. The purified water is typically used for drinking or other applications where pure water is needed, while the concentrate stream may be discharged or further treated. In terms of water softening, RO can be effective in removing dissolved minerals such as calcium and magnesium, which cause water hardness. However, the process is not always the most cost-effective solution for water softening, and other treatment methods such as ion-exchange may be preferred in certain situations. Additionally, RO can produce a significant amount of wastewater due to the concentrate stream, which may be a concern in areas with water scarcity.

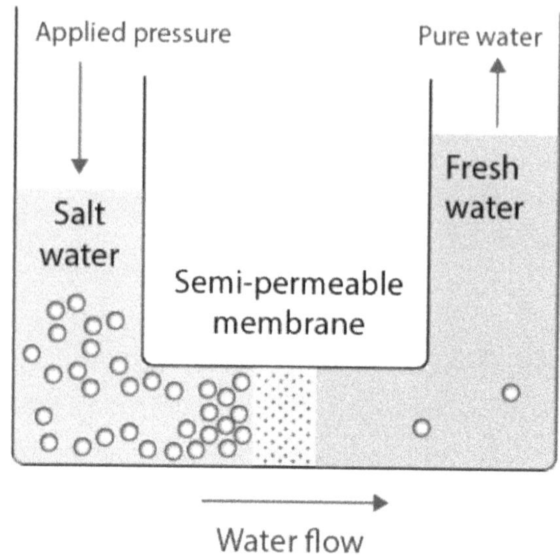

Figure 1.3: *Reverse Osmosis Process*

i.   In this process, pure water is separated from salt water. 15-40 kg/cm² pressure is applied for separating the water from its contaminants.

ii. The dilute solution can be replaced by fresh water to get fresh water effectively from impure or seawater. Thus, in Reverse Osmosis (RO), the solvent/water is separated from the contaminants (solution).

iii. The membranes used are cellulose acetate, polymethacrylate, polyamide, polysulfone, etc.

Advantages:

- RO effectively removes dissolved solids, minerals, and contaminants, providing high-quality purified water.
- Suitable for various water sources, including tap water, well water, and brackish water.
- RO systems come in compact sizes, making them suitable for both residential and commercial use.
- Requires minimal maintenance compared to other water treatment methods.
- RO systems can operate using relatively low energy consumption.
- Unlike some other water treatment methods, RO does not require the use of chemicals for purification.

Disadvantages:

- RO systems produce a significant amount of wastewater, which can be wasteful in areas with water scarcity.
- RO requires energy to operate the pressure pumps, making it relatively energy-intensive compared to other water treatment methods.
- RO removes minerals from water, which can lead to demineralisation and affect the taste and health benefits of water.
- RO systems can be expensive to purchase and install, especially for larger-scale applications.
- RO membranes require regular cleaning and replacement, adding to the overall maintenance costs.

1.8 BOILER FEED WATER

Water is largely used in boilers (as feed) for the production of steam. The presence of impurities in a water sample makes it hard (and corrosive too in some cases), and any water sample cannot be used as boiler feed as it may pose the problems of corrosion, embrittlement of the boiler vessel, etc. Water with some specifications used in boilers for steam generation is called boiler feed water.

Requisites of Boiler Feed Water:

- Hardness in water, caused by dissolved minerals like calcium and magnesium, should be minimised to prevent scale formation on boiler surfaces, which reduces efficiency and increases maintenance requirements.
- Boiler feed water should be free from impurities such as suspended solids, dissolved solids, organic matter, and gases. Impurities can cause corrosion, scale formation, and carryover in the boiler system.
- Boiler feed water should have sufficient alkalinity to prevent acidic corrosion and to maintain the desired pH level in the boiler water.
- Minimised to prevent scale formation on boiler surfaces.
- The level of dissolved oxygen in boiler feed water should be minimised to prevent oxygen pitting corrosion in the boiler system.

1.8.1 Scale and Sludge Formation:

In boilers, water undergoes evaporation and transforms into steam. As water volume decreases during this process, it reaches a saturation point, causing dissolved salts to precipitate. When these salts reach their saturation point, they precipitate out of the water, forming deposits on the inner walls of the boiler. If the precipitation results in loose, slimy, and non-adhering deposits, it's termed as sludge. Conversely, if the precipitated matter creates a hard, firmly attached coating on the inner walls, it's referred to as scale. Both boiler scale and sludge pose common challenges, leading to reduced efficiency, higher maintenance expenses, and potential equipment breakdowns.

Sludge formation occurs due to the accumulation of suspended particles in the feedwater, including dirt, rust, and debris. These particles settle within the boiler, forming a sludge-like substance capable of obstructing pipes and reducing flow rates. Furthermore, sludge accumulation can lead to localised overheating and equipment failures if it builds up in critical boiler areas.

e.g., $MgCO_3$, $MgCl_2$, $CaCl_2$, $MgSO_4$, etc.

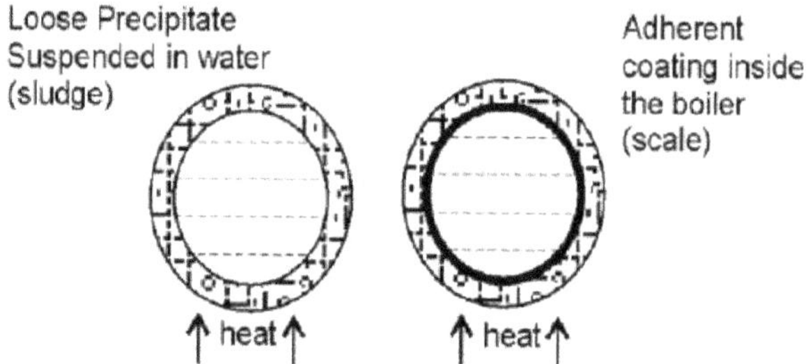

Disadvantages of Sludge Formation:

1. **Reduced Efficiency**: Decreases heat transfer efficiency and increases energy consumption.

2. **Increased Maintenance Costs**: Requires frequent cleaning, leading to higher operational expenses.

3. **Corrosion**: Accelerates corrosion of boiler components, risking leaks and equipment failures.

4. **Shortened Lifespan**: Reduces the lifespan of boiler parts, requiring premature replacements.
5. **Water Quality Issues**: Contaminates boiler water, posing health hazards and affecting downstream processes.
6. **Poor Steam Quality**: Impurities in steam affect product quality and downstream operations.

Prevention of Sludge Formation:
1. **Proper Water Treatment**: Implementing effective water treatment processes to remove impurities and control dissolved solids.
2. **Regular Maintenance**: Conducting regular boiler inspections and cleaning to remove existing sludge deposits and prevent their accumulation.
3. **Optimising Operation**: Operating the boiler within recommended parameters to minimise the risk of sludge formation and corrosion.
4. **Chemical Treatment**: Adding corrosion inhibitors and antiscalants to the boiler water to prevent sludge formation and reduce the likelihood of corrosion.

Scales:
Scale formation is caused by the buildup of mineral deposits on the internal surfaces of the boiler, such as the heat transfer surfaces, pipes, and tubes. This buildup is often caused by the presence of dissolved minerals in the feedwater, such as calcium, magnesium, and silica. When the water is heated and evaporated, these minerals are left behind and can form a hard, crusty layer of scale on the boiler surfaces. This layer reduces the heat transfer rate, making the boiler less efficient and increasing the risk of overheating and equipment failure.

Scales are the main source of troubles. Formation of scales may be due to the presence of salts like $Mg(HCO_3)_2$, $Mg(OH)_2$, $Ca(HCO_3)_2$, $CaSO_4$.

(1) Decomposition of calcium bicarbonate

$$Ca(HCO_3)_2 \rightarrow CaCO_3 \downarrow + H_2O + CO_2 \uparrow \text{ Scale}$$

However, scale composed chiefly of calcium carbonate is soft and is the main cause of scale formation in low-pressure boilers. But in high-pressure boilers, CaCO3 is soluble.

$$CaCO_3 + H_2O \rightarrow Ca(OH)_2 \text{ (soluble)} + CO_2 \uparrow$$

2. **Deposition of Calcium Sulphate:**

    The solubility of calcium sulphate in water decreases with the rise of temperature. Thus, the solubility of $CaSO_4$ is 3,200 ppm at 15°C, and it reduces to 55 ppm at 230°C and 27 ppm at 320°C. In other words, $CaSO_4$ is soluble in cold water but almost completely insoluble in superheated water. Consequently, $CaSO_4$ gets precipitated as hard scale on the heated portions of the boiler. This is the main cause of scales in high-pressure boilers. Calcium sulphate scale is quite adherent and difficult to remove even with the help of a hammer and chisel.

3. **Hydrolysis of magnesium salts:** Dissolved magnesium salts undergo hydrolysis (at prevailing high temperature inside the boilers), forming magnesium hydroxide precipitate, which forms a soft type of scale, e.g.,
    $$MgCl_2 + 2 H_2O \rightarrow Mg(OH)_2 \downarrow + 2HCl \uparrow$$

4. **Presence of silica (SiO_2),** even present in small quantities, deposits as calcium silicate ($CaSiO_3$) and/or magnesium silicate ($MgSiO_3$). These deposits stick very firmly on the inner side of the boiler surface and are very difficult to remove. One important source of silica in water is the sand filter

Disadvantages of Scale Formation:

*   **Reduced Efficiency:** Scale acts as an insulating barrier on heat transfer surfaces, hindering the transfer of heat from combustion gases to the water. This reduces the overall efficiency of the boiler, as more fuel is required to achieve the desired temperature and pressure.

*   **Increased Energy Consumption:** The reduced efficiency caused by scale formation necessitates higher energy consumption to maintain

desired operating conditions. This leads to increased fuel or electricity costs, resulting in higher operational expenses.

- **Equipment Damage**: Scale buildup can lead to overheating of boiler components such as tubes, pipes, and heat exchangers. This thermal stress can cause warping, cracking, or even catastrophic failure of the affected parts, requiring costly repairs or replacements.

- **Corrosion Risk**: Scale deposits create localised areas of high concentration where corrosive reactions can occur. This can lead to pitting corrosion and deterioration of boiler surfaces, further compromising the integrity of the system and increasing maintenance requirements.

- **Water Treatment Challenges**: Scale formation complicates water treatment processes as it reduces the effectiveness of chemical treatments and requires more frequent and aggressive methods to control scaling. This increases the complexity and cost of water treatment operations.

- **Reduced Steam Quality**: Scale contamination in boiler systems can lead to impurities in the steam, affecting the quality of steam produced. This can result in reduced efficiency and reliability of downstream processes and equipment reliant on high-quality steam.

Prevention of Scales:

- **Water Treatment**: Implementing effective water treatment processes, such as softening, demineralisation, or reverse osmosis, helps remove or reduce the concentration of dissolved minerals in the feedwater. This prevents scale formation and extends the lifespan of boiler components.

- **Chemical Treatment**: Adding scale inhibitors or antiscalant chemicals to the boiler feedwater can help prevent the precipitation of minerals and the formation of scale. These chemicals inhibit the crystallisation and deposition of scale-forming compounds, keeping boiler surfaces clean.

- **Blowdown Control**: Proper control of boiler blowdown, which involves regularly removing a portion of the boiler water to control the concentration of dissolved solids, helps prevent the buildup of scale-forming minerals. Regular blowdown removes concentrated impurities before they have a chance to precipitate and form scale.

- **Scale Monitoring**: Regular monitoring of boiler water quality, including the concentration of dissolved solids and the presence of scale-forming minerals, helps detect and address potential scale formation issues before they escalate. This allows for timely adjustments to water treatment and chemical dosing programmes as needed.

1.8.2   Caustic Embrittlement:

Caustic embrittlement of boilers is a specific instance of caustic embrittlement that occurs in the steel components of industrial boilers. Boilers are used in a variety of industries to generate steam for heating, power generation, and other applications. They are typically made of steel, which is susceptible to caustic embrittlement when exposed to certain caustic agents.

The caustic agents that are most commonly associated with caustic embrittlement of boilers are concentrated alkaline solutions such as sodium hydroxide (NaOH) or potassium hydroxide (KOH). These solutions are commonly used to remove scale and other deposits from the interior surfaces of boilers. However, if the solutions are not properly handled or if the equipment used for cleaning is not adequately rinsed, the solutions can come into contact with the metal components of the boiler.

When steel is exposed to a caustic solution, the solution can dissolve the protective oxide layer on the surface of the steel, allowing hydrogen to be absorbed into the metal. The hydrogen can then diffuse into the grain boundaries of the steel, causing internal stresses that can lead to cracking and ultimately failure of the metal.

The effects of caustic embrittlement of boilers can be severe and can lead to catastrophic failures if not properly addressed. Symptoms of caustic embrittlement in boilers may include cracking, flaking, and other signs of material degradation. If left unchecked, these symptoms can lead to leaks or even ruptures of the boiler components.

To prevent caustic embrittlement of boilers, it is important to use appropriate cleaning procedures that minimise contact between the caustic solutions and the metal components. It is also important to use materials with high resistance to caustic embrittlement and to monitor boiler components for signs of material degradation. Regular inspections and maintenance can help identify and address potential issues before they lead to catastrophic failures.

Caustic embrittlement can be avoided:

1. By using sodium phosphate as a softening agent, instead of sodium carbonate;
2. by adding tannin or lignin to boiler water, since these block the hair-cracks, thereby preventing infiltration of caustic soda solution in these;
3. by adding sodium sulphate to boiler water. Na_2SO_4 also blocks hair-cracks, thereby preventing infiltration of caustic soda solutions. It has been observed that caustic cracking can be prevented if Na_2SO_4 is added to boiler water so that the ratio $\dfrac{[Na_2SO_4 \text{ concentrations}]}{[NaOH] \text{concentration}}$ is kept as 1:1:2:1 and 3:1 in boilers working respectively at pressures up to 10, 20, and above 20 atmospheres.

1.8.3 Boiler Corrosion

Boiler corrosion is the decay or destruction of boiler material by a chemical or electrochemical attack from its environment. The main reasons for boiler corrosion are:

- Dissolved oxygen.
- Dissolved carbon dioxide.
- Dissolved salts like magnesium chloride.

(A) Dissolved oxygen:

When water containing dissolved oxygen is fed into boilers, the following reaction occurs, corroding the boiler material (rust formation).

$2\,Fe + 2H_2O + O_2$	$\rightarrow$	$2\,Fe(OH)_2$
$4\,Fe(OH)_2 + O_2$	$\rightarrow$	$2\,(Fe_2O_3 \cdot 2H_2O)$
Ferrous hydroxide		Rust

Removal of dissolved oxygen:

(1) By adding a calculated quantity of sodium sulphite, hydrazine, or sodium sulphide. Thus;

$$2\,Na_2SO_3 + O_2 \rightarrow 2\,Na_2SO_4$$
$$N_2H_4 + O_2 \rightarrow N_2 + 2\,H_2O$$

Hydrazine

$$Na_2S + 2\,O_2 \rightarrow Na_2SO_4$$

(2) By mechanical de-aeration, i.e., water spraying in a perforated plate-fitted tower, heated from sides and connected to a vacuum pump. High temperature, low pressure, and a large, exposed surface (provided by perforated plates) reduce the dissolved oxygen in water.

(B) Dissolved carbon dioxide:

CO_2 react with water to convert carbonic acid.

$$CO_2 + H_2O \rightarrow H_2CO_3$$

which has a slow corrosive effect on the boiler material. Carbon dioxide is also released inside the boiler. If water used for steam generation contains bicarbonate, for example,

$$Mg(HCO_3)_2 \rightarrow MgCO_3 + H_2O + CO_2$$

Removal of CO_2:

(1) By adding a calculated quantity of ammonia. Thus,

$$2NH_4OH + CO_2 \rightarrow (NH_4)_2CO_3 + H_2O$$

(2) By mechanical aeration process along with oxygen.

(C) Acids from dissolved salts:

Water containing dissolved magnesium salts liberate acids on hydrolysis, e.g.,

$$MgCl_2 + 2H_2O \rightarrow Mg(OH)_2 + 2HCl$$

The liberated acid reacts with iron (of the boiler) in chain like reactions producing HCI again and again. Thus

$$Fe + 2HCI \rightarrow FeCl_2 + H_2$$
$$FeCl_2 + 2H_2O \rightarrow Fe(OH)_2 + 2HCl$$

Consequently, the presence of even a small amount of $MgCl_2$ will cause corrosion of iron to a large extent.

1.8.4 Priming and Foaming

Priming and foaming are two related phenomena that can occur in boilers and can have serious consequences for the safety and efficiency of the equipment. Priming is the process by which water is carried over into the steam produced by the boiler. This can occur when the water level in the boiler is too high, causing water to be carried over into the steam space. When this occurs, the steam that is produced can contain droplets of water, which can lead to erosion of the turbine blades and other components downstream of the boiler.

Foaming, on the other hand, is the formation of bubbles in the boiler water that can rise up and carry water droplets into the steam space. This can occur when the boiler water contains high levels of dissolved and suspended solids, such as oils, grease, or other contaminants, that can cause the surface tension of the water to be reduced, leading to the formation of foam.

Both priming and foaming can have serious consequences for the safety and efficiency of the boiler. In addition to the erosion of downstream components, priming and foaming can cause the level control of the boiler to become unstable, leading to fluctuations in water level and the potential for the boiler to become overheated or even to run dry.

To prevent priming and foaming, it is important to maintain appropriate water chemistry in the boiler, including control of dissolved and suspended solids, p^H, and alkalinity. Additionally, the water level in the boiler should be carefully controlled to prevent the level from becoming too high, and appropriate controls and safety systems should be in place to prevent the boiler from becoming overheated or running dry. Regular maintenance and inspections can help identify and address potential issues before they lead to catastrophic failures.

1.9   NUMERICAL BASED ON HARDNESS OF WATER

The concentrations of hardness as well as non-hardness-constituting ions are usually expressed in terms of the equivalent amount of $CaCO_3$.

- The choice of $CaCO_3$, in particular, is due to its molecular weight of 100 (equivalent weight=50), and it is the most insoluble salt that can be precipitated in water treatment.
- KCl, $NaCl$, SiO_2, Na_2SO_4, K_2SO_4, Fe_2O_3, etc. are not contributing towards hardness; hence, while calculating hardness, it is ignored.
- Conversion factors cause some impurities in water which commonly come across as shown below.

Sr.No.	Salts	Multiplication factor to convert $CaCO_3$ Equivalent
1	$CaCO_3$	100/100
2	$MgCO_3$	100/84
3	$Ca(HCO_3)_2$	100/162
4	$Mg(HCO_3)_2$	100/146
5	$CaSO_4$	100/136
6	$MgSO_4$	100/120
7	$CaCl_2$	100/111
8	$MgCl_2$	100/95
9	$Ca(NO_3)_2$	100/164
10	$Mg(NO_3)_2$	100/148

1. A sample of water is found to contain the following dissolving salts in milligrams per litre.

    $Mg(HCO_3)_2$ = 73, $CaCl_2$ = 111, $Ca(HCO_3)_2$ = 81, MgSO4 = 40 and $MgCl_2$ = 95. Calculate temporary and permanent hardness and total hardness.

    Solution: Convert all impurities into $CaCO_3$ equivalent.

Salts	Amount (ppm)	Multiplication factor	Amount equivalent to $CaCO_3$ (ppm)
$Mg(HCO_3)_2$	73	100/146	73 x 100/146 = 50
$CaCl_2$	111	100/111	111 x 100/111 = 100
$Ca(HCO_3)_2$	81	100/162	81 x 100/162 = 50
$MgSO_4$	40	100/120	40 x 100/162 = 33.3
$MgCl_2$	95	100/95	95 x 100/92 = 100

1. Temporary hardness
    $= Mg(HCO_3)_2 + Ca(HCO_3)_2$
    $= 50 + 50 = 100$ mg/L or ppm

2. Permanent hardness
    $= CaCl_2 + MgSO_4 + MgCl_2$
    $= 100 + 33.3 + 100 = 233.3$ mg/L or ppm

3. Total hardness
    $=$ Temporary hardness + Permanent hardness.
    $= 100 + 233.3 = 333.3$ mg/L or ppm

2. A sample of water is found to contain the following dissolving salts in milligrams per litre.

    $Mg(HCO_3)_2$ = 16.8, $MgCl_2$ = 12.0, $MgSO_4$ = 29.6 and NaCl = 5.0. Calculate temporary and permanent hardness of water.

    Solution: Convert all impurities into $CaCO_3$ equivalent,

Salts	Amount (ppm)	Multiplication factor	Amount equivalent to CaCO3 (ppm)
$Mg(HCO_3)_2$	16.8	100/146	16.8 x 100/146 = 11.50
$MgCl_2$	12	100/95	12 x 100/95 = 12.63
$MgSO_4$	29.6	100/120	29.6 x 100/120 = 24.66
NaCl	5	NaCl does not contribute hardness to water; hence, it is ignored.	

Temporary hardness = $Mg(HCO_3)_2$ = 11.50 mg/L.

Permanent hardness = $MgCl_2$ + $MgSO_4$ = 12.63 + 24.66 = 37.29 mg/L

3. Calculate the temporary and permanent hardness of water having impurities;

$Ca(HCO_3)_2$ = 40.5 ppm, $Mg(HCO_3)_2$ = 36.5 ppm, $MgSO_4$ = 30 ppm, $CaSO_4$ = 34.00 ppm, $CaCl_2$ = 27.75 ppm, NaCl = 12 ppm.

solution:

Salts	Amount	Multi factor	Amount equivalent to CaCO3 (ppm)
$Ca(HCO_3)_2$	40.5 ppm	100/162	25 ppm
$Mg(HCO_3)_2$	36.5 ppm,	100/146	25 ppm
$MgSO_4$	30 ppm	100/120	25 ppm
$CaSO_4$	34.00 ppm	100/136	25 ppm
$CaCl_2$	27.75 ppm,	100/111	25 ppm
NaCl	12 ppm	ignored	———

Temporary hardness: $[Ca(HCO_3)_2 + Mg(HCO_3)_2]$ = [25 + 25] = 50 ppm

Permanent hardness: $[MgSO_4 + CaSO_4 + CaCl_2]$ = [25 + 25 + 25] = 75 ppm

1.10 NUMERICAL BASED ON ZEOLITE PROCESS

1. The hardness of 10,000 litres of water was removed by passing it through a zeolite softener. The softener then required 100 litres of NaCl solution (brine solution) containing 150g/l of NaCl for regeneration.

   Solution: NaCl containing 200 litres of solution = 150 g/litre x 200 litres.

   = 30,000 g

   The CaCO3 equivalent of 30000 g of NaCl = 30000 x 100 / 2 x 58.5

   = 25641 g of NaCl in $CaCO_3$ Equivalent

   = 25641 x 103 mg of NaCl in $CaCO_3$ equivalent

   25641 x 103 mg of NaCl in $CaCO_3$ equivalent is required for regeneration of the softener that softens 10000 litres of water.

   10,000 litres of water = 25,641 x 103 mg of NaCl in $CaCO_3$ Equivalent

1 litre of water = 25641 x 103/10000

Hardness of water = 2564.1 mg/l

2. An exhausted zeolite softener is regenerated by passing 150 litres of NaCl solution having a strength of 150 gm/litre of NaCl. If the hardness of water is 600 ppm, calculate the total volume of water.

   Solution: NaCl containing 150 litres of solution = 150 g/litre x 150 litres.

   = 22500 g

   The $CaCO_3$ equivalent of 22500 g of NaCl = 22500 x 100 / 2 x 58.5

   = 19230.76 g of NaCl in $CaCO_3$ Equivalent

   = 19230.76 x 103 mg of NaCl in $CaCO_3$ Equivalent

   We can say that water has hardness of 600 ppm containing 19230.76 x 103 mg of NaCl in $CaCO_3$ equivalent.

   Total volume of water = 19,230.76 x 103 / 600

   = 32.06 x 103 lit

IMPORTANT QUESTIONS:

1. What is Hardness of water? Explain Types of hardness of water with units.

2. Describe Ion-Exchange process of Water softening

3. What is water softening? Explain the process of Zeolite for water softening.

4. Explain the EDTA method for determination of hardness of water.

5. Explain 1. Scale and sludge formation 2. Boiler corrosion

6. Explain 1. Priming & Foaming 2. Caustic Imbrittlement

7. What is softening of water? Discuss the Zeolite Process of water softening. Give their advantages and disadvantages

8. Discuss the deionisation process of water softening. Give their advantages and disadvantages.

9. What is scale and sludge formation? What are causes and disadvantages of scale formation?

10. What is reverse osmosis? Discuss RO Method for softening of sea water with neat sketch.

11. What is reverse osmosis? How reverse osmosis use for desalination of water?

12. Named the methods for water softening? Describe Zeolite process for water softening.

13. What is softening of water? Discuss zeolite process for water softening. Give its advantages, disadvantages.

14. Explain Scale and Sludge Formation in boilers with disadvantages and prevention.

15. What is demineralisation of water? Explain the chemical reaction involved and the method for it.

16. Define temporary and permanent hardness of water with examples.

17. What is caustic embrittlement? How it can be prevented?

18. Differentiate between scale and sludge. How these can be removed from boiler?

19. Discuss the principle of ion-exchange process for softening of hard water.

20. Explain the Permutit process of water softening.

21. Discuss in details of priming and Foaming.

22. Describe the principle involved in determination of hardness by EDTA method.

23. What is scale? What are disadvantages of scale formation?

24. Calculate temporary, permanent and hence total hardness of water sample containing following impurities in ppm $Ca(HCO_3)_2$=36.5, $MgCO_3$=21, $MgSO_4$=30, $CaSO_4$=34, $MgCl_2$=23.75, KCl=12.8

25. The water contains the following impurities in mg/l.
    $Mg(HCO_3)_2$ = 7.3, $CaSO_4$ = 6.8, $MgCl_2$= 9.5, $MgSO_4$= 6.0 ppm, $NaCl$ = 4.0, K_2SO_4 =1.8, Al_2O_3= 13.2. Calculate temporary & permanent hardness.

26. What is Hardness and calculate a sample of water is found to contain the following analytical data in milligrams per litre: $Mg(HCO_3)_2$ = 14.6, $MgCl_2$ = 9.5, $MgSO_4$ = 6.0, and $Ca(HCO_3)_2$ = 16.2. Calculate the temporary and permanent hardness of water in parts per million, Degree Clarke's, and Degree French.

27. The Zeolite softener was completely exhausted and was regenerated by passing 150 litres of NaCl solution contains 75 grams per litre of NaCl.

How many litres of water havening hardness of 400 ppm can be soften using this softener.

28. An exhausted zeolite softener was regenerated by passing 150 lits. of NaCl solution having a strength of 100g/l of NaCl. How many lit. of water sample having hardness of 200 ppm can be softened using this softener.

29. The hardness of 10,000 litres of water sample was removed by zeolite softener. The zeolite softener required 200 litres of NaCl solution containing 2.5 gm/litre of NaCl. Calculate hardness in ppm.

30. The hardness of 4000 dm^3 of water samples was completely removed by zeolite softener. The zeolite had required 125 dm^3 of NaCl solution, containing 2000 mg/ dm^3 of NaCl for regeneration. Calculate hardness of the water sample.

31. An exhausted zeolite softener was regenerated by passing 150 litres of NaCl solution, having strength of 150g/L of NaCl. How many litres of hard water sample having hardness of 600ppm can be softened by using this softener, if it is 50% exhausted?

CHAPTER 2

NANOMATERIALS

2.1 BASICS OF NANOCHEMISTRY

Nanochemistry is the branch of science which deals with designing and synthesis of materials of nanoscale (1-100 nm) dimension. It includes large organic molecules, inorganic cluster compounds, and metallic or semiconductor particles.

"Nanotechnology is based upon the manipulation of individual atoms and molecules to build structures to complex atomic specifications."

OR

"The design, characterisation, production, and application of structures, devices, and systems by controlled manipulation of size and shape at the nanometre scale (atomic, molecular, and macromolecular scale) that produces structures, devices, and systems with at least one novel/superior characteristic or property".

Nanotechnology is the creation of functional materials, devices, and systems through control of matter on the nanometer (1 to 100+ nm) length scale and the exploitation of novel properties and phenomena developed at that scale. Nanotechnology products are mostly gradually improved products where some form of nanotechnology-enabled material (such as carbon nanotubes, nanocomposite structures, or nanoparticles of a particular substance) is used in the manufacturing process.

Examples: Red blood cells are 7000 nm in diameter and 2000 nm in height. White blood cells are 10000 nm in diameter. A virus is 100 nm, etc.

Sr.No.	Name	Range
1	Nanoparticles range	1-100 nm
2	Fullerenes (C90/Buckyballs)	1 nm
3	Quantum dots	8 nm
4	DNA (Width)	2 nm
5	proteins	5-50 nm
6	Viruses	75-100 nm
7	Bacteria range	1000-10000 nm

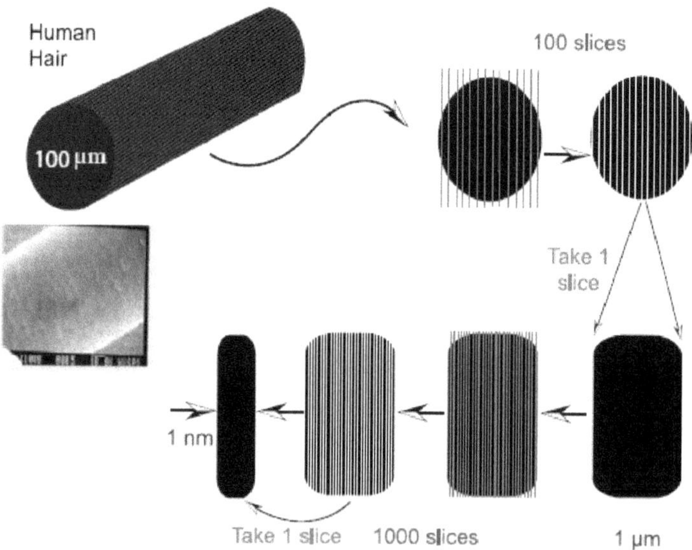

Figure 2.1: *Cross-sectional area of human hair*

2.2 NANOMATERIALS

Nanocrystalline materials are materials possessing grain sizes on the order of a billionth of a metre. They manifest extremely fascinating and useful properties, which can be exploited for a variety of structural and non-structural applications. All materials are composed of grains which in turn comprise many atoms. These are usually invisible to the naked eye, depending on their size. Conventionally, materials have grains varying in size anywhere from 100 µm to millimetres. A micron is micrometres or millionths (10^{-6}) of a metre. An average human hair is about 100 µm in diameter. A nanometer is even smaller in dimension than a µm and a billionth (10^{-9}) of a metre. A nanocrystalline material has a grain size on the order of 1-100 nm.

Nanoparticles are particles that have one dimension that is 100 nanometers or less in size. The properties of many conventional materials change when formed from nanoparticles. This is typically because nanoparticles have a greater surface area per weight than larger particles; this causes them to be more reactive to certain other molecules. Nanomaterials have a relatively larger surface area when compared to the same mass of material produced in a larger form. This can make materials more chemically reactive and affect their strength or electrical properties. Quantum effects can begin to dominate the behaviour of matter at the nanoscale, affecting the optical, electrical, and magnetic behaviour of materials. Materials can be produced that are nanoscale in one dimension (for example, very thin surface coatings), in two dimensions (for example, nanowires and nanotubes) or in all three dimensions (for example, nanoparticles).

2.3 PROPERTIES OF NANOMATERIALS

Nanomaterials exhibit unique properties that differ significantly from their bulk counterparts due to their small size and high surface area. There are some important properties of nanomaterials:

1. **Large Surface Area to Volume Ratio**: Nanomaterials have a high surface area relative to their volume, which enhances their reactivity and interaction with other materials.

2. **Quantum Effects**: At the nanoscale, quantum mechanical effects become significant, affecting the electrical, optical, and magnetic properties of the materials.

3. **Mechanical Strength**: Nanomaterials often exhibit enhanced mechanical properties, such as increased strength and hardness, due to their reduced defect density and size.

4. **Electrical Conductivity**: Some nanomaterials, like carbon nanotubes and graphene, have exceptional electrical conductivity, making them useful in electronics and energy applications.

5. **Optical Properties**: Nanomaterials can exhibit unique optical properties, such as quantum dots displaying size-tunable fluorescence, which is useful in imaging and display technologies.

6. **Chemical Reactivity**: The increased surface area and high reactivity of nanomaterials make them ideal for catalytic applications.

7. **Thermal Conductivity**: Nanomaterials can have significantly different thermal conductivity compared to their bulk forms, which can be either higher or lower depending on the material and structure.

8. **Magnetic Properties**: Magnetic nanomaterials can exhibit superparamagnetism, where they show magnetic properties only in the presence of an external magnetic field.

2.4   CARBON NANOTUBES (CNT):

A carbon nanotube (CNT) is a miniature cylindrical carbon structure that has hexagonal graphite molecules attached at the edges. Nanotubes look like a powder or black soot, but they're actually rolled-up sheets of graphene that form hollow strands with walls that are only one atom thick. Nanotubes, which are sometimes called bulky tubes, were developed from the Fullerene, a structure that is similar to the geodesic domes.

Nanotubes can be characterised by their number of concentric cylinders, cylinder radius, and cylinder length. Some nanotubes have a property called chirality, an expression of longitudinal twisting. Multiple nanotubes can be assembled into microscopic mechanical systems called nanomachines.

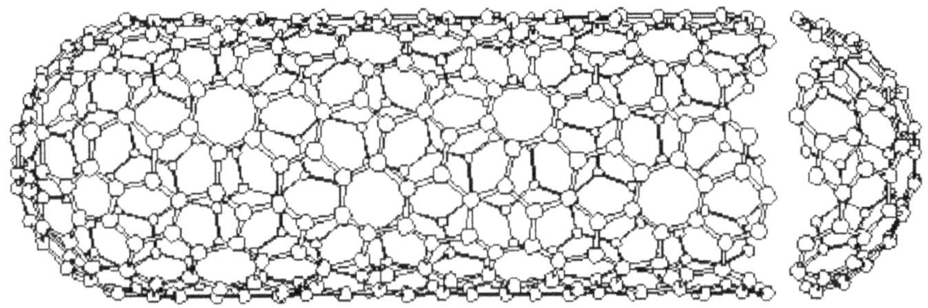

Figure 2.2: *Carbon nanotube*

Properties of Carbon Nanotubes

- **Mechanical Properties**
  - ○ High Strength: About 100 times stronger than steel, yet only a fraction of the weight.
  - ○ Elasticity: Can stretch up to approximately 18% of their original length without breaking.
  - ○ Flexibility: Can be bent significantly without damage.
  - ○ Tensile Strength: Extremely high tensile strength, allowing them to withstand substantial forces.
- **Electrical Properties**
  - ○ Conductivity: Can be either metallic or semiconducting, offering superior electrical conductivity.
  - ○ Field Emission: Excellent electron field emitters due to their sharp tips and high aspect ratio.
- **Thermal Properties**
  - ○ Conductivity: Possess high thermal conductivity, making them effective heat conductors.
  - ○ Expansion: Exhibit a low thermal expansion coefficient, maintaining structural integrity across temperature variations.
- **Chemical Properties**
  - ○ Stability: Chemically inert and resistant to many chemical reactions, enhancing their durability.

○ Functionalization: Surface can be chemically modified to improve compatibility with other materials or introduce specific functionalities.

Applications of Carbon Nanotubes

Carbon nanotubes (CNTs) are cylindrical molecules with extraordinary mechanical, electrical, thermal, and chemical properties, making them suitable for a wide range of applications.

- Making transistors smaller and faster than traditional silicon.
- Used in touch screens, displays, and solar cells due to excellent electrical conductivity and transparency.
- Replacing copper or aluminium interconnects in integrated circuits.
- Enhancing the mechanical strength of polymers, metals, and ceramics.
- Creating lightweight, strong, and conductive fabrics for smart clothing and protective gear.
- Improving energy density, charge/discharge rates, and lifespan.
- Enhancing efficiency and durability of electrodes.
- Delivering drugs to specific cells or tissues.
- Detecting biomolecules with high sensitivity.
- Creating scaffolds that support cell growth and tissue regeneration.
- Removing contaminants from water.
- Detecting environmental toxins and pollutants.
- Reducing friction and wear in mechanical systems.

2.5 APPLICATIONS OF NANOMATERIALS

Nanomaterials, characterised by their extremely small size and unique properties, have a wide range of applications across various fields. There are some key applications of nanomaterials:

1. **Medicine and Healthcare:**

   ○ **Drug Delivery:** Nanoparticles enable targeted drug delivery, enhancing efficacy and reducing side effects.

   ○ **Medical Imaging:** Quantum dots and other nanomaterials improve resolution and contrast in imaging techniques.

- ○ **Diagnostics**: Nanoscale biosensors detect diseases early with high sensitivity.
2. **Electronics**:
   - ○ **Transistors and Semiconductors**: Nanomaterials like graphene and carbon nanotubes enable smaller, faster, and more efficient transistors.
   - ○ **Display Technologies**: Quantum dots are used for brighter, more energy-efficient displays.
   - ○ **Flexible Electronics**: Nanomaterials allow for the creation of bendable electronic devices.
3. **Energy**:
   - ○ **Solar Cells**: Nanomaterials enhance light absorption and charge separation, improving solar cell efficiency.
   - ○ **Batteries**: Nanomaterials in electrodes increase energy density and charging speed.
   - ○ **Supercapacitors**: Nanomaterials improve the performance of supercapacitors for rapid energy storage and release.
4. **Environmental Protection**:
   - ○ **Water Treatment**: Nanomaterials remove contaminants through filtration, adsorption, and catalytic degradation.
   - ○ **Air Purification**: Nanomaterials are used in filters and catalytic converters to remove air pollutants.
   - ○ **Soil Remediation**: Nanoparticles detoxify contaminated soils.
5. **Catalysis**:
   - ○ **Chemical Reactions**: Nanocatalysts enhance reaction efficiency and selectivity, reducing the need for harsh conditions.
   - ○ **Fuel Cells**: Nanomaterials improve the catalytic activity and durability of fuel cell electrodes.
6. **Materials Science**:
   - ○ **Strengthening Materials**: Nanomaterials are added to composites to improve strength, toughness, and lightweight properties.
   - ○ **Protective Coatings**: Nanocoatings provide enhanced protection against corrosion, wear, and UV radiation.

7. **Consumer Products:**
   - **Cosmetics**: Nanomaterials are used in sunscreens and cosmetics for better UV protection and improved texture.
   - **Textiles**: Nanomaterials impart stain resistance, antibacterial properties, and improved durability.
   - **Food Packaging**: Nanomaterials enhance barrier properties, extending the shelf life of food products.

2.6 SYNTHESIS OF NANOMATERIALS

Top-down and bottom-up are two distinct methods for product manufacturing. The Foresight Institute first introduced these terms in 1989 in the context of nanotechnology to differentiate between molecular manufacturing, which aims to produce large, atomically precise objects, and conventional manufacturing, which produces large objects without atomic precision. The bottom-up approach involves assembling smaller, typically molecular components into more complex structures, whereas the top-down approach uses larger, externally controlled tools to construct nanoscale devices.

In the top-down approach, traditional workshop techniques or microfabrication methods are employed, where tools are externally controlled to cut, mill, and shape materials into the desired forms. Techniques like photolithography and inkjet printing are examples of this approach. Conversely, bottom-up methods leverage the chemical properties of individual molecules to either self-organise or self-assemble into functional structures or rely on positional assembly. These methods are based on principles of molecular self-assembly and molecular recognition, as seen in supramolecular chemistry. Bottom-up approaches have the potential to produce devices more cost-effectively and in parallel compared to top-down methods, although they may face challenges as the size and complexity of the assemblies increase.

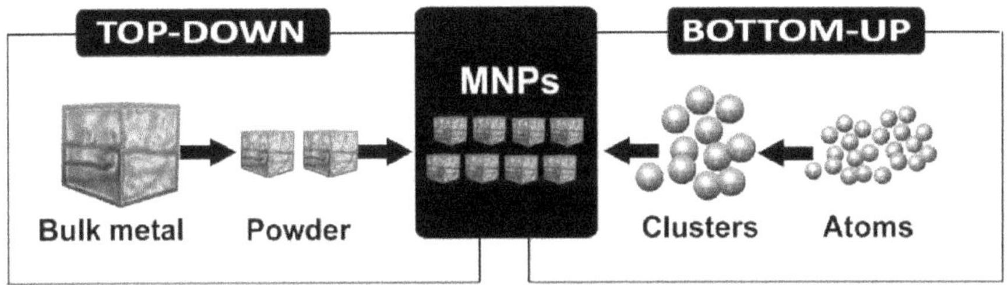

Figure 2.3: Synthesis of nanomaterial

2.6.1   Sol-gel Processes

Sol-gel processes principle is the conversion of precursor solution into a gel via hydrolysis and condensation reactions. The following steps are involved in the synthesis of nanomaterials by the sol-gel process.

Examples: Zinc oxide nanoparticles, TiO_2 nanoparticles can be synthesised by this method.

a) **Preparation of sol:** In this method, metal alkoxide is used as a precursor to synthesize nanoparticles of a metal oxide. Metal alkoxide is dissolved in alcohol and then water is added under acidic, neutral, or basic conditions. Addition of water leads to hydrolysis in which the alkoxide ligand is replaced with a hydroxyl ligand.

$$MOR + H_2O \rightarrow MOH + ROH \text{ (hydrolysis)}$$

b) **Conversion of sol to gel:** The polycondensation reaction between MOH and MOR results in the formation of an oxide (O^-) or alcohol (OH^-) bridged network (gel).

$$MOH + ROM \rightarrow M\text{-}O\text{-}M + R\text{-}OH \text{ (Polycondensation)}$$

c) **Ageing of the gel:** The reaction mixture is allowed to continue polycondensation reactions until the gel transforms into a solid mass, accompanied by contraction of the gel network and expulsion of solvent from gel pores.

d) Removal of a solvent: The water and other volatile liquids are removed from the gel network. If isolated by thermal evaporation, the resulting product is termed a xerogel. If the solvent is extracted under supercritical conditions, the resulting product is termed an aerogel.

e) **Heat treatment:** The sample obtained is calcined at high temperature (800°C) to obtain nanoparticles. Nanoparticles formed by the sol-gel process commonly have a size ranging from 1 to 100 nm.

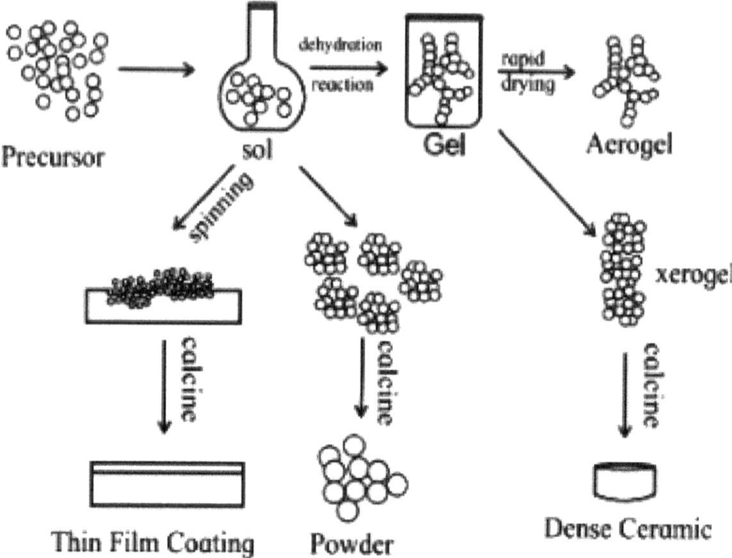

Figure 2.4: *Sol-Gel Process*

Advantages of Sol-gel Process

- It produces thick coating to provide corrosion protection performance.
- It easily shapes materials into complex geometries in a gel state.
- It has low-temperature sintering capability, usually 200-800°C.
- It provides a simple, economical, and effective method to produce high-quality coatings.

Applications of Sol-gel Process

- Used in ceramics manufacturing for investment casting and producing thin films of metal oxides.
- Sol-gel materials have applications in optics, electronics, energy, space, sensors, medicine (e.g., controlled drug release), and separation technologies (e.g., chromatography).
- Important for zeolite synthesis.

- Can incorporate other metals and metal oxides, creating stable silicalite sol.
- Produces ceramic membranes for microfiltration, ultrafiltration, nanofiltration, and reverse osmosis.

2.6.2 Chemical Vapour Deposition Method

Chemical vapour deposition (CVD) is a chemical process used to produce high-purity, high-performance solid materials. The process is often used in the semiconductor industry to produce thin films. In typical CVD, the wafer (substrate) is exposed to one or more volatile precursors, which react and/or decompose on the substrate surface to produce the desired deposit. Frequently, volatile by-products are also produced, which are removed by gas flow through the reaction chamber.

Microfabrication processes widely use CVD to deposit materials in various forms, including: monocrystalline, polycrystalline, amorphous, and epitaxial. These materials include: silicon, carbon fibre, carbon nanofibers, fluorocarbons, filaments, carbon nanotubes, SO_2, silicon germanium, tungsten, silicon carbide, silicon nitride, silicon oxynitride, titanium nitride, and various high-k dielectrics. CVD is also used to produce synthetic diamonds.

Chemical Vapour Deposition (CVD) is a versatile and widely used technique for producing high-quality, high-performance solid materials by depositing a thin film onto a substrate through the chemical reactions of vapour-phase precursors. Here is a detailed description of the CVD method:

Advantages:
- Versatile: CVD can deposit any element or compound.
- CVD produces high-density films.
- Economical in production since many products can be coated at a time.
- Used for coatings or freestanding structures.
- Fabricates net or near-net complex shapes.
- Self-cleaning—extremely high-purity deposits (>99.99% purity)
- Conforms homogeneously to contours of the substrate surface.
- Controllable thickness and morphology.

Applications:

- It is used to prepared nanotubes and nanowires.
- It produces hard coatings and metal films for microelectronics.
- It is used to prepare semiconducting devices, dielectrics, and energy conversion devices.
- Applied to aircraft and turbine blades, automotive timing chain pins, gas cooker grills, and chemical plant items for resistance to carbon, oxygen, and sulphur.
- Improves photo resist adhesion for semiconductor wafers and silane/substrate adhesion for microarrays.
- Coats biosensors to reduce performance drift.
- Provides anti-corrosive coating.

IMPORTANT QUESTIONS:

1. Explain the term nanochemistry and nanomaterials.
2. Give applications of nanomaterials.
3. What are nanomaterials? Give their properties and applications.
4. Explain the sol-gel method of synthesis of nanomaterials.
5. Explain the Chemical Vapour Deposition method of synthesis of nanomaterials.
6. What are Carbon nanotubes? Write their properties and applications.

CHAPTER 3

LUBRICANTS

3.1 INTRODUCTION

Lubricants are substances that are strategically placed between two surfaces that are moving, sliding, or rolling against each other to reduce the friction and resistance between them. This process, known as lubrication, plays a critical role in enhancing the efficiency and longevity of mechanical systems.

When two surfaces interact, whether they are moving, sliding, or rolling, they inevitably rub against each other. This rubbing action generates resistance known as friction. Friction is an inherent force that opposes the motion of the surfaces in contact, leading to several undesired effects. The primary consequence of friction is the wear and tear on the surfaces involved. Over time, this wear can lead to damage and degradation of the components, affecting the overall performance and reliability of the machinery.

In addition to physical wear, friction generates heat as a byproduct. This heat results from the conversion of mechanical energy into thermal energy due to the resistance encountered during surface contact. The excess heat produced can be problematic as it not only increases the risk of overheating but also contributes to the loss of operational efficiency. Elevated temperatures can lead to the degradation of materials, reduction in lubrication effectiveness, and potential failure of the components.

Lubrication, through the application of lubricants, addresses these issues by forming a protective layer between the surfaces. This layer reduces direct contact between the surfaces, thereby decreasing friction and minimising the resultant wear. By lowering friction, lubricants also help in controlling the temperature by dissipating heat more effectively. This results in smoother operation, enhanced efficiency, and prolonged lifespan of the machinery.

3.2 FUNCTION OF LUBRICANTS

Lubricants form a protective layer between moving parts, reducing friction and wear.

- They dissipate heat generated by friction, preventing overheating and component damage.
- Lubricants inhibit corrosion by forming a barrier against moisture and contaminants.
- Lubricants seal gaps between parts, preventing leaks and protecting against dirt and debris.
- By reducing wear and tear, lubricants help prolong the lifespan of machinery and equipment.
- It enhances the efficiency of mechanical systems by reducing energy losses due to friction.
- It reduces the rate of corrosion.
- It also acts as a seal in internal combustion engines.

3.3 CHARACTERISTICS OF A LUBRICANT

It should have enough viscosity and oiliness.

- It should have flash and fire points higher than the operating temperature of the machine.
- It should be chemically inert.
- It should not come out of the surface under pressure.
- It should not evaporate easily.
- It should stick on the surface.

- It should leave low carbon residue.
- It should not form emulsion with water.
- It should have cloud and pour points lower than the operating temperature of the machine.
- The volatility of the lubricating oil should be low.

3.4 CLASSIFICATION OF LUBRICANTS:

On the basis of consistency, lubricants are classified as three types:

Solid lubricants, liquid lubricants, and semisolid lubricants:

1. **Solid Lubricants:**
   - These lubricants are in solid form at room temperature.
   - Examples: Graphite, molybdenum disulphide (MoS_2), boron nitride (BN)x, mica, $CoCl_2$, Ag_2SO_4, PbI_2, etc.
   - Solid lubricants are often used in applications where liquid lubricants are not suitable, such as high-temperature environments or where contamination is a concern.

2. **Liquid Lubricants:**
   - These lubricants are in liquid form at room temperature.
   - They include mineral oils, synthetic oils, and vegetable oils.
   - Liquid lubricants are commonly used in various mechanical systems, including engines, gearboxes, and hydraulic systems, where they provide smooth lubrication and dissipate heat efficiently.

3. **Semisolid Lubricants:**
   - Also known as grease, semisolid lubricants have a consistency between that of solid and liquid lubricants.
   - Grease consists of a base oil thickened with a soap or other thickening agent.
   - Semisolid lubricants are used in applications where a more adhesive lubricant is needed, such as in bearings, seals, and open gears. They provide excellent sealing properties and resistance to water washout.

3.5 APPLICATIONS OF LUBRICANTS

Lubricants are primarily used to reduce the friction between two moving surfaces.

- Rust and corrosion inhibitors.
- Used in the soap and paint industries.
- Liquid lubricants are used in medicines.
- Lubricants are also used as cutting fluid in cutting, grinding, and drilling of metals.
- Used as anti-wear, antioxidants, and antifoaming agents.

3.6 PROPERTIES OF LUBRICANTS

The properties of lubricants need to be well studied so that selection of the best lubricants for particular applications can be made. Some of the important properties are as follows.

3.6.1 Viscosity and Viscosity Index

This is the most important property of lubricants. Viscosity is the property of a fluid by virtue of which it offers resistance to its own flow. Viscosity is a measure of the internal resistance to motion of a liquid or a fluid. It is due to the intermolecular force of attraction between fluid molecules. The lower the viscosity, the greater the flow ability. Viscosity helps in the selection of good lubricating oil. Light oils have low densities and easy flow abilities and are used on parts moving at high speed. Heavy oils are used on parts moving at slow speed under heavy loads.

In lubrication, the relative viscosity is determined. Relative viscosity is the time required in seconds to pass through a capillary of fixed length and diameter at a constant temperature. The results are usually expressed in terms of the time in seconds taken by the oil to flow through the standard orifice of the particular apparatus like Redwood viscometer no. 1, Redwood viscometer no. 2, Engler's viscometer, Seybolt viscometer, etc.

Viscosity Index

When lubricating oil is heated, the intermolecular forces of attraction of fluid molecules break. Due to a decrease in such force of attraction, the viscosity of the fluid decreases. Hence, the viscosity of lubricating oil decreases with an increase in temperature and vice versa. When lubricant is introduced between moving bodies, the oil temperature increases as operating temperature increases. With the increase in temperature, the oil becomes thinner as the viscosity of the oil decreases. If there is a much more significant change in viscosity of oil with a change in temperature, the oil may not maintain a fluid film between the sliding bodies. Hence, this change in viscosity with temperature should be as minimal as possible.

Viscosity index (V.I.) is a measure of the rate of change of viscosity with temperature. The viscosity of oil decreases readily with increases in temperature; it has a low V.I. While if viscosity decreases slowly with an increase in temperature, it has a high V.I. For all lubricating oils, a scale of 0-100 is considered.

The naphthalene-based Gulf oils are found to contain rapid change in viscosity with respect to temperature. Hence, the oils in the series of Gulf oils are considered as low viscosity standard oils with V.I. = 0. The paraffinic-based Pennsylvanian oils are found to contain the least change in viscosity with respect to temperature. Hence, these oils are considered as high viscosity standard with V.I. = 100. All other oils are placed between 0-100.

3.6.2   Flash Points and Fire Point

Lubricants are subjected to high temperatures when they are used. Due to this high temperature, they have a tendency to volatilise, causing a loss of lubricants. A good lubricant should not volatilise under the conditions of lubrication. If they volatise, the vapours formed should not catch fire under the temperature conditions of lubrication. A good lubricant should form inflammable vapours only at a temperature beyond the working temperature of the lubricants.

- **Flash Point:** It is defined as the lowest temperature at which the lubricating oil gives off enough vapours that ignite for a moment when a small flame of standard dimension is brought near it.
- **Fire Point:** It is defined as the minimum temperature at which the oil gives off enough vapours that burn continuously for five seconds when even a small flame is brought near it.

In most cases, the fire point is higher than the flash point by 5-40°C. Good lubricating oil should have a flash point and fire point higher than the working temperature. This ensures safety against fire hazards not only during the use of lubricant but also during storage and transportation.

Flash point and fire point are determined by either closed cup or open cup apparatus. In the open cup apparatus, the oil is heated with its upper surface exposed to the atmosphere. Cleveland's apparatus is an example of an open cup apparatus. The flash point obtained by the open cup apparatus is generally about 10 to 30°F higher than that obtained by the closed cup apparatus. Thus, the flash point obtained by the closed cup apparatus is more correct. The closed cup apparatus commonly used are Abel apparatus and Pensky-Martens apparatus.

3.6.3 Cloud Point and Pour Point

The lubricating oils obtained from petroleum contain dissolved paraffin wax and asphaltic or resinous impurities that separate out of the oil at low temperatures. Further solidification of the lubricant causes jamming of the machine.

- **Cloud point:** When oil is cooled slowly, the temperature at which it becomes cloudy or hazy in appearance is called its cloud point.
- **Pour point:** When oil is cooled slowly, the temperature at which it ceases to flow or pour is called its pour point.

The cloud and pour points indicate the suitability of lubricants in cold conditions. In machines working at low temperatures, the lubricants that are used should have low pour points. Examples are refrigerator plants and aircraft engines, which are required to start and operate at sub-zero temperatures.

Examples: Refrigerator plants and aircraft engines, which may be required to start and operate at subzero temperatures.

3.6.4   Acid Value

The acid value is a measure of the amount of free fatty acids present in a substance, typically a fat or oil. It is expressed as the quantity of potassium hydroxide (KOH) in milligrams required to neutralise the free acids present in one gram of the sample. The acid value is an important parameter in the characterisation of fats and oils, as it provides information about their quality, purity, and degree of degradation.

Acid value serves as an indicator of the quality and purity of fats and oils. Higher acid values may suggest lower quality due to increased levels of free fatty acids, which can result from improper handling, storage, or processing.

IMPORTANT QUESTIONS:

1. Define lubricants. Discuss the classification of lubricants with suitable examples.
2. How are lubricants classified? Give examples.
3. Define lubricants and lubrication. What are the functions of lubricants?
4. Define lubricant. Discuss the important properties of a good lubricant and its significance.
5. Write short notes on the following properties of lubricants: (a) Cloud and Pour point (b) Flash and Fire point.
6. What are viscosity & viscosity index of lubricating oil?
7. Define the following terms, 1. Flash point and Fire point 2. Acid value

CHAPTER 4

CORROSIONS AND CORROSION CONTROL

4.1 INTRODUCTION

Chemical corrosion is the deterioration or degradation of a material due to chemical reactions with its environment. Corrosion can occur in various materials including metals, polymers, and ceramics. The damage caused by corrosion can lead to the failure of the material and the structures made from it.

The corrosion process involves the transfer of electrons from one material to another through an electrochemical reaction. This occurs when a material comes into contact with an electrolyte, such as a liquid or gas that can conduct electricity, and an anode and cathode are formed. The anode is the site where corrosion occurs, and the cathode is the site where the electrons are consumed. The losses due to corrosion are significant, so it is essential to protect the metal from corrosion. The choice of the metal depends on the environment to which the metal is exposed.

"It is not possible to stop corrosion; it can be controlled to a great extent by effective chemical techniques."

Most of the metals except noble metals occur in the form of their stable compounds such as oxides, sulphides, carbonates, chlorides, and silicates.

During the extraction process, they are reduced to their metallic state and the surface of metals begins to decay when exposed to the environment. This type of metallic destruction takes place due to the direct chemical attack by the environment or electrochemical attack. Hence, the process of destruction of metal due to the action of the surrounding medium is called corrosion.

4.2   CLASSIFICATION OF CORROSION

Corrosion is classified on the basis of its occurrence.

Mainly, corrosion is of two types.

1)   Atmospheric corrosion/dry corrosion/direct chemical corrosion.
2)   Electrochemical corrosion/immersed or wet corrosion.

1. Atmospheric Corrosion

Atmospheric corrosion is a type of corrosion that occurs on the surface of metals when they are exposed to the environment. It is a complex electrochemical process that involves the interaction between metal, oxygen, water, and various other environmental factors. The atmosphere contains many different gases, such as oxygen, carbon dioxide, and nitrogen, which can react with the metal surface. The most common reaction involved in atmospheric corrosion is the reaction of oxygen with the metal surface to form metal oxides. For example, iron reacts with oxygen to form iron oxide, which is commonly known as rust.

It can be further classified as:

a)   Corrosion due to oxygen.
b)   Corrosion due to other gases.

a) Corrosion Due to Oxygen:

Oxidation corrosion, also known as dry corrosion, is a type of corrosion that occurs when a metal is exposed to oxygen and moisture in the environment. In this process, the metal undergoes a chemical reaction with the oxygen in the air, forming an oxide layer on the surface of the metal. This oxide layer can be protective or non-protective, depending on its thickness, composition, and adhesion to the underlying metal surface.

The oxidation process can occur in two ways: homogeneous and heterogeneous. In homogeneous oxidation, the metal is uniformly corroded throughout the surface area, while in heterogeneous oxidation, only certain areas of the metal are corroded, leaving the rest of the surface unaffected.

The corrosion process starts with the formation of a thin layer of metal oxide on the surface of the metal. This layer can act as a protective barrier, preventing further oxidation. However, if the oxide layer is not dense or uniform, it can allow moisture and oxygen to penetrate and react with the underlying metal surface, causing further corrosion.

In addition to oxygen and moisture, other factors can also contribute to oxidation corrosion. These include temperature, pH, and the presence of contaminants such as salts and acids. High temperatures can accelerate the corrosion process, while low temperatures can slow it down. Acids and salts can also accelerate the corrosion process by creating an electrolytic environment that promotes the flow of electrons between the metal and the environment. When a metallic surface comes in contact with atmospheric oxygen, it undergoes oxidation to form a thin film of oxide, which may be stable, porous, nonporous, unstable, and volatile.

$$2M + O_2 \longrightarrow 2MO$$
$$\text{Metal} \qquad \text{Metal oxide}$$

Mechanism: When the metallic surface comes in contact with atmospheric oxygen, it undergoes an oxidation reaction to form the metallic ion with the loss of e-.

$$M \longrightarrow M^{n+} + 2ne^- \text{ (oxidation)}$$

Whatever electrons are lost are picked up by the atmospheric oxygen to form oxide ions.

$$n\tfrac{1}{2} O_2 + 2\,ne^- \longrightarrow O^{2-} \text{ (Reduction)}$$

Hence, the net reaction.

$$M \rightarrow M^{n+} + 2e^-$$
$$\tfrac{1}{2} O_2 \; 2e^- \rightarrow O^{2-}$$
$$M + \tfrac{1}{2} O_2 \rightarrow M^{n+} + O^{2-} \rightarrow MO$$
Metal oxide

Where; M represents metal.

M^{n+} represents metal ions.

nO^{2-} represents oxide ions

MO represents metal oxides.

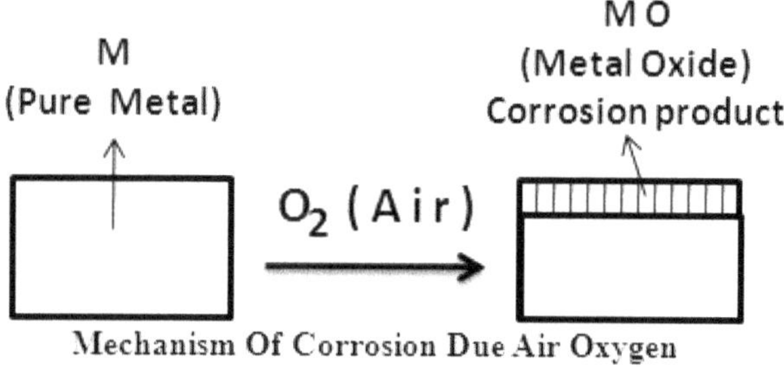

Mechanism Of Corrosion Due Air Oxygen

When oxidation starts, a thin layer of oxide is formed on the metal surface, and depending upon the nature of the metal oxide, corrosion is protective or destructive.

i)   Stable

ii) Unstable

iii) Volatile

iv) Porous.

i)   When a stable layer is formed, it behaves as a protective coating in nature and thus shields the metal surface. Hence, such a film can cut off penetration of attracting oxygen to the underlying metal.

Eg. The oxide layer formed in Al, Sn, Pb, Ca, Pd, etc. is stable & non-porous; consequently, further oxidation corrosion is prevented.

ii) When an unstable oxide layer is formed, the decomposition of metal oxide into metal and oxygen takes place. Hence, the metal does not undergo oxidation corrosion. e.g. Noble metals like Ag, Au, Pt & Pd do not undergo oxidation corrosion.

iii) The oxide layer volatilises as soon as it is formed, thereby leaching the underlying metal surface exposed for further attack. This causes rapid and continuous corrosion leading to excessive corrosion, e.g. Molybdenum oxide is volatile.

$$2Mo + 3O_2 \rightarrow 2MoO_3$$

iv) The oxide layer formed on Fe has pores; in such a case, atmospheric oxygen has access to the underlying surface of the metal, thereby the corrosion continues.

Metal $+ O_2 \rightarrow$ Porous Metal oxide (further attack through pores)

b) Corrosion due to other gases

Some gases like CO_2, Cl_2, H_2S, H_2 cause the corrosion of metal. The degree of attack depends on the formation of protective and non-protective layers on the metal surfaces.

For examples;

Corrosion due to CO_2: Atmospheric CO_2 causes the corrosion of metal in the presence of water. In this case, the formation of carbonates & hydroxide of metal takes place on its surface.

$$Fe + H_2O + CO_2 \rightarrow FeCO_3 + H_2\uparrow$$
$$4\ FeCO_3 + 6\ H_2O + O_2 \rightarrow 4\ Fe(OH)_3 + 4CO_2\uparrow$$

Corrosion due to Cl_2: - When dry chlorine gas is passed over silver metal, a protective film of silver chloride (AgCl) is formed, thus protecting the metal from further corrosion. In some cases, the film formed is porous; therefore, it is non-protective and gets corroded.

$$2Ag + Cl_2 \rightarrow 2AgCl$$

Corrosion due to H_2S: Hydrogen sulphide gas forms a layer of sulphide on the surface of the metal.

$$Fe + H_2S \rightarrow FeS + H_2\uparrow$$

Corrosion due to H_2: In this process, atomic hydrogen is formed by the thermal decomposition of H_2.

$$\text{i.e. } H_2 \rightarrow H + H$$

This atomic hydrogen is very reactive. It diffuses into the metal and combines with the elements which are present in it. When atomic hydrogen comes in contact with a steel sheet, it diffuses into the sheet & reacts with carbon to form methane gas. Due to this, the percentage of carbon in steel decreases, ultimately reducing the strength of the steel & causing brittleness.

2. Electrochemical Corrosion/Immersed/Wet Corrosion:

Electrochemical corrosion, also known as wet corrosion, is the process by which a metal degrades and deteriorates due to its reaction with its environment, particularly in the presence of an electrolyte. This process occurs as a result of electrochemical reactions that take place between two metals or between a metal and its environment.

Electrochemical corrosion is caused by the presence of two dissimilar metals in an electrolyte, which creates a flow of electrical current between them. This current flow leads to the formation of an anode and a cathode. The anode is the metal that corrodes, while the cathode is the metal that does not corrode. The anode is oxidised, and the cathode is reduced.

The rate of corrosion depends on several factors, including the types of metals involved, the properties of the electrolyte, and the conditions of the environment. Corrosion can be accelerated by factors such as temperature, p^H, salinity, and the presence of pollutants.

The anode gives off electrons in the solution, which results in the formation of ions and hence gets corroded. On the other hand, the cathode receives the electrons and forms a protective coating and hence it is not corroded. Thus, corrosion, which is brought about through ionic reactions in the presence of moisture or a solution when two dissimilar metals are in contact with each other, is called electrochemical corrosion. It is also known as immersed corrosion as it occurs in metal when they are immersed or dipped in the same solution.

The anodic area, oxidation reaction i.e. liberation of free electrons takes place, so anodic metal is destroyed by either dissolution or forming a combined state such as oxide, etc. Thus, corrosion occurs at the anodic area.

$$M \rightarrow M^{n+} \text{ (Oxidation)}$$

Whereas, at cathodic areas, reduction reaction i.e. gain of electrons takes place. At the cathodic part, dissolved constituents in the conducting medium gain the electrons to form some ions like OH^-, O^{2-}

The electrochemical corrosion is further classified as
1.   Galvanic cell corrosion
2.   Concentration cell corrosion

1.   Galvanic Cell Corrosion

Galvanic cell corrosion is a type of electrochemical corrosion that occurs when two dissimilar metals come into contact with each other in the presence of an electrolyte, which could be a liquid, gas, or solid. This process is also known as bimetallic corrosion or dissimilar metal corrosion. Galvanic corrosion is driven by a chemical reaction that occurs at the interface of the two metals, resulting in the transfer of electrons from the more active metal (the anode) to the less active metal (the cathode). The transfer of electrons causes the anode to corrode, and the cathode to be protected from corrosion.

To understand how galvanic cell corrosion works, we can look at the basic structure of a galvanic cell. A galvanic cell consists of two electrodes, an anode and a cathode, which are connected by a conductive material called an electrolyte. The anode is the metal that is more active and will corrode in the presence of an electrolyte, while the cathode is the metal that is less active and will be protected from corrosion.

When the two metals are in contact with each other, an electrochemical reaction occurs at the interface between them. This reaction is driven by the potential difference between the two metals, which is caused by the difference in their electronegativities. The more electronegative metal (the anode) loses electrons to the less electronegative metal (the cathode) through the electrolyte, creating a flow of current between the two metals.

The anode corrodes because it loses electrons, which causes it to dissolve in the electrolyte. The cathode, on the other hand, gains electrons, which causes it to become more stable and less likely to corrode. Over time, the anode can become completely consumed, while the cathode remains relatively unaffected.

Galvanic cell consists of two containers: one contains $ZnSO_4$ solution in which a Zn rod is immersed, and the other contains $CuSO_4$ solution in which a copper rod is immersed. The solutions are in contact by a KCl salt bridge, and electrical contact is made by means of a wire (Zn^{++} -0.76V, Cu^{++} +0.34)

The following reaction takes place because the oxidation potential of Zn is lower than that of Cu. Hence, the Zn- rod starts to dissolve in its salt to form Zn^{++} ions due to oxidation reaction and the process of corrosion takes place.

$$Zn \rightarrow Zn^{+2} + 2e^- \text{ Oxidation anodic}$$

Whatever $e^\ominus$ formed is passed through the circuit into the second beaker & is accepted by Cu^{2+} ions present in the solution & forms neutral copper. These atoms are deposited on a copper rod hence it does not undergo the corrosion process.

$$Cu^{2+} + 2e^- \rightarrow Cu^0 \text{ Reduction (cathodic)}$$

Hence net reaction

$$Zn \rightarrow Zn^{2+} + 2e^- \text{ oxidation (anodic)}$$
$$Cu^{2+} + 2e^- \rightarrow Cu^0 \text{ Reduction}$$
$$Zn + Cu^{2+} \rightarrow Zn^{2+} + Cu^0$$

2. Concentration cell corrosion:

Concentration cell corrosion, also known as electrolytic or concentration corrosion, is a type of corrosion that occurs when there are differences in the concentration of electrolytes in two or more areas of a metal surface. This type of corrosion is a form of electrochemical corrosion, in which metal ions are oxidised at one location and reduced at another location, leading to a transfer of electrons and the deterioration of the metal.

In a concentration cell, the differences in the concentration of electrolytes cause an electrochemical potential to develop between the two regions. This electrochemical potential drives the movement of metal ions from the area of higher concentration to the area of lower concentration. The flow of metal ions generates an electrical current, which accelerates the corrosion process.

If a metal (Zn) is partially immersed in a dilute solution of neutral salt (like NaCl) & the solution is not agitated properly, then the parts above and adjacent to the water line are more strongly aerated because of the easy access of oxygen & hence become cathodic. On the other hand, parts immersed to a greater depth, which have less access of oxygen, show a lower oxygen concentration & thus become anodic, so a difference of potential is created. This causes a flow of current between the two differentially aerated areas of the same metal. Zn will dissolve at the anodic areas & oxygen will take up $e^\ominus$ at the cathodic areas to form hydroxyl ions.

$$Zn \rightarrow Zn^{2+} + 2e^- \text{ oxidation}$$
$$\tfrac{1}{2} O_2 + H_2O + 2e^- \rightarrow 2\,OH^- \text{ Reduction.}$$
$$Zn + \tfrac{1}{2} O_2 + H_2O \rightarrow Zn^{2+} + 2\,OH^- \rightarrow Zn(OH)_2 \downarrow \text{(Net Reaction)}$$

The circuit is completed by migration of ions through the electrolyte and flow of electrons through the metal from anode to cathode.

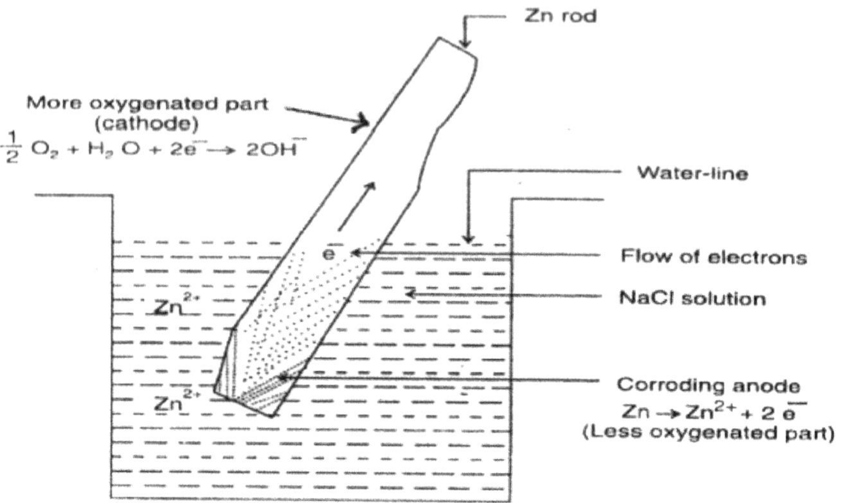

Figure 4.1: *Concentration Cell Corrosion*

4.3 MECHANISM OF ELECTROCHEMICAL CORROSION

Electrochemical corrosion is a process in which a metal undergoes a chemical reaction with its environment, leading to its degradation over time. This process occurs when a metal is exposed to an electrolyte, which is a solution containing ions that can conduct electricity. The metal serves as one electrode of an electrochemical cell, with the electrolyte serving as the other electrode.

Electrochemical corrosion involves the flow of electrons between anode and cathode. The anodic area is where oxidation takes place, and metal atoms lose electrons to the environment and pass into the solution.

$$M \rightarrow M^{n+} + ne^-$$

The cathodic area oxidation takes place where electrons are consumed with either the evolution of hydrogen or absorption of oxygen, which depends on the nature of the corrosive environment.

1. Evolution of hydrogen:

This type of corrosion occurs in an acidic medium and in the absence of oxygen. Considering the metal Fe, the anodic reaction is the dissolution of iron as ferrous ions with the liberation of electrons.

$$\text{At anode: Fe} \rightarrow \text{Fe}^{2+} + 2e^- \text{ (Oxidation)}$$

The electrons released flow through the metal from anode to cathode, whereas H+ ions of the acidic solution are eliminated as hydrogen gas.

$$\text{At cathode: 2H+ + 2}e^- \rightarrow \text{H}_2 \uparrow \text{(Reduction)}$$
$$\text{The overall reaction is Fe + 2H}^+ \rightarrow \text{Fe}^{2+} + \text{H}_2.$$

This type of corrosion causes displacement of hydrogen ions from the solution by metal ions. All metals above hydrogen in the electrochemical series have a tendency to get dissolved in an acidic solution with the simultaneous evolution of H_2 gas. The anodes are large areas, whereas cathodes are small areas.

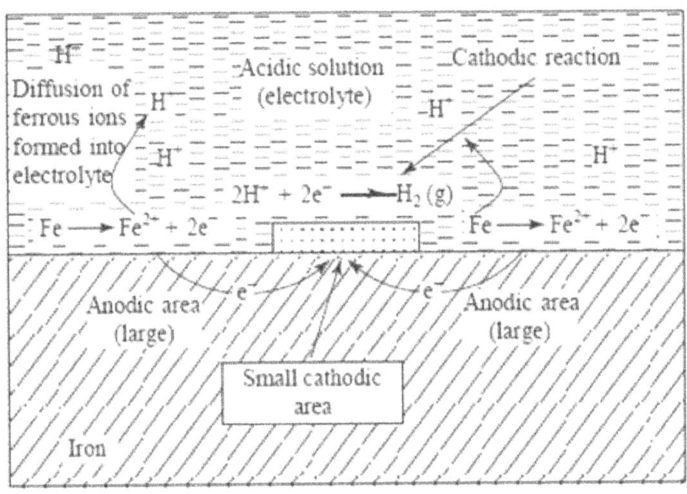

Figure 4.2. Mechanism of Evolution of Hydrogen

2. Absorption of oxygen:

This type of corrosion reaction takes place in the presence of atmospheric oxygen. For example, rusting of iron in a neutral aqueous solution. The surface of iron is usually coated with a thin film of iron oxide. If the film develops cracks, anodic areas are created on the surface, while the metal parts act as cathodes. It shows that anodes are small areas, while the rest of the metallic part forms large cathodes. The released electrons flow from anode to cathode through the iron metal.

At anode: $Fe \rightarrow Fe^{2+} + 2e\text{-}$ (Oxidation)

At the cathode: $\frac{1}{2} O_2 + H_2O + 2e^- \rightarrow 2OH^-$ (Reduction)

Overall reaction is $Fe^{2+} + 2OH^- \rightarrow Fe(OH)_2$.

If oxygen is in excess, ferrous hydroxide is easily oxidised to ferric hydroxide.

$$4Fe(OH)_2 + O_2 + 2H_2O \rightarrow 4Fe(OH)_3 \text{ or } Fe_2O_3.3H_2O \text{ (Rust)}$$

$Fe(OH)$ corresponds to rust, which is hydrated iron (III) oxide of variable composition, $Fe_2O_3.nH_2O$. The degree of hydration of the iron (III) oxide affects the color of the rust, which may vary from black (Fe_2O_4) to yellow or reddish-brown ($Fe_2O_3.H_2O$).

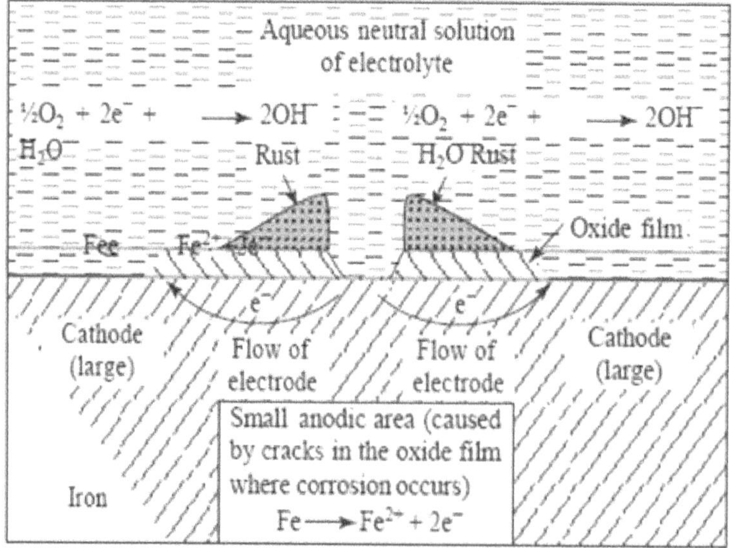

Figure 4.3: *Mechanism of absorption of oxygen*

4.4 IMPORTANT TYPES OF CORROSION

4.4.1 Pitting Corrosion:

Pitting corrosion is a localised form of corrosion that occurs on metal surfaces, resulting in small, irregularly shaped holes or pits. It is caused by a combination of factors such as the presence of a corrosive environment, the chemical composition of the metal, and the presence of impurities or defects in the metal.

Pitting corrosion typically starts with the formation of a small, localised anode on the metal surface. An anode is a region where the metal undergoes oxidation, releasing electrons and forming metal ions. In the case of pitting corrosion, this anode is often associated with a small defect or impurity on the metal surface, such as a scratch, a pit, or a grain boundary. Once the anode is formed, the surrounding metal becomes the cathode, where reduction reactions occur. The electrons released from the anode migrate towards the cathode, resulting in the formation of a local electric current. This current causes the metal ions to dissolve, leaving behind a pit or cavity on the metal surface.

Pitting corrosion can occur in a wide range of metal alloys, including stainless steel, aluminium, copper, and brass. The severity of pitting corrosion can vary depending on the specific alloy and the nature of the corrosive environment. In some cases, pitting corrosion can lead to rapid metal loss and structural failure, while in other cases, it may progress slowly over a long period of time.

Fe metal will dissolve at the anodic areas, and oxygen will take up $e^{\ominus}$ at the cathodic areas to form hydroxyl ions. Thus, the corrosion product $Fe(OH)_2$ forms near the cavity (pits). Hence, corrosion is known as Pitting Corrosion.

$$Fe \rightarrow Fe^{2+} + 2e^{-} \text{ (oxidation)}$$
$$\tfrac{1}{2} O_2 + H_2O + 2e^{-} \rightarrow 2\,OH^{-} \text{ (Reduction)}$$
$$Fe + \tfrac{1}{2} O_2 + H_2O \rightarrow Fe^{2+} + 2\,OH^{-} \rightarrow Fe(OH)_2 \downarrow \text{ (Net Reaction)}$$

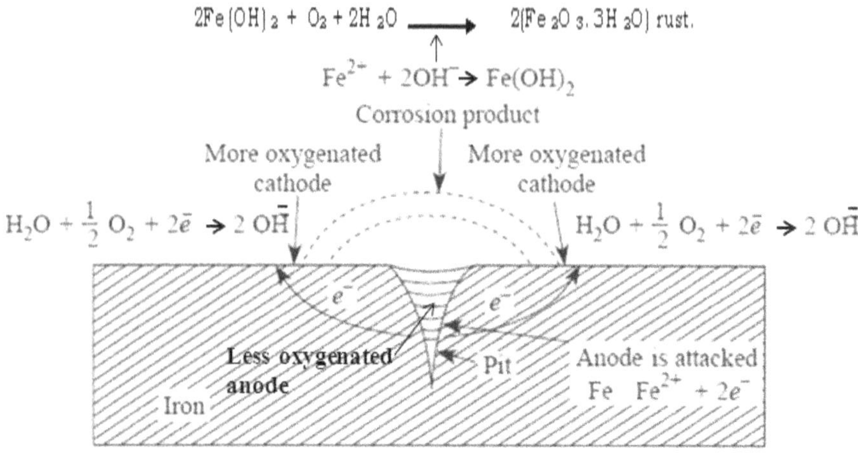

Figure 4.4: *Pitting corrosion*

4.4.2 Waterline corrosion:

Waterline corrosion is a type of corrosion that occurs on metal surfaces in contact with air and water. This type of corrosion is commonly found in marine and coastal environments where metal structures are exposed to a combination of salt water, moisture, and oxygen.

The corrosion process begins when saltwater droplets or moisture in the air come into contact with the metal surface. The salt in the water reacts with the metal surface, causing the formation of metal salts, such as iron oxide or copper chloride. These salts are more brittle and less durable than the original metal, which can cause the metal to weaken and degrade over time.

Waterline corrosion is often seen as a distinctive "tide mark" on the metal surface, where the corrosion is more concentrated at the waterline due to the continuous exposure to moisture and air. The extent and severity of waterline corrosion depend on various factors such as the type of metal, the level of salinity in the water, the amount of dissolved oxygen, and the temperature and humidity of the environment.

When water is stored in a steel tank, it is generally found that the maximum amount of corrosion takes place just beneath the level of the water meniscus. The area above the waterline, highly oxygenated, acts as the cathode and is completely unaffected by corrosion. However, the area below the waterline is less oxygenated and gets corroded.

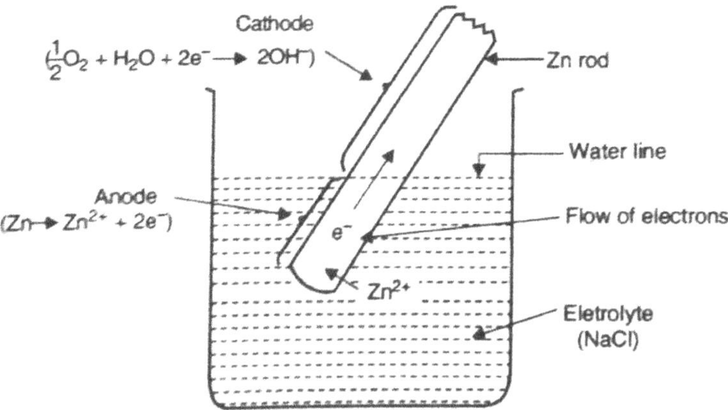

Figure 4.5: *Waterline corrosion*

Fe metal will dissolve at the anodic areas & oxygen will take up $e^\ominus$ at the cathodic areas to form hydroxyl ions. Thus, the corrosion product Fe(OH)2 forms below the waterline. Hence, corrosion is known as waterline corrosion.

$$Fe \rightarrow Fe^{2+} + 2e^- \text{ oxidation}$$
$$\frac{1}{2} O_2 + H_2O + 2e^- \rightarrow 2\ OH^- \text{ Reduction}$$
$$Fe + \frac{1}{2} O_2 + H_2O \rightarrow Fe^{2+} + 2\ OH^- \rightarrow Fe(OH)_2 \downarrow \text{(Net Reaction)}$$

To prevent waterline corrosion, various corrosion protection measures can be employed such as regular cleaning and maintenance, coatings and paints that create a barrier between the metal surface and the environment, cathodic protection which uses an electrical current to protect the metal surface, or the use of more corrosion-resistant metals or alloys. The most commonly affected metals by waterline corrosion are steel, aluminium, and copper alloys, which are widely used in marine applications such as ship hulls, piers, offshore oil rigs, and other coastal structures. Corrosion of these metal surfaces can lead to significant structural damage, reduction of strength, and even catastrophic failure in extreme cases.

4.4.3   Intergranular Corrosion:

Intergranular corrosion (IGC) is a type of corrosion that occurs at the grain boundaries of metals and alloys. It is a localised form of corrosion that can result in the failure of metal components, particularly in applications where the metal is exposed to a corrosive environment.

In metals and alloys, the grain boundaries are the regions where the crystals of the metal meet. These regions can be more susceptible to corrosion than the bulk of the metal due to several factors, including changes in chemical composition, micro-structure, and the presence of impurities.

IGC occurs when the grain boundaries of a metal are preferentially corroded compared to the bulk of the metal. This can result in the formation of deep pits or cracks along the grain boundaries, which can weaken the metal and ultimately lead to failure.

The susceptibility of a metal to IGC depends on several factors, including the composition of the metal, the type of corrosive environment, and the temperature of the metal. In general, metals and alloys that contain a high concentration of certain elements, such as carbon, phosphorus, or sulphur, are more susceptible to IGC. Similarly, certain environments, such as acidic or alkaline solutions, can increase the likelihood of IGC.

Preventing IGC requires careful selection of materials and design considerations, as well as proper maintenance and monitoring of metal components. This may involve using corrosion-resistant alloys, applying protective coatings or inhibitors, controlling the pH of the environment, or adjusting the temperature of the metal to reduce the risk of corrosion. In some cases, it may also be necessary to inspect metal components regularly for signs of corrosion and to repair or replace damaged parts as needed.

For example, in stainless steel (an alloy of Fe, C, and Cr), chromium carbide precipitate is formed at the grain boundaries during welding. Thus, the composition of Cr is less in the region adjacent to grain boundaries, but the grain centre and grain boundaries are richer in Cr. Hence, the region just adjacent to grain boundaries is more anodic and corroded.

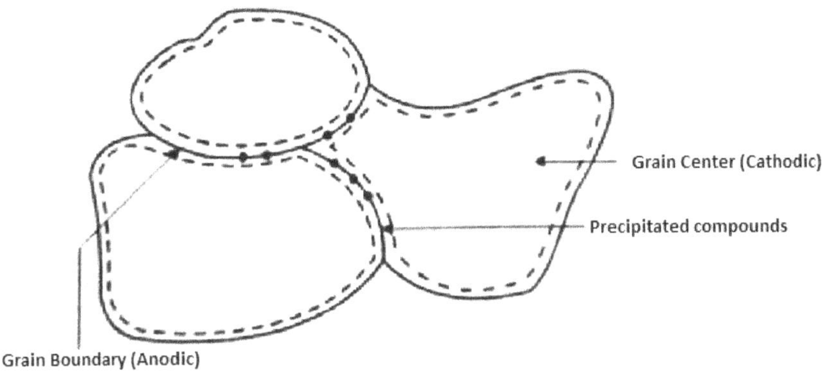

Figure 4.6: *Intergranular corrosion*

4.4.4 Stress Corrosion:

Stress corrosion is a phenomenon where a material experiences significant degradation when subjected to both tensile stress and a corrosive environment. The degradation occurs in the form of cracking, pitting, or other forms of damage and can eventually lead to failure of the material. Stress corrosion typically occurs in metals and alloys, although it can also occur in ceramics and polymers. The type of corrosion that occurs in stress corrosion is different from typical corrosion because it is influenced by both the stress and the corrosion environment.

The corrosion environment typically includes a corrosive substance, such as water, acid, or a salt solution. The presence of this substance can weaken the material and increase its susceptibility to cracking or other forms of damage. In addition, the stress on the material can be introduced in several ways, including mechanical loading, thermal cycling, or residual stress from manufacturing processes.

The combination of these factors leads to a unique type of corrosion, where the material degrades more quickly than it would in a corrosive environment without stress. This is because the stress can accelerate the initiation and propagation of cracks, and the cracks can then provide sites for the corrosive substance to attack the material.

Stress corrosion can occur in a wide range of applications, including pipelines, pressure vessels, aircraft components, and structural materials.

It is important to take steps to prevent stress corrosion, as it can lead to catastrophic failures and significant safety risks.

Preventive measures include selecting materials that are resistant to stress corrosion, designing structures with low stress concentrations, controlling the environment to minimise the presence of corrosive substances, and monitoring for signs of corrosion and cracking. Additionally, proper maintenance and inspection can help identify and address stress corrosion before it leads to failure.

4.5   CORROSION CONTROL

Corrosion is a natural process that occurs when metals are exposed to the environment. It is the gradual deterioration of metal by chemical or electrochemical reactions with its surroundings. Corrosion can lead to a significant decrease in the strength and integrity of metal structures, and it can cause serious safety and economic problems. Therefore, corrosion control is essential to prevent or mitigate the effects of corrosion.

Corrosion control involves several techniques that can be applied to prevent or mitigate corrosion. The most commonly used techniques are discussed below:

- **Protective Coatings:** One of the most effective ways to control corrosion is to apply a protective coating on the metal surface. The coating acts as a barrier between the metal and the environment, preventing the metal from coming into contact with corrosive agents. Coatings can be made from a variety of materials, including paints, epoxies, and polyurethanes. The type of coating used depends on the type of metal, the environment, and the level of protection required.

- **Cathodic Protection:** This technique involves making the metal to be protected the cathode in a corrosion cell, which effectively stops corrosion from occurring. Cathodic protection can be achieved by two methods: sacrificial anode cathodic protection and impressed current cathodic protection. In sacrificial anode cathodic protection, a more active metal is attached to the metal to be protected, and it corrodes preferentially, sacrificing itself to protect the main metal. In impressed current cathodic protection, an external power supply is used to provide a current that forces the metal to be protected to become the cathode.

- **Design Modification:** Corrosion control can also be achieved by modifying the design of the metal structure to make it less susceptible to corrosion. This can include the use of corrosion-resistant alloys, designing for easy access and maintenance, and providing adequate drainage.

- **Corrosion Inhibitors:** These are chemicals that are added to the environment to prevent or slow down the corrosion process. Inhibitors work by forming a protective film on the metal surface or by changing the environment's chemistry to make it less corrosive. Inhibitors can be added to water or oil systems, fuel tanks, or cooling systems.

- **Environmental Modification:** Corrosion control can be achieved by modifying the environment in which the metal is located. This can include controlling the pH, temperature, and humidity of the environment, and removing or reducing the amount of corrosive agents present.

Corrosion control is a crucial aspect of maintaining the integrity and safety of metal structures. The choice of corrosion control method depends on the type of metal, the environment, and the level of protection required. Protective coatings, cathodic protection, design modification, corrosion inhibitors, and environmental modification are all effective techniques that can be used to prevent or mitigate the effects of corrosion.

4.6 MATERIAL SELECTION AND PROPER DESIGN

Corrosion is a common problem that affects the integrity and durability of materials, particularly in industrial environments where exposure to corrosive agents is common. To prevent corrosion, it is important to select the right materials and design structures that can withstand the effects of corrosion. Selection of the right type of material is one of the main factors for corrosion control. Cost, structure, chemical & physical properties of the metal are the factors important for material selection. Noble metals have almost nil corrosion, but they cannot be selected for general & economical purposes because of high cost. The next choice is to use the purest possible metal; even minute amounts of some impurities may lead to corrosion.

1. Material Selection:

The process of selecting materials for corrosion control involves a thorough understanding of the operating environment, including the type and concentration of corrosive agents, temperature, humidity, and other factors that can impact material performance. The following factors should be considered when selecting materials for corrosion control:

i.   Corrosion resistance: The material's resistance to corrosion is the primary factor to consider when selecting materials for corrosion control. Materials that are naturally resistant to corrosion, such as stainless steel, aluminium, or plastics, are often preferred.

ii. Strength and durability: The material's strength and durability are important to ensure that it can withstand the stresses of the operating environment.

iii. Cost: The cost of the material is an important consideration, particularly for large structures or projects. Choosing cost-effective materials that meet the performance requirements is often preferred.

iv. Availability: The availability of the material, particularly in the required quantity and size, is an important factor to consider when selecting materials.

v.   Maintenance requirements: The maintenance requirements of the material, including cleaning and surface treatment, should be considered when selecting materials.

2. Protection by Proper Design:

To protect against corrosion, proper design of the equipment plays a significant role. Some of the factors that should be considered for proper design are:

- The contact between different metals and alloys should not be made, especially if they are far apart in the galvanic series. Where it cannot be avoided, an efficient electrical insulator should be used. If this is not followed, then the more active metal gets corroded, causing local corrosion.

- The rate of corrosion also depends on the relative sizes of the anode and cathode. As far as possible, if two dissimilar metals are in contact, the combination of a small anode and a large cathode should be avoided.

- If two dissimilar metals are to be used in the same article, they should be selected so that they are as near as possible in the galvanic series (minimum potential difference).

- The equipment, which has localised stresses, sharp bends, and lap joints, because these parts become more anodic and corrode.

- Each metal has a minimum corrosion rate at a specific pH. Therefore, corrosion can be controlled by suitably adjusting the acidity or alkalinity of the environment.

- The presence of crevices between adjacent parts of the structure, even in the case of the same metal, should be avoided. The welded butt joints of the same metal/alloy should be used instead of riveted or bolted joints; otherwise, crevice corrosion may result. Tanks & pipelines should be free from crevices. They should not have loosely or badly riveted seams.

- Sharp corners and recesses should be avoided because dust or solid particles may accumulate, leading to corrosion due to different aeration.

- The equipment should be supported with stands to allow air circulation. Dirt should not be accumulating in the corner of the base.

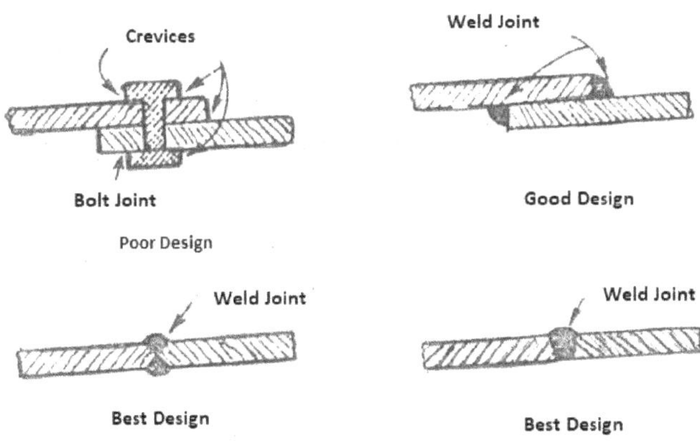

Figure 4.7: Lap joint with Rivet

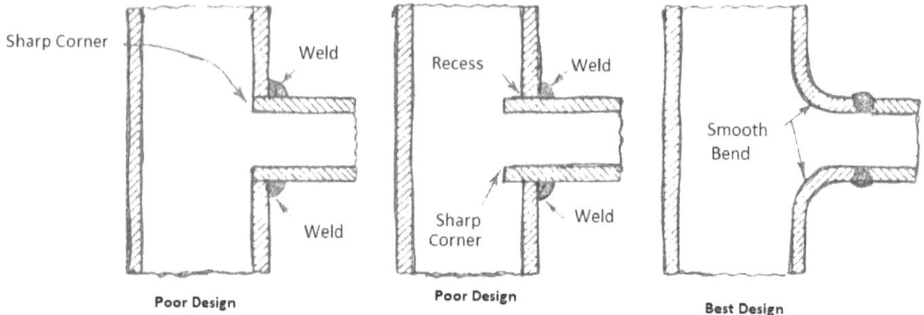

Figure 4.8: *Prevention of corrosion by design*

4.7   CATHODIC PROTECTION OF METAL

Cathodic protection is a technique used to protect metals from corrosion by making them the cathode of an electrochemical cell. It works by providing an electrical current to the metal, which reduces the potential difference between the metal and its environment, preventing the electrochemical reactions that cause corrosion.

The principle involved in cathodic protection is to force the metal (to be protected) to behave like a cathode, thereby preventing corrosion.

Cathodic protection can be achieved by 1. Connecting a metal (to be protected) to a more anodic (active and high-sop) metal, i.e. by sacrificial protection method, and 2. By applying impressed current to convert corroding metal from anode to cathode, i.e. by impressed current protection method.

1.   Sacrificial Anode Cathodic Protection:

In this type of cathodic protection, a more reactive metal is attached to the metal to be protected. This more reactive metal acts as the anode, sacrificing itself to protect the protected metal from corrosion. The anode is typically made of a metal that has a more negative potential than the protected metal, such as zinc, magnesium, or aluminium. The anode corrodes in place of the protected metal and is periodically replaced to ensure continued protection.

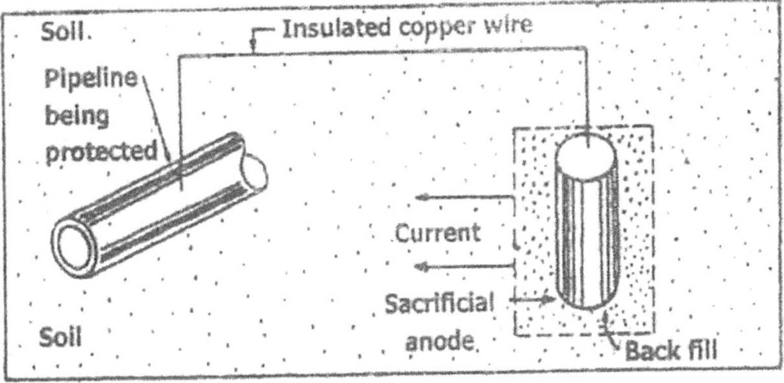

Figure 4.9: *Sacrificial Anode Cathodic Protection*

Uses:

1. Protection from soil corrosion of underground cables, buried iron pipelines, etc., by connecting to Mg block.
2. Protection from marine corrosion, like marine structures, ship hulls, water tanks, and boilers, by connecting to Zn plates.

2. Impressed Current Cathodic Protection:

In this type of cathodic protection, an external power source is used to provide a direct current to the metal to be protected. This direct current creates a cathodic polarisation that reduces the potential difference between the metal and its environment, thereby reducing the rate of corrosion. The power source is typically a rectifier that converts alternating current (AC) from the power grid to direct current (DC) suitable for cathodic protection. The anode material can be graphite, titanium, or high silicon iron.

The effectiveness of cathodic protection depends on several factors, including the type of metal being protected, the environment in which it is located, and the type of cathodic protection being used. The potential difference between the metal and its environment must be reduced below the corrosion potential for corrosion to be prevented. The level of current required for cathodic protection depends on the size and shape of the metal object and the resistivity of the surrounding environment.

Cathodic protection is commonly used to protect metal structures in harsh environments, such as pipelines, storage tanks, offshore platforms, and ship hulls. It is also used to protect historic structures and artefacts made of metal, as well as to extend the life of bridges, piers, and other infrastructure made of steel or reinforced concrete. The cost of cathodic protection varies depending on the size and complexity of the structure, as well as the type of cathodic protection used. However, it is generally considered to be a cost-effective method of preventing corrosion and extending the life of metal structures.

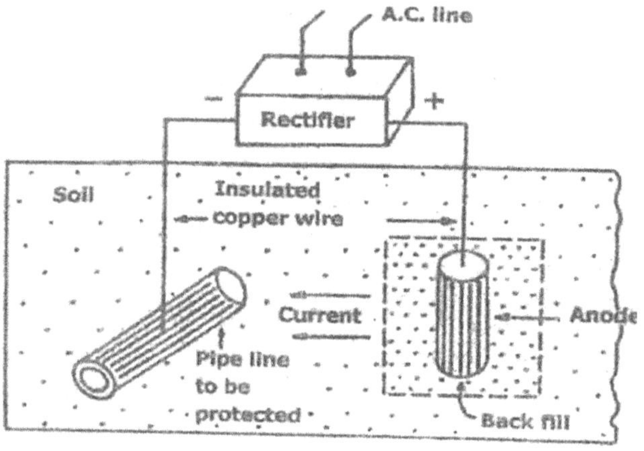

Figure 4.10: *Impressed Current Cathodic Protection*

Uses:

1. The method can be applied for the protection of open water box coolers, water tanks, buried oil or water pipelines, condensers, transmission lines, towers, etc.
2. It is used for large structures and long-term operation.

4.8 HOT-DIPPING

This is a significant method for corrosion control. In this process, the metal to be coated is submerged in a molten bath of the coating metal. The base metal must have a high melting point, while the coating metal should have a low melting point. This technique is commonly used to apply coatings of metals and alloys with low melting points, such as zinc (Zn), antimony (Sb), and lead (Pb).

4.8.1   Galvanising Process:

The process of coating of zinc over iron or steel articles to prevent them from corrosion is called galvanising. Galvanising or hot-dipping zinc coating protects steel products where they are to be exposed to the atmosphere or soil. Materials which are galvanised are sheets, pipes, wire, strips, etc. In this process, the iron or steel sheet is first cleaned with 7 to 8% dilute H_2SO_4 at 60-90°C for 15-20 minutes. This process is known as pickling. This process not only cleans articles but also helps in removing any rust or impurities if present on it. Then it is washed with water in a water bath and dried by passing through a drying chamber. It is then dipped in a bath of molten zinc, maintained at a temperature of 425-460°C. The surface of the bath is covered with flux of ammonium chloride to prevent the oxidation of zinc. The article coated with a zinc layer is then taken out of the bath and passed through hot rollers which remove excess zinc. This results in only a thin layer of zinc on the article. Finally, it is annealed at a temperature of 650°C and then slowly cooled. It is shown in the figure 4.11.

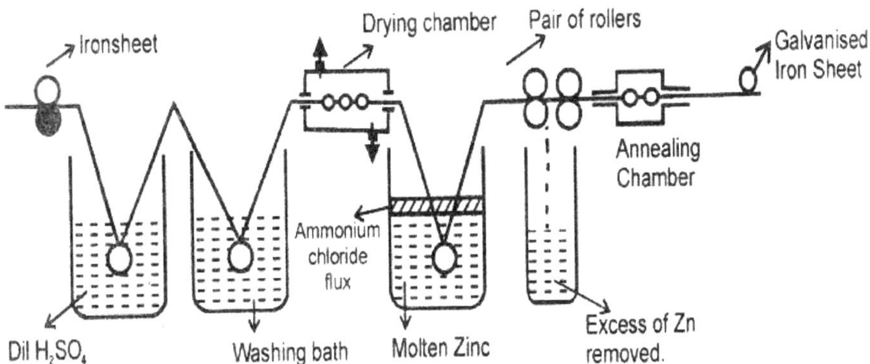

Figure 4.11: *Galvanising Process*

Applications:

- **Construction:** Used for steel beams, columns, and other structural components to prevent rust and extend the lifespan of buildings and bridges.
- **Automotive Industry:** Protects car bodies and frames from corrosion, enhancing durability and safety.
- **Agriculture:** Galvanised steel is used in fencing, gates, and farm equipment to resist weathering and wear.
- **Utility Infrastructure:** Employed in the production of utility poles, streetlights, and guardrails to ensure long-term durability and safety.
- **Household Appliances:** Coat washing machines, refrigerators, and air conditioners to prevent rust and improve longevity.

4.8.2 Tinning Process:

The process of coating tin on iron or steel articles to prevent them from corrosion is called tinning. Tinning is very similar to galvanising.

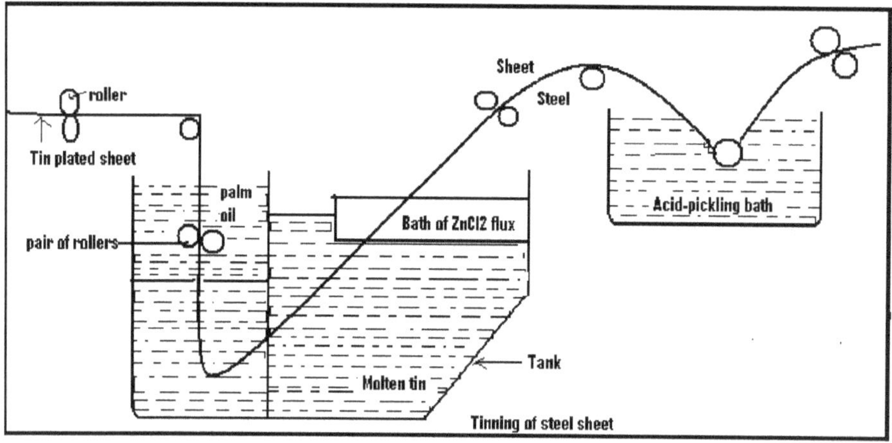

Figure 4.12: Tinning process.

In the tinning process, the iron or steel sheet is first cleaned with a solution of dilute H_2SO_4 (4-8%) at about 70-80°C for 3 to 5 minutes to remove unwanted materials present on the metal surface. This process is known as pickling. The tinning vessel has two compartments separated by a partition below the surface of the molten tin. A molten layer of zinc chloride flux floats over the molten tin in the first compartment, while a palm oil bath floats on the molten tin in the second compartment. After this, the sheet is passed through a bath of zinc chloride solution, which helps the molten metal adhere to the metal sheet. The sheet is then passed through a tank of molten tin and through a series of hot rollers immersed in a palm oil bath. The palm oil protects the tin coating surface from oxidation. The rollers remove any excess tin and produce a thin film of uniform thickness on the iron or steel sheet.

Applications:
- **Food Packaging:** Used in tin-plated cans to prevent corrosion and contamination.
- **Electronics:** Enhances solderability of wires and circuit board contacts, ensuring reliable electrical connections.
- **Plumbing:** Tinned copper pipes and fittings prevent corrosion and enhance durability.
- **Automotive Industry:** Protects components like fasteners and connectors from rust and ensures conductivity.
- **Household Items:** Coats, cooking utensils, and bakeware to prevent rust and provide a safe, non-reactive surface.

IMPORTANT QUESTIONS:
1. What is dry corrosion? Explain the mechanism of oxidation corrosion and the nature of oxide films.
2. Explain the following: i) Pitting corrosion, ii) Intergranular corrosion.
3. Explain the following: i) Water-line corrosion. ii) Stress corrosion.
4. Discuss the wet corrosion mechanism by H_2 evolution and O_2 absorption.
5. Explain Intergranular and Stress corrosion.
6. What is galvanic corrosion? How to prevent it?
7. What is corrosion? Discuss different types of corrosion.
8. Describes chemical and electrochemical corrosion.
9. Explain the mechanism of wet corrosion.

10. What is electrochemical corrosion? Discuss the mechanism of electrochemical corrosion involving the absorption of oxygen.
11. Explain the mechanism of wet corrosion in the presence of dissolved oxygen in a neutral or alkaline medium.
12. Describe the design and material selection parameters for corrosion control.
13. What is cathodic protection? Explain the impressed current method.
14. Discuss the process of tinning. Give points of comparison with galvanising.
15. How will you control corrosion by proper material selection and design?
16. Explain the galvanizing and tinning processes for corrosion control.
17. Explain how corrosion can be controlled by applying various principles of design and material selection.
18. Discuss the Tinning process used for corrosion control.

CHAPTER 5

E-Waste, Recycling and Green Computing

5.1 METAL EXTRACTION FROM E-WASTES

During the last two decades, technological advancement has rapidly happened, causing obsolete and end-of-life electronic devices to become electronic waste (e-waste). For instance, the lifespan of a computer has reduced from 4-6 years in 1992 to 2-3 years in 2015.

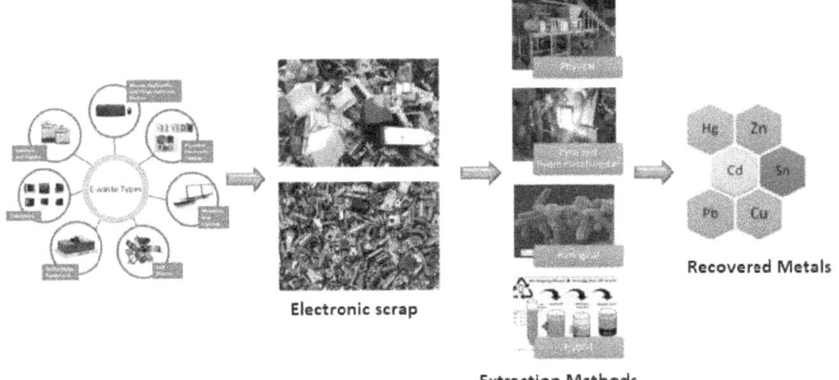

Figure 5.1: *Metal extraction process*

In 2016, global e-waste generation reached approximately 44.7 million tons, equivalent to 6.1 kg per inhabitant, with an annual increase rate of 3%-5%. E-waste not only poses a problem in terms of quantity but also contains up to 1000 toxic substances, including toxic metals and metalloids like arsenic, barium, beryllium, cadmium, cobalt, chromium, copper, iron, lead, mercury, nickel, and zinc. Without appropriate management procedures, these toxicants can cause significant environmental and health issues. Disposal methods such as landfilling and incineration quicken the release of toxic substances, particularly in older landfills lacking proper liners or barriers.

Despite being categorised as hazardous waste, e-waste holds significant potential for value recovery. It contains valuable materials such as iron, copper, aluminium, plastics, and precious metals like gold, silver, platinum, and palladium, making e-waste a feasible urban mine. For instance, 11% of the global gold production (2,770 tons) came from mines in 2013, while about 300 tons of gold were recovered from e-waste in 2014 (USGS, 2014). E-waste is typically recycled through both formal and informal procedures. However, the contamination hazards of e-waste to the environment including soil, sediment, water, and air have become serious issues in many countries, such as China. This chapter explores the constraints and opportunities associated with hazardous substances in e-waste and various e-waste treatment strategies.

Constraints

1) **Complexity of E-waste Composition:** E-waste consists of a variety of materials, including plastics, metals, and ceramics, making the extraction process complex. Different electronic devices contain varying amounts and types of metals, requiring tailored extraction processes.

2) **Technological Limitations:** Current extraction technologies may not be efficient or cost-effective for recovering metals from e-waste. Many technologies also struggle to achieve high-purity levels, which are necessary for the recycled metals to be reused in high-quality applications.

3) **Economic Viability:** The cost of extracting metals from e-waste can be high, particularly when compared to traditional mining methods. Market prices for recovered metals can fluctuate, impacting the economic feasibility of recycling operations.

4) **Environmental and Health Risks:** Improper recycling methods can lead to the release of hazardous substances, posing environmental and health risks. Informal recycling sectors, particularly in developing countries, often lack the necessary infrastructure and regulations to safely manage e-waste.

Opportunities

1) **Resource Recovery:** E-waste contains valuable metals such as gold, silver, platinum, and rare earth elements, presenting a significant resource recovery opportunity. Efficient extraction methods can reduce the need for mining raw materials, conserving natural resources and reducing environmental impacts.

2) **Technological Advances:** Innovations in extraction technologies, such as bioleaching and hydrometallurgical processes, offer more efficient and environmentally friendly methods for recovering metals from e-waste. Advancements in automation and robotics can improve the precision and safety of the recycling process.

3) **Economic Benefits:** Establishing a strong e-waste recycling industry can create jobs and stimulate economic growth. Recycled metals can be sold at a profit, providing a revenue stream for recycling companies.

4) **Regulatory Support and Public Awareness:** Strong regulatory frameworks and incentives can promote proper e-waste management and recycling practices. Increased public awareness about the importance of recycling e-waste can drive consumer participation and support for recycling programmes.

5.2   CHEMICAL EXPOSURE AND CONTAMINATION

Chemicals: Each semiconductor used in computer chips and electronics devices includes hundreds (no kidding) of hazardous chemicals, which can contribute to a variety of physical problems in children and adults.

- **Lead (Pb):** Cathode-ray tube (CRT) monitors contain lead and other hazardous metals. The glass of the screens, when broken, releases a dust that is harmful as well. Lead in the environment can cause respiratory problems and cognitive development issues.
  - **Sources:** Found in solder, batteries, and CRT monitors.
  - **Health Risks:** Lead exposure can cause neurological damage, particularly in children, and lead to cognitive and developmental issues.
  - **Environmental Impact:** Lead can contaminate soil and water, posing risks to wildlife and ecosystems.
- **Mercury (Hg):** Liquid-crystal display (LCD) monitors contain mercury (also used in cellphones, MP3 players, and television sets), which can damage the brain, nervous system, reproductive system, kidneys, and lungs.
  - **Sources:** Present in LCD screens, switches, and some types of batteries.
  - **Health Risks:** Mercury exposure can affect the nervous system, digestive system, and immune system, and is particularly harmful to pregnant women and young children.
  - **Environmental Impact:** Mercury can bioaccumulate in the food chain, particularly in aquatic ecosystems, leading to long-term ecological damage.
- **Cadmium (Cd):** It is released as a powder while crushing and milling plastics, CRTs, and circuit boards.
  - **Sources:** Used in batteries, pigments, coatings, and as a stabiliser in plastics.
  - **Health Risks:** Cadmium exposure can lead to kidney damage, bone deterioration, and is classified as a human carcinogen.
  - **Environmental Impact:** Cadmium can persist in the environment, contaminating soil and water, and entering the food chain.

- **Chromium (Cr):** Used to protect metal housings and plates in a computer from corrosion.
  - **Sources:** Found in metal plating, corrosion protection, and pigments.
  - **Health Risks:** Hexavalent chromium (Cr VI) is highly toxic and can cause lung cancer, respiratory issues, and skin irritation.
  - **Environmental Impact:** Chromium can contaminate water sources, leading to toxic effects on aquatic life and potentially affecting human water supplies.

Strategies to Mitigate Chemical Exposure and Contamination

Improved Recycling Practices: Employing advanced technologies to safely divide and process e-waste can reduce the release of hazardous substances. Implementing best practices for handling and storing e-waste helps prevent environmental contamination.

Research and Development:

Investing in research to develop safer and more efficient methods for metal extraction from e-waste. Exploring alternatives to hazardous materials in electronics manufacturing to reduce the presence of toxic substances in e-waste.

5.3   GREEN CHEMISTRY

The limitations of a command-and-control system for the environment have become more obvious even as the system has become more successful. In industrialised societies with good, well-enforced regulations, most of the easy and inexpensive measures that can be taken to reduce environmental pollution and exposure to harmful chemicals have been implemented. Therefore, small increases in environmental protection now require relatively large investments in money and effort. Is there a better way? There is, indeed. The better way is through the practice of green chemistry.

"Green chemistry can be defined as the practice of chemical science and manufacturing in a manner that is sustainable, safe, and non-polluting and that consumes minimum amounts of materials and energy while producing little or no waste material."

The practice of green chemistry begins with recognition that the production, processing, use, and eventual disposal of chemical products may cause harm when performed incorrectly. In accomplishing its objectives, green chemistry and green chemical engineering may modify or totally redesign chemical products and processes with the objective of minimising wastes and the use or generation of particularly dangerous materials. Those who practice green chemistry recognise that they are responsible for any effects on the world that their chemicals or chemical processes may have. Green chemistry is about increasing profits and promoting innovation while protecting human health and the environment. To a degree, we are still finding out what green chemistry is. That is because it is a rapidly evolving and developing sub-discipline in the field of chemistry. And it is a very exciting time for those who are practitioners of this developing science. Basically, green chemistry harnesses a vast body of chemical knowledge and applies it to the production, use, and ultimate disposal of chemicals in a way that minimises consumption of materials, exposure of living organisms, including humans, to toxic substances, and damage to the environment. And it does so in a manner that is economically feasible and cost-effective.

In one sense, green chemistry is the most efficient possible practice of chemistry and the least costly when all of the costs of the practice of chemistry, including hazards and potential environmental damage, are taken into account. Green chemistry is sustainable chemistry.

Green Chemistry is an innovative approach that aims to design chemical products and processes that reduce or eliminate the use and generation of hazardous substances. It is a proactive philosophy that seeks to prevent pollution at its source rather than dealing with its consequences. For engineering students, understanding the principles and applications of green chemistry is crucial for developing sustainable technologies and processes. The principle of green chemistry covers such concepts as:

1) The strategy processes to maximise the amount of raw material that ends up in the final product.

2) Using safe, environmentally benign substances, including solvents, whenever possible.

3) Designing energy-efficient processes.

4) Implementing the best form of waste disposal: preventing waste creation in the first place.

5.4 TWELVE PRINCIPLES OF GREEN CHEMISTRY

The principles of Green Chemistry are a significant beginning for the chemical profession in dealing with this novel concept for the betterment of the environment. The twelve principles of Green Chemistry proposed by Paul Anastas and John Warner encompass all aspects on the product and the production level from prevention to the design of more efficient synthesis, from the design of less hazardous substances to the use of renewable feedstocks.

1. It is better to prevent waste than to treat or clean up waste after it is formed.

2. Synthetic methods should be designed to maximise the incorporation of all materials used in the process into the final product.

3. Whenever practicable, synthetic methodologies should be designed to focus and generate substances that possess little or no toxicity to human health and the environment.

4. Chemical products should be designed to preserve efficiency of function while reducing toxicity.

5. The use of auxiliary substances (solvents, separation agents, etc.) should be made unnecessary whenever possible, and when used, it is harmless.

6. Energy requirements should be recognised for their environmental and economic impacts and should be minimised. Synthetic methods should be conducted at ambient temperature and pressure.

7. A raw material or feedstock should be renewable rather than depleting whenever technically and economically practicable.

8. Unnecessary assumption (blocking deprotection, temporary group protection, modification of physical/chemical processes) should be avoided whenever possible.

9. Catalytic reagents (as selective as possible) are superior to stoichiometric reagents.

10. Chemical products should be designed so that at the end of their function, they do not persist in the environment and instead break down into harmless degradation products.

11. Analytical methodologies need to be further developed to allow for real-time in-process monitoring and control prior to the formation of hazardous substances.

12. Substances and the form of a substance used in a chemical process should be chosen so as to minimise the potential for chemical accidents, including releases, explosions, and fires.

5.5   GREEN COMPUTING

Green computing is the practice of using computing resources efficiently. [The goals are to reduce the use of hazardous materials, maximise energy efficiency during the product's lifetime, and promote recyclability or biodegradability of expired products and factory waste.] Such practices include the implementation of energy-efficient central processing units (CPUs), servers and peripherals as well as reduced resource consumption and proper disposal of electronic waste (e-waste). In 1992, the U.S. Environmental Protection Agency launched Energy Star, a voluntary labelling programme which is designed to promote and recognise energy efficiency in monitors, climate control equipment, and other technologies. This resulted in the widespread adoption of sleep mode among consumer electronics. The term "green computing" was probably coined shortly after the Energy Star programme began; there are several USENET posts dating back to 1992 which use the term in this manner.

Green computing is the study and practice of using computing resources efficiently. The primary objective of such a programme is to account for an expanded spectrum of values and criteria for measuring organisational (and societal) success. Modern IT systems rely upon a complicated mix of people, networks, and hardware; as such, a green computing initiative must be systemic in nature and address increasingly sophisticated problems. Elements of such a solution may comprise items such as end-user satisfaction, management restructuring, regulatory compliance, disposal of electronic waste, and telecommuting.

5.6 ROLE OF GREEN COMPUTING IN ENVIRONMENT AND RESEARCH

Green Computing refers to the practice of designing, manufacturing, using, and disposing of computers, servers, and associated subsystems efficiently and effectively with minimal or no impact on the environment. It encompasses a broad range of practices that aim to improve the energy efficiency and environmental sustainability of IT operations.

Role in the Environment

1) **Reducing Energy Consumption:** Green computing aims to reduce the energy consumption of computers and data centres, which in turn decreases the carbon footprint associated with power generation. This includes the use of energy-efficient components, power management techniques, and virtualisation to optimise server usage.

   Example: Implementation of energy-efficient processors and power supplies in servers.

2) **Minimising Electronic Waste:** By promoting the recycling and proper disposal of electronic devices, green computing helps in reducing e-waste. It also encourages the use of recyclable materials and the design of devices for longer lifespans and easier disassembly.

   Example: E-waste recycling programmes and take-back initiatives by companies like Apple and Dell.

3) **Utilising Renewable Energy:** Integrating renewable energy sources, such as solar or wind power, into data centres and IT operations reduces dependence on fossil fuels and lowers greenhouse gas emissions.

   Example: Google's data centres running on 100% renewable energy.

4) **Reducing Harmful Emissions:** Green computing reduces the emissions of harmful substances such as carbon dioxide (CO_2), sulphur dioxide (SO_2), and nitrogen oxides (NOx) by optimising energy use and implementing cleaner energy sources.

   Example: Adoption of low-power and energy-efficient devices across organisations.

5) **Promoting Sustainable Practices:** Encouraging sustainable practices in manufacturing, usage, and disposal of IT products helps in conserving resources and reducing environmental pollution.

   Example: Designing products with eco-friendly materials and ensuring compliance with environmental standards such as RoHS (Restriction of Hazardous Substances).

Role in Research

1) **Innovation in Energy Efficiency:** Green computing drives research into new technologies and methodologies to improve the energy efficiency of hardware and software. This includes the development of low-power processors, energy-efficient algorithms, and innovative cooling techniques for data centres.

   Example: Research on energy-efficient multi-core processors and dynamic power management techniques.

2) **Advancement in Virtualisation and Cloud Computing:** Research in green computing has led to significant advancements in virtualisation and cloud computing, which allow for more efficient utilisation of computing resources and reduced energy consumption.

   Example: Development of hypervisor technologies like VMware vSphere and Microsoft Hyper-V.

3) **Data Centre Optimisation:** Research in green computing focuses on optimising data centre operations through better design, advanced

cooling methods, and intelligent resource management to reduce energy consumption and environmental impact.

Example: Implementation of advanced cooling solutions like liquid cooling and free cooling in data centres.

4) **Sustainable Software Development:** Green computing encourages the development of software that is optimised for energy efficiency, which can significantly reduce the power consumption of applications and systems.

   Example: Algorithms designed to minimise computational complexity and energy usage.

5) **Interdisciplinary Research:** Green computing fosters interdisciplinary research combining computer science, electrical engineering, environmental science, and economics to create comprehensive solutions for sustainable IT practices.

   Example: Collaborative research projects between universities and industry to develop eco-friendly computing technologies.

6) **Environmental Impact Assessment:** Research in green computing includes assessing the environmental impact of IT products and services throughout their lifecycle, from production to disposal, to identify areas for improvement.

   Example: Life cycle assessment (LCA) studies on the environmental impact of data centres and electronic devices.

5.7 GREEN DEVICES

Green Devices refer to electronic devices that are designed, manufactured, and operated with a focus on reducing their environmental impact. This includes minimising energy consumption, using eco-friendly materials, and ensuring that the devices are recyclable or biodegradable at the end of their life cycle.

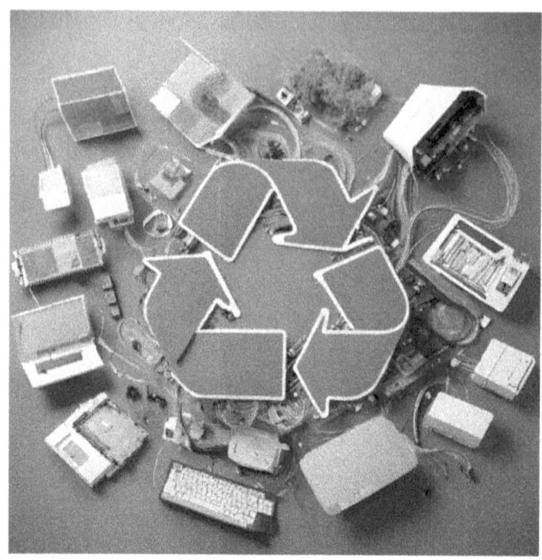

Key Aspects of Green Devices:

1) **Energy Efficiency:** Devices are designed to consume less power during operation and standby modes. This includes using energy-efficient components and optimising software for lower power consumption.

   Examples: Energy Star-rated computers, LED monitors, and smartphones with power-saving modes.

2) **Eco-friendly Materials:** Utilising materials that are less harmful to the environment, such as recyclable plastics, lead-free solder, and non-toxic chemicals.

   Examples: Biodegradable phone cases, laptops with recycled aluminium chassis.

3) **Lifecycle Management:** Ensuring that devices are designed for longevity, easy repair, and eventual recycling. This reduces e-waste and promotes a circular economy.

   Examples: Modular smartphones like Fairphone, which are designed for easy repair and upgrades.

4) **Sustainable Manufacturing:** Implementing manufacturing processes that reduce waste, lower carbon emissions, and minimise water and energy use.

   Examples: Factories powered by renewable energy, use of water-based solvents.

5) **End-of-Life Disposal:** Designing products for easier disassembly and recycling, and providing programmes for proper disposal of electronic waste.

   Examples: Take-back programmes by companies like Apple and Dell.

Importance for Engineering Students:

1) **Innovation:** Encourages the development of new materials and designs that are both efficient and environmentally friendly.

2) **Regulatory Compliance:** Understanding green devices helps in adhering to environmental regulations and standards.

3) **Sustainability:** Contributes to global sustainability goals by reducing the environmental footprint of electronic products.

4) **Market Demand:** Growing consumer demand for sustainable products makes knowledge of green devices crucial for future engineers.

5.8   GREEN DATA SERVERS

Green Data Servers are servers designed to operate with maximum energy efficiency and minimal environmental impact. As data centres consume significant amounts of energy, optimising these servers is essential for reducing the overall carbon footprint of IT operations.

Key Aspects of Green Data Servers:

1) **Energy Efficiency:** Using energy-efficient processors, memory, and storage solutions that reduce power consumption.

   Examples: Low-power CPUs, SSDs instead of HDDs for storage.

2) **Virtualisation and Cloud Computing:** Maximising server utilisation through virtualisation, which allows multiple virtual servers to run on a single physical server, reducing the number of physical servers needed.

   Examples: VMware, Microsoft Hyper-V.

3) **Efficient Cooling Solutions:** Implementing advanced cooling technologies to minimise the energy required to keep servers cool.

   Examples: Liquid cooling, free cooling (using outside air).

4) **Renewable Energy Sources:** Powering data centres with renewable energy sources such as solar, wind, or hydroelectric power.
   Examples: Google and Apple data centres running on 100% renewable energy.

5) **Efficient Data Centre Design**: Designing data centres with energy efficiency in mind, such as using energy-efficient lighting, optimising airflow, and implementing power management techniques.
   Examples: LEED-certified data centres, use of hot and cold aisle containment.

6) **Resource Optimisation:** Optimising server workloads to ensure that resources are used efficiently, reducing idle power consumption.
   Examples: Dynamic provisioning, automated load balancing.

Importance for Engineering Students:

1) **Technical Expertise:** Provides knowledge of cutting-edge technologies and practices in data centre management and server design.

2) **Sustainability:** Promotes the development and adoption of sustainable IT infrastructure.

3) **Cost Savings:** Understanding energy-efficient technologies can lead to significant cost savings in data centre operations.

4) **Industry Demand:** With increasing focus on sustainability, expertise in green data servers is highly sought after in the tech industry.

Advantages of Green Computing:

1) Reduced energy usage from green computing techniques translates into lower carbon dioxide emissions, stemming from a reduction in the fossil fuel used in power plants and transportation.

2) Conserving resources means less energy is required to produce, use, and dispose of products.

3) Saving energy and resources saves money.

4) Green computing even includes changing government policy to encourage recycling and lowering energy use by individuals and businesses.

5) Reduce the risk existing in the laptops, such as chemicals known to cause cancer, nerve damage, and immune reactions in humans.

6) System-Wide Green Computing and Individual Green Computing are the best possible ways to practice Green Computing.

7) Companies implementing System-Wide Green Computing, and employees and individuals practising individual green computing techniques, help in a long way in creating an impact to save the planet.

IMPORTANT QUESTIONS:

1. Name three toxic metals found in e-waste.
2. What are the four main constraints associated with metal extraction from E-waste?
3. List two valuable metals that can be recovered from e-waste.
4. What is bioleaching in the context of e-waste recycling?
5. What is green chemistry?
6. What are the benefits of implementing green chemistry in chemical processes?
7. What is the primary objective of green computing?.
8. Name two goals of green computing that are similar to those of green chemistry.
9. List three key areas that a green computing initiative must address.
10. How does green computing aim to reduce energy consumption?
11. What role does green computing play in minimising electronic waste?
12. Explain how one-way green computing can reduce harmful emissions.
13. What are green devices designed to minimise?
14. Mention one example of sustainable manufacturing in green computing.
15. Discuss the environmental and health risks associated with improper e-waste recycling methods.
16. Explain the opportunities for resource recovery from e-waste and how they can reduce the need for traditional mining.
17. Describe the technological advances that can improve the efficiency and environmental friendliness of E-waste recycling.

18. Identify the major hazardous substances found in E-waste and discuss their sources, health risks, and environmental impacts.

19. Define the concept of green chemistry and discuss its importance in sustainable chemical engineering.

20. Discuss the concept of green computing and its goals in reducing the environmental impact of electronic devices.

21. Discuss the role of green computing in reducing energy consumption and its impact on the environment. Provide specific examples.

22. Explain how green computing contributes to minimising electronic waste and promoting recyclability.

23. Explain the importance of research in advancing virtualization and cloud computing as part of green computing initiatives.

24. Describe how green computing practices can lead to reduced harmful emissions and support environmental sustainability.

25. Identify and explain the key aspects of green devices, including energy efficiency, eco-friendly materials, and lifecycle management.

26. Discuss the role of green data servers in optimising data centre operations and reducing environmental impact.

27. Outline the advantages of green computing for both the environment and businesses, focusing on energy conservation and cost savings.

28. Explain the concept of green computing and its relevance to engineering students in terms of innovation, regulatory compliance, and market demand.

CHAPTER 6

ENERGY SCIENCE

6.1 INTRODUCTION

Energy serves as the driving force behind modern society, energising everything from residential and transportation needs to industrial and communication systems. Among the various energy sources, chemical fuels are particularly significant and widely used. This chapter explores the science behind chemical fuels, focusing on their role in fulfilling our energy needs, the fundamental principles of their combustion, and their environmental and economic impacts.

Fuel technology is a dynamic and promising field within modern science and engineering. In rapidly developing countries like India, industrial growth has led to a steadily increasing demand for power. As the sixth-largest consumer of fuel globally, India's energy needs are substantial.

Chemical fuels are used not only for heating but also in locomotives, mechanical operations, metallurgy, power generation, and the chemical industry.

6.2 CHEMICAL FUEL

A fuel is defined as any combustible substance which, on burning in air, gives a large amount of heat that can be used economically for domestic and industrial purposes.

During the process of combustion of a fuel, the atoms of carbon, hydrogen, etc., combine with oxygen with simultaneous liberation of heat at a rapid rate.

$$\text{Fuel} + O_2 \rightarrow \text{By-products} + \text{Heat}$$
$$\text{(More energy content)}$$

Fuels, in the broad sense, include stored fuels that are available in the earth's crust, i.e. fossil fuel.

Classification of Fuels is classified as
1. **Primary fuels** which occur in nature as such, e.g. coal, petroleum, and natural gas.
2. **Secondary fuels** which are derived from the primary fuels, e.g. coke, gasoline, coal.
    gas, etc.

Both primary and secondary fuels may be further classified based on their physical state as (i) solid fuels, (ii) liquid fuels, and (iii) gaseous fuels.
1. **Solid Fuels:** Coal, Wood, Charcoal, etc.
2. **Liquid Fuels:** Petroleum (Crude Oil), Ethanol, Biodiesel, Gasoline, Diesel, Kerosene, etc.
3. **Gaseous Fuels:** Natural Gas, Propane, Hydrogen, Biogas, LPG, CNG, etc.

6.3 PROPERTIES OF FUELS:

Properties of fuels vary depending on their chemical composition and intended use. Here are some key properties commonly associated with fuels:
1. **Energy Content**: The amount of energy released per unit mass or volume when the fuel undergoes combustion. Typically measured in joules per kilogram (J/kg) or megajoules per liter (MJ/L).
2. **Octane Number (Gasoline) / Cetane Number (Diesel)**: Indicates the fuel's resistance to knocking (gasoline engines) or its ignition quality

(diesel engines). Indicates better resistance to knocking (gasoline) or quicker ignition (diesel).

3. **Density**: Mass per unit volume of the fuel. Affects the volumetric efficiency of storage and transportation.

4. **Viscosity**: Resistance to flow; thickness or stickiness of the fuel. Affects atomisation during combustion and flow characteristics in fuel systems.

5. **Flash Point**: Lowest temperature at which the fuel can vaporize to form an ignitable mixture in air. Higher flash points are safer as they reduce the risk of accidental ignition.

6. **Autoignition Temperature**: Temperature at which the fuel spontaneously ignites without a spark or external flame. Indicates better resistance to premature ignition.

7. **Pour Point**: Lowest temperature at which the fuel remains fluid enough to flow or be pumped. Critical for storage and use in cold climates.

8. **Sulfur Content**: Amount of sulfur present in the fuel. Higher sulphur content leads to increased emissions of sulphur dioxide (SO_2), contributing to air pollution.

9. **Water Content**: Amount of water present in the fuel. Can cause corrosion in fuel systems and reduce combustion efficiency.

10. **Ash Content**: Residue left after complete combustion of the fuel. Can cause fouling in engines and affect emissions.

11. **Heating Value**: Amount of heat released when a specific amount of fuel is burned completely.

6.4 CHARACTERISTICS OF GOOD FUEL:

1. **High Energy Content:**

    It provides a significant amount of energy per unit mass or volume, enhancing efficiency in combustion processes.

2. **Low Volatility:**

    It maintains stability and consistency in storage and handling, reducing evaporation losses.

3. **High Octane Number (Gasoline) / Cetane Number (Diesel)**:

   It indicates resistance to knocking (gasoline) or quick ignition (diesel), thereby improving engine performance and efficiency.

4. **Low Sulfur Content**:

   It minimises emissions of sulphur oxides (SOx), reducing environmental impact and helping comply with emissions regulations.

5. **Good Lubricating Properties**:

   It lubricates engine components, reducing wear and friction, and extends engine life while improving efficiency.

6. **Clean Burning**:

   It produces minimal ash and particulate matter during combustion, thereby reducing engine deposits and emissions of pollutants.

7. **Stable Combustion Characteristics**:

   It ensures consistent ignition and combustion under varying conditions, ensuring reliable engine operation.

8. **Compatibility with Engine Components**:

   It does not cause corrosion or damage to fuel system components, maintaining engine reliability and longevity.

9. **Environmentally Friendly**:

   It has low emissions of greenhouse gases and pollutants, supporting environmental sustainability goals.

10. **High Calorific Value**:

    It releases substantial heat energy when burnt completely, maximising energy efficiency in various applications.

6.5 CALORIFIC VALUE OF FUEL

The calorific value of fuel is defined as the amount of heat liberated by the complete combustion of a unit mass or volume of the fuel. This is an important property of fuel on which its efficiency is judged.

Units of Heat:

- **Calorie** is the amount of heat required to raise the temperature of one gram of water through one degree Centigrade (15-16°C).

- **Kilocalorie** is equal to 1,000 calories. It may be defined as 'the quantity of heat required to raise the temperature of one kilogram of water through one degree Centigrade. Thus; 1 kcal = 1,000 cal
- **British Thermal unit (B.T.U.)** is defined as "the quantity of heat required to raise the temperature of one pound of water through one degree Fahrenheit (60-61°F). This is the English system unit.

---

1 B.T.U. = 252 cal = 0.252 kcal

1 kcal = 3.968 Btu.

Classification of Calorific Values:

A) Gross or Higher Calorific Value (GCV or HCV)

Gross Calorific value is the total amount of heat produced when a unit mass or volume of fuel is burnt completely, and the products of combustion have been cooled to room temperature (i.e. 15 °C).

Almost all fuels contain hydrogen, and when the calorific value of hydrogen-containing fuel is determined experimentally, the hydrogen is converted into steam. If the products of combustion are condensed to room temperature, then the latent heat of condensation of steam also gets included in the measured heat.

B) Lower or Net Calorific Value

Net calorific value is defined as the net heat produced when a unit mass or volume of fuel is burnt completely, and the products of combustion are allowed to escape into the atmosphere.

In actual use of any fuel, the water vapour and moisture produced due to the combustion of hydrogen are not condensed and allowed to escape as such along with hot combustion gases. Hence, a lesser amount of heat is available.

Net calorific value (NCV) or Low Heat Value (LHV)

LCV = HCV – Latent heat of water vapour formed

LCV = HCV – mass of [H] X 0.09 X 587 Kcal/kg

[Since 1 part by weight of hydrogen gives 9 parts by weight of water. The latent heat of steam is 587 cal/g (or kcal/kg).] Thus

---

Net calorific value = Gross calorific value - 0.09H x 587 cal/g

Where H is the% of hydrogen in the fuel.

6.6 ANALYSIS OF COAL

In order to assess the quality of coal, the following two types of analysis are made.

1. **Proximate Analysis** It includes the determination of moisture, volatile matter, ash and fixed carbon. This gives quick and valuable information regarding commercial classification and determination of suitability for a particular industrial use.

2. **Ultimate Analysis** It includes the determination of carbon, hydrogen, nitrogen, sulfur and oxygen in coal. Since it is used for the determination of elements present in the coal, it is also called elemental analysis. This analysis gives exact results and are useful in calculating the calorific value of coal using Dulong's formula.

6.6.1 Proximate Analysis of Coal

It is a fundamental procedure in fuel analysis that provides a comprehensive understanding of a fuel's composition by determining four key components: moisture, volatile matter, ash, and fixed carbon.

(1) **Moisture:** Moisture refers to the water content present in coal. About 1 g of finely powdered air-dried coal sample is weighed in a silica crucible. The silica crucible is placed inside an electric hot air oven, maintained at 105-110°C. The crucible is allowed to remain in the oven for 1 hour and then taken out, cooled in a desiccator, and weighed. Loss in weight is reported as moisture (on a percentage basis).

Percentage of moisture = Loss in weight x 100 / Wt. of coal taken

---

(2) **Volatile matter**: Volatile matter consists of the compounds in coal that are released as gases or vapours when the coal is heated in the absence of air. The dried sample of coal left in the crucible in (1) is then covered with a lid and placed in a muffle furnace, maintained at 925-950°C. The crucible is taken out of the oven after 7 minutes of heating. The crucible is cooled first in air, then inside a desiccator, and weighed again. The loss in weight is reported as volatile matter on a percentage basis.

Percentage of volatile matter = Loss in weight x 100 / Wt. of coal sample taken

(3) **Ash:** Ash is the inorganic residue that remains after coal combustion, consisting of minerals and other non-combustible materials. The residual coal in the crucible in (2) is then heated without a lid in a muffle furnace at 700 ± 50°C for 1/2 *hour*. The crucible is then taken out, cooled first in air, then in a desiccator and weighed. Heating, cooling, and weighing are repeated until a constant weight is obtained. The residue is reported as ash on a percentage basis.

Percentage of ash = Wt. of ash left x 100 / Wt. of coal taken

(4) **Fixed carbon**: Fixed carbon is the solid, combustible residue that remains after the volatile matter has been driven off. It represents the portion of coal that burns in the solid state.

Percentage of fixed carbon = 100 -% of (moisture + volatile matter + ash).

Importance of proximate analysis: Proximate analysis provides the following valuable information in assessing the quality of coal:

(1) **Moisture:** High moisture content can decrease the calorific value of coal and increase transportation costs. During combustion, more energy is required to evaporate the water, reducing the overall efficiency.

(2) **Volatile matter**: A high-volatile matter containing coal burns with a long flame, high smoke, and has low calorific value. Hence, the lesser the volatile matter, the better the rank of the coal. Higher volatile content in coal is undesirable. A high-volatile matter content means that a high proportion of fuel will be distilled and burned as a gas or

vapour. The volatile matter present in the coal may be combustible gases (such as methane, hydrogen, carbon monoxide, and other hydrocarbons) or non-combustible gases (like CO_2 and N_2). Volatile matter content is of special significance in coal gas manufacture and in carbonization plants, particularly when byproduct recovery is the main object. Thus, high-volatile matter containing coals do not cake well; whereas medium-volatile matter content coals are capable of yielding hard and strong coke on carbonisation.

(3) **Ash** is a useless, non-combustible matter, which reduces the calorific value of coal. Moreover, ash causes hindrance to the flow of air and heat, thereby lowering the temperature. Also, it often causes trouble during firing by forming clinker, which blocks the interspaces of the grate. This in turn causes obstruction to air supply; thereby, the burning of coal becomes *irregular*. Hence, the lower the ash content, the better the quality of coal. The presence of ash also increases transporting, handling, and storage costs. The presence of ash also causes early wear of furnace walls, burning of apparatus and *feeding* mechanism.

(4) **Fixed carbon**: The higher the percentage of fixed carbon, the greater its calorific value and the better the quality of coal. The greater the percentage of fixed carbon, the smaller the percentage of volatile matter. This also represents the quantity of carbon (in coal) that can be burnt by a primary current of air drawn through the hot bed of a fuel. Hence, a high percentage of fixed carbon is desirable.

6.6.2   Ultimate Analysis of Coal:

It is a detailed chemical analysis that determines the elemental composition of coal. This analysis provides critical information on the percentages of carbon (C), hydrogen (H), sulphur (S), nitrogen (N), oxygen (O), and ash. Understanding these elements is essential for evaluating coal's combustion properties, heating value, and environmental impact.

1. **Carbon and Hydrogen:**

    About 1-2 g of accurately weighed coal sample is burnt in a current of oxygen in a combustion apparatus. C and H of the coal are converted into CO_2 and H_2 respectively. The gaseous products of combustion are absorbed respectively in KOH and $CaCl_2$ tubes of known weights. Increase in weight of these gives the amount of carbon and hydrogen present in the coal.

$$C + O_2 \rightarrow CO_2$$
$$H_2 + 1/2\ O_2 \rightarrow H_2O$$
$$2KOH + CO_2 \rightarrow K_2CO_3 + 2H_2O$$
$$CaCl_2 + 7H_2O \rightarrow CaCl_2.7H_2O$$

% of Carbon = [increase in weight of KOH tube x 12 x 100] / [weight of coal sample x 44]

% of Hydrogen = [increase in wt of $CaCl_2$ tube x 2 x 100] / [wt of coal sample x 18]

1. **Nitrogen:.**

   About 1 g of accurately weighed powdered coal is heated with concentrated H_2SO_4 along with K_2SO_4 (catalyst) in a long-necked flask (called Kjeldahl's flask). After the solution becomes clear, it is treated with an excess of KOH and the liberated ammonia is distilled over and absorbed in a known volume of standard acid solution. The unused acid is then determined by back titration with standard NaOH solution. From the volume of acid used by ammonia liberated, the percentage of N in coal is calculated as follows.

   % of Nitrogen = [vol. of acid used x 1.4 x normality] / wt of coal sample.

2. **Sulphur:** 1 g of coal sample is burnt in a bomb calorimeter. Sulphur is oxidised to H_2SO_4 vapours, which on cooling turn into liquid sulfuric acid. Then the H2SO4 solution is treated with $BaCl_2$ solution, and $BaSO_4$ is formed.

   $$BaCl_2 + H_2SO_4 \rightarrow BaSO_4 + 2HCl$$

The ppt is then filtered, washed, dried, and heated until a constant mass is obtained. Then it is cooled and its weight noted down.

$$\% \text{ of } S = [\text{mass of BaSO}_4 \text{ ppt x 32 x 100}] / [\text{wt of coal sample x 233}]$$

3.   **Ash:** 1 g of dry coal is taken in a silica crucible and heated in a muffle furnace at a temperature of 700-750 °C for 30 minutes, until a constant mass of residue is obtained. Then it is cooled in desiccators and its weight is noted again. The loss in weight is the ash present in the coal sample.

$$\% \text{ of ash: (constant wt. of residue left x 100) / wt of coal sample.}$$

4.   **Oxygen:**

$$\% \text{ of Oxygen: 100 - } [\% \text{ of C \& H } +\% \text{ of N } +\% \text{ of S } +\% \text{ of ash}].$$

Significance of Ultimate Analysis:

(1) **Carbon and hydrogen**: Greater the percentage of carbon and hydrogen, the better the coal in quality and calorific value. However, hydrogen is mostly associated with the volatile matter and hence, it affects the use to which the coal is put. Also, a higher percentage of carbon in coal reduces the size of the combustion chamber required. The amount of carbon, the major combustible constituent of coal, depends on the type of coal and its percentage increases with rank from lignite to anthracite. Thus, the percentage of carbon forms the basis of classification of coal.

(2) **Nitrogen** has no calorific value and hence, its presence in coal is undesirable; thus, a good quality coal should have very little nitrogen content.

(3) **Sulfur** although contributes to the heating value of coal, yet on combustion produces acids (SO_2 and SO_3), which have harmful effects of corroding the equipment and also cause atmospheric pollution. Sulfur is usually present to the extent of 0.5 to 3.0% and derived from

ores like iron pyrites, gypsum, etc., mined along with the coal. The presence of sulfur is highly undesirable in coal to be used for making coke for the iron industry, since it is transferred to the iron metal and badly affects the quality and properties of steel. Moreover, oxides of sulfur (formed as combustion products) pollute the atmosphere and lead to corrosion.

(4) **Oxygen** content decreases the calorific value of coal. High oxygen content coals are characterised by high inherent moisture, low calorific value, and low coking power. Moreover, oxygen is in combined form with hydrogen in coal and thus, hydrogen available for combustion is less than the actual amount. An increase in 1% oxygen content decreases the calorific value by about 1.7% and hence, oxygen is undesirable. Thus, a good quality coal should have a low percentage of oxygen.

6.7   PETROLEUM:

Petroleum is derived from the Latin word (petra means rock and oleum means oil). It is a dark greenish-brown viscous oil found deep in the earth's crust; hence, it is also called mineral oil. It is a complex mixture of alkanes, alkenes, and aromatic hydrocarbons with small quantities of organic compounds containing oxygen, nitrogen, and sulfur. Petroleum or crude oil has a composition that varies within a narrow range as below.

Element	C	H	N	S	O
Percentage	80-87	11.1.- 15.0	0.4-0.9	0.1 – 3.5	0.1 -0.9

The primary liquid fuel is crude Petroleum Oil; it is extracted by digging wells deep down in the earth. Depending upon the proportions in which the paraffinic, olefin, and aromatic hydrocarbons are present in crude oil, it is classified as:

• Paraffin-based: This petroleum oil mainly consists of paraffinic hydrocarbons together with small amounts of naphthalenes and aromatic hydrocarbons.

- Asphaltic-based: This petroleum oil consists of non-paraffinic hydrocarbons such as aromatic and naphthenic hydrocarbons.
- Mixed base: It contains both paraffinic and naphthenic-based hydrocarbons in varying proportions.

Refining of Petroleum

Mining of Petroleum

Petroleum oil is extracted from deep down in the earth's crust. The oil is extracted from the earth's crust by drilling holes, and pipes are sunk up to the oil-bearing rock. Oil generally rushes out to the surface itself because of hydrostatic pressure of natural gas. But when the pressure becomes very low, oil is extracted with pumps.

Refining of Petroleum

Crude oil coming out of the well generally consists of many impurities like dirt, water, and other impurities. After the removal of these impurities, oil is subjected to fractional distillation (separation of liquids by virtue of the difference in boiling points). Fractional distillation of petroleum is carried out in a specially designed tall fractionating tower. It is provided with a large number of horizontal stainless-steel trays. Each tray is provided with a number of small chimneys covered with loose caps.

The crude oil is heated to about 400°C in an iron retort, and hot vapours of oil are introduced into the fractionating tower from the bottom of the tower. The tower is hot at the lower end and comparatively cooler towards the upper end. As the vapours of oil rise up in the fractionating tower, they get cooled gradually, and the fractional condensation takes place, and various liquids are separated by virtue of their boiling points. The oil fraction having the highest boiling point gets condensed first at the bottom and the lowest boiling fraction at the top. The uncondensed gases escape from the top. The residues left in the iron retort are a black tarry mass known as asphalt or pitch, which can be used for making roads, paints, etc. It is also used as a preservative for wood and metals.

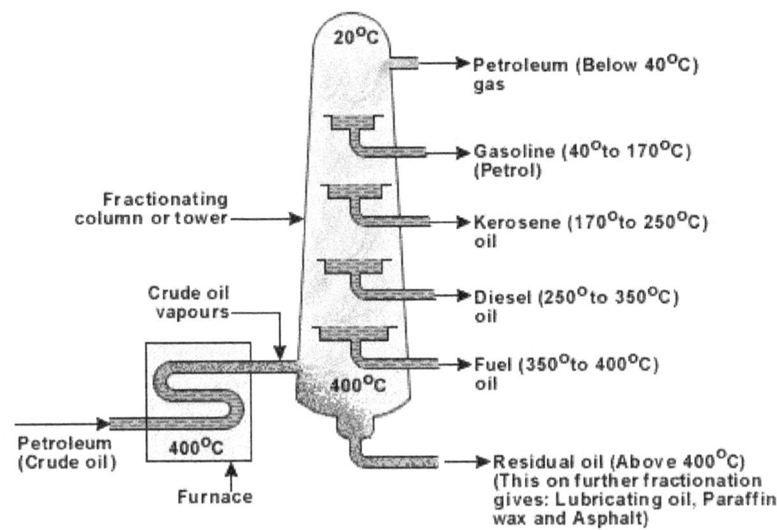

Figure 6.1: *Fractional distillation of crude petroleum.*

Table: Fractions by Distillation of Crude

Sr. No.	Name of Fraction	Boiling range	Approximate composition in terms of hydro-carbons containing carbon atoms	Uses
1	Uncondensed gas	Below 30°C	C_1 to C_4	As domestic and industrial fuel - LPG
2	Petroleum ether.	30 – 70 °C	$C_5 - C_7$	As a solvent.
3	Gasoline or petrol or motor spirit.	40 – 120 °C	$C_5 - C_9$	As motor fuel, solvent, and in dry cleaning.
4	Naphtha or solvent spirit.	120 –180 °C	$C_9 - C_{10}$	As a solvent in dry cleaning.
5	Kerosene oil	180 – 250 °C	$C_{10} - C_{16}$	As an illuminant, jet engine fuel is used for preparing laboratory gas.

Sr. No.	Name of Fraction	Boiling range	Approximate composition in terms of hydro-carbons containing carbon atoms	Uses
6	Diesel oil, fuel oil, or gas oil	250 – 320 °C	$C_{10} - C_{18}$	Diesel engine fuel.
7	Heavy oil.	320 – 400 °C	$C_{17} - C_{30}$	For obtaining gasoline through the cracking process.

6.8 CRACKING OF OIL:

An average grade of crude oil on fractionation yields about 20–30% of gasoline, 30–45% of intermediate oil, and 25–50% of residual fuel oil. Among these fractions, the gasoline fraction obtained (straight run gasoline) has the highest demand in the automobile industry. Also, the quality of straight run gasoline is not up to the mark; hence, heavy boiling fractions are converted to lower fractions by a process called cracking. Cracking is defined as the decomposition of bigger hydrocarbon molecules into smaller, low-boiling hydrocarbons of lower molecular weight.

This process is suitable for those oils that readily vapourize. It requires less time than the liquid phase method. The petrol obtained has better antiknock properties.

Cracking

e.g. $C_{10}H_{22} \rightarrow$ $C_5 H_{12} + C_5 H_{10}$

n-pentane   n - pentane

There are two methods of cracking in use.

i) **Thermal Cracking**: - The heavy oils are subjected to high temperature and pressure where bigger hydrocarbon molecules break down to give smaller molecules of paraffins, olefins & some hydrogen. There are two types of thermal cracking.

a) **Liquid Phase Cracking**:

In this type, the cracking oil is kept in the liquid form by applying high pressure, 15 to 100 kg/ cm² at 475 to 530°C. The octane rating of gasoline obtained is 65 to 70.

b) **Vapour Phase Cracking**:

The cracking oil is first vaporized and then cracked at 600 °C – 650 °C and under low pressure of 10–20 Kg/ cm².

2) **Catalytic Cracking**:

The quality and petrol obtained by cracking can be improved by using a suitable catalyst like Aluminium silicate $Al_2(SiO_3)$ & Alumina Al_2O_3. Advantages: - The yield of petrol is higher; quality of petrol produced is better. Petrol possesses better antiknock properties. Energy consumed in catalytic cracking is much less than in thermal cracking process.

6.8.1 Fixed-Bed Catalytic Cracking

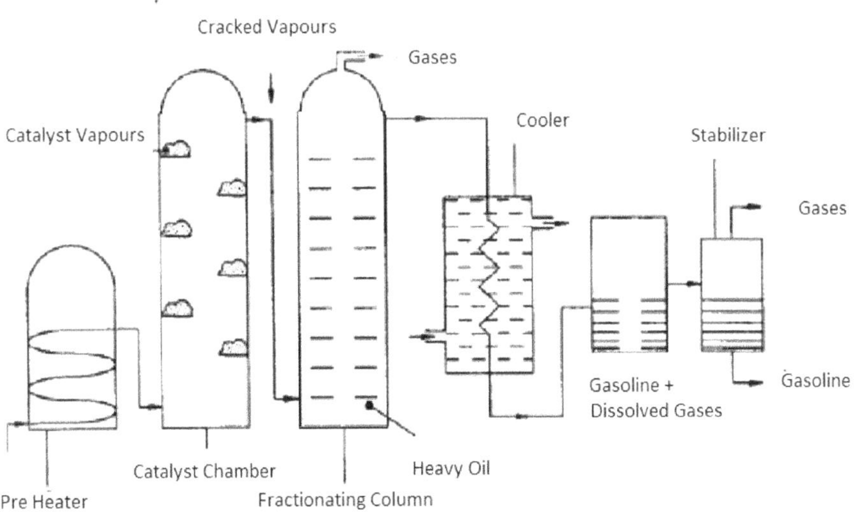

Figure 6.2: *Fixed-bed catalytic cracking process*

The heavy oil is passed through the preheater, where the oil is vaporised and heated to 400 to 500°C, and then forced through a catalytic chamber containing the catalyst of silica-alumina gel (SiO_2, Al_2O_3) or bauxite, is mixed with clay and zirconium oxide maintained at 400 to 500°C and 1.5 kg/cm²pressure. During its passage through the tower, cracking takes place; about 30-40% of the charge is converted into gasoline, and about 2-4% carbon is formed, which gets deposited on the catalytic bed.

The vapours produced are then passed through a fractionating column, where heavy oil fractions condense. The vapours are then admitted into a cooler, where some of the gaseous products are condensed along with gasoline, and uncondensed gases move on.

The gasoline containing some dissolved gases is then sent to a stabiliser, where the dissolved gases are removed, and pure gasoline is obtained. When a substantial amount of carbon is deposited on the catalyst bed during cracking, the catalyst stops functioning. It is reactivated by burning off the deposited carbon in a stream of hot air. During the reactivation of the catalyst, the vapours are diverted through another catalyst chamber.

6.8.2   Moving Bed Catalytic Cracking:

Moving Bed Catalytic Cracking (MBCC) is a process used in the refining of crude oil to convert heavy hydrocarbons into lighter, more valuable products such as gasoline, diesel, and other petrochemicals. It involves the use of a catalyst in a moving bed reactor, which enhances the cracking process by facilitating the breaking of long-chain hydrocarbons into shorter, more useful molecules.

In this process, the solid catalyst is very finely powdered so that it behaves almost as a fluid, which can be circulated in a gas stream. Hence, it is also known as the Fluid Bed Catalytic Cracking Process.

The heavy oil charge is passed through a preheater where the oil is vaporized and heated to 400 to 500 °C. The silica-alumina gel (SiO_2 Al_2O_3) or Bauxite catalyst is mixed with clay and zirconium oxide and introduced in the catalyst regenerator. Cracking takes place during the passage of the catalyst with oil vapours from the regenerator to the reactor. The cracked vapours are separated from the catalyst by a centrifugal separator and then passed through a fractionating column, finally sent to a cooler where gasoline is condensed. The exhausted catalyst is continuously removed from the reactor and forced into the regenerator. The deposited carbon and tarry material are burnt off in the regenerator. The regenerated catalyst is again circulated with vapours of heavy oil.

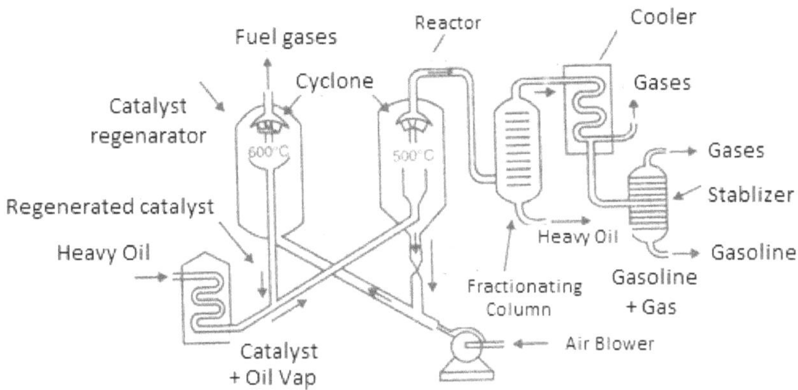

Figure 6.3: Moving-bed type catalytic cracking

6.9   KNOCKING

The gasoline and diesel oil are used as fuel in an internal combustion engine. In an internal combustion engine, a mixture of fuel (gasoline or diesel) is ignited in the cylinder. The ignition is brought about by means of an electrical spark (in a petrol engine) or by compression of air (in a diesel engine).

The whole process consists of four strokes in a petrol engine.

In an internal combustion engine, a mixture of air and gasoline vapours is introduced into the cylinder, a process known as the suction stroke. Following this, the fuel-air mixture is compressed, referred to as the compression stroke. The primary chemical reaction occurring is the oxidation of hydrocarbons. An electrical spark then ignites the mixture. The combustion produces hot gases that increase the pressure in the cylinder, which is called the power stroke. After combustion is complete, the exhaust gases are expelled, reducing the pressure in the cylinder, known as the exhaust stroke. This cycle then repeats. For efficient operation, the fuel-air mixture must burn smoothly and rapidly; once initiated by a spark, the flame should spread quickly and uniformly through the gas mixture to ensure the expanding gas drives the piston down the cylinder smoothly.

The ratio of gaseous volume at the end of the suction stroke to the volume at the end of the compression stroke of the piston is known as the Compression Ratio. The efficiency of the engine depends on the ratio. The higher the compression ratio, the higher the efficiency of the engine. However, if the compression ratio is above a certain limit, the fuel-air mixture gets heated to a high temperature and spontaneous combustion occurs even before sparking. This is known as pre-ignition. Furthermore, it may happen that the last portion of the fuel-air mixture gets spontaneously self-ignited, resulting in an explosive violence.

In certain situations, due to the presence of specific constituents in the gasoline, the rate of oxidation becomes so high that portions of the fuel-air mixture ignite spontaneously, producing an explosive sound known as knocking. Knocking not only reduces the engine's efficiency but also leads to significant energy loss and potential damage to the piston and cylinder.

6.10 CHEMICAL STRUCTURE AND KNOCKING:

The phenomenon of knocking in internal combustion engines is closely related to the chemical structure of the fuel used. Knocking occurs when the fuel-air mixture in the engine's cylinder ignites prematurely, causing a sharp and damaging increase in pressure. Understanding how the chemical structure of gasoline influences knocking is crucial for designing fuels that minimise this issue.

Gasoline is a complex mixture of hydrocarbons, primarily composed of:

- **Alkanes (Paraffins)**: Straight-chain or branched hydrocarbons (e.g., octane, iso-octane).
- **Cycloalkanes (Naphthenes)**: Ring-shaped hydrocarbons (e.g., cyclohexane).
- **Aromatics**: Hydrocarbons containing benzene rings (e.g., toluene, xylene).

The knocking of a fuel engine is closely related to the chemical structure of the fuel used.

1. The knocking tendency decreases as the molecular structure becomes more compact, contains double bonds (alkenes), or forms cyclic structures.

   Examples: Alkenes of the same carbon chain length generally exhibit better antiknocking properties than corresponding alkanes due to the presence of double bonds, which enhance stability and reduce the likelihood of premature ignition under compression.

2. In straight-chain alkanes (normal alkanes), the anti-knocking property typically decreases with increasing hydrocarbon chain length.

   Example: n-Butane shows better anti-knocking properties compared to n-pentane, n-hexane, and n-Cetane (n-octane).

3. **Branched Chain Alkanes**: Branched-chain alkanes generally have better anti-knocking properties than straight-chain alkanes.

   Example: Iso-alkanes (branched alkanes) exhibit enhanced antiknocking tendencies, with the degree of improvement increasing with the number and strategic placement of branches. For instance, 2,2-dimethylpentane demonstrates higher antiknocking properties than 2-methylhexane due to its more compact and branched structure.

4. **Alkenes**: The anti-knocking tendency in alkenes increases when the double bond is closer to the centre of the carbon chain.

   Example: CH_3-CH=CH-CH_3 (2-butene) exhibits better antiknocking properties than CH_3-CH_2-CH=CH_2 (1-butene) because the double bond is positioned closer to the centre, enhancing stability and reducing the tendency for premature combustion.

5. **Aromatic Compounds**: Aromatic hydrocarbons like benzene, toluene, and naphthalene possess high antiknocking tendencies and high octane numbers. The stable ring structure of aromatic compounds resists combustion under high pressure conditions, contributing to their superior antiknocking properties.

6.11 OCTANE NUMBER AND CETANE NUMBER:

Octane Number:

Knocking is mainly due to spontaneous ignition of the last portion of the charge, giving a detonating shock wave. The knocking tendency of fuels may be determined by measuring their highest useful compression ratios in a standard engine run under set conditions. In order to classify the fuels according to their knocking properties, an arbitrary scale has been established by Edger (1926), known as octane rating or octane number. It was found that the hydrocarbon Iso-octane (2,2,4-trimethylpentane) has very good combustion characteristics and exhibits very little tendency to knocking. Hence, its Octane number is taken as 100. On the other hand, the straight-chain hydrocarbon n-heptane (C_7H_{16}) knocks very readily, and hence its octane number is taken as zero.

$$CH_3\text{-}CH_2\text{-}CH_2\text{-}CH_2\text{-}CH_2\text{-}CH_2\text{-}CH_3$$

$$\begin{array}{ccccc} & CH_3 & & CH_3 & \\ & | & & | & \\ CH_3- & C - CH_2 & - & CH & - CH_3 \\ & | & & & \\ & CH_3 & & & \end{array}$$

<table>
<tr><td align="center">n- Heptane
Anti-knocking value = 0</td><td align="center">Iso- Octane
Anti-knocking value = 100</td></tr>
</table>

Definition: The octane number of a given fuel is defined as the percentage of iso-octane in a mixture of iso-octane and n-heptane which has the same knocking tendency in a standard engine run under standard conditions.

Thus, the gasoline with an octane number of 90, its knocking property matches with a 90:10 mixture of iso-octane & n-heptane. The greater the octane number, the greater the antiknocking property of the fuel.

Cetane Number:

The knocking propensity of diesel fuel is quantified using the cetane number, which measures how easily the fuel ignites under compression. Cetane number contrasts with octane number used for gasoline, focusing on different aspects of ignition behaviour in internal combustion engines.

The cetane number indicates the fuel's ignition quality: higher numbers denote quicker ignition, minimising ignition delay. Cetane (hexadecane) serves as the benchmark with a cetane number of 100, igniting promptly upon compression. Conversely, α-methyl naphthalene, an aromatic hydrocarbon, has a cetane number of 0 due to its extended ignition delay compared to standard diesel fuels.

Examples: A cetane number of 60 for diesel fuel means it ignites similarly to a blend containing 60% cetane and 40% α-methyl naphthalene. This standardised comparison ensures consistent engine performance by aligning the ignition characteristics of different diesel fuels.

In petrol engines, knocking results from spontaneous combustion of residual fuel-air mixtures. Diesel engines experience knocking due to delayed ignition of the initial fuel volume. Fuels with high octane numbers used in petrol engines typically exhibit low cetane numbers, and vice versa, reflecting their differing combustion characteristics.

Understanding the cetane number helps in selecting diesel fuels that optimise engine performance by ensuring efficient combustion initiation and minimising ignition delay, thereby enhancing overall engine efficiency and reliability.

6.12   DIESEL ENGINE FUEL

The diesel engine, also known as a Compression Ignition Engine (IC Engine), operates by igniting fuel through heat and pressure rather than a spark.

Unlike gasoline engines, diesel engines rely on high compression to ignite the fuel-air mixture. Air is drawn into the cylinder during the intake or suction stroke, followed by compression during the compression stroke. Compression ratios typically range from 15:1 to 20:1, resulting in pressures of about 30 to 50 kg/cm². The compression process raises the temperature of the air inside the cylinder to approximately 500 to 600°C.

During the compression stroke, diesel fuel is injected into the highly compressed, hot air in the form of a fine spray. The fuel droplets vapourize and mix with the hot air, reaching temperatures where spontaneous ignition occurs. This ignition initiates the power stroke, where the rapid combustion of the fuel-air mixture generates high pressure, driving the piston downward.

Diesel fuels are selected based on their ignition characteristics, requiring an ignition temperature at least 300°C lower than the temperature achieved during compression. This ensures that ignition occurs reliably and efficiently under the high pressures and temperatures present in the engine cylinder. After the power stroke, the exhaust stroke begins where the piston moves upward, expelling the combustion gases through the exhaust valve. The cycle then repeats, with each stroke occurring in sequence: intake (suction), compression, power (ignition), and exhaust.

Key Differences from Gasoline Engines:
- **Ignition Method**: Diesel engines use compression ignition, while gasoline engines use spark ignition.
- **Fuel Type**: Diesel engines use diesel fuel, which is less volatile than gasoline and requires higher compression for ignition.
- **Efficiency**: Diesel engines typically achieve higher thermal efficiency due to the compression ignition process and leaner fuel-air mixtures.

Applications:
- **Automotive**: Diesel engines are commonly used in heavy-duty vehicles, trucks, buses, and industrial equipment where high torque and fuel efficiency are advantageous.
- **Industrial**: They are also used in stationary applications such as generators and pumps where reliable and efficient power is required.

IMPORTANT QUESTIONS

1. What is chemical fuel? Giving examples, explain how fuels are classified?
2. Define calorific value. What are the Higher and Lower calorific values?
3. Explain the gross and net calorific value of coal. Give its relationship.
4. What is the proximate analysis of coal? Explain the determination of constituents and give its significances.
5. What is the ultimate analysis of coal? Explain the determination of C&H, S & N. and give its significances.
6. What is Catalytic cracking? Explain Fixed-Bed catalytic cracking.
7. What is cracking? Compare thermal and catalytic cracking.
8. What is cracking? Explain Moving Bed Catalytic Cracking.
9. Explain the terms "octane number" and "cetane number".

CHAPTER 7

ENERGY STORAGE SYSTEM

7.1 INTRODUCTION

A battery is a device that converts chemical energy into electrical energy, which can be used to power electronic devices. It is a collection of one or more cells that are interconnected in a specific way to generate a voltage. Batteries come in many different shapes and sizes, and they are used in a wide range of applications, including mobile phones, laptops, cars, and even large-scale energy storage systems.

The basic components of a battery are the anode, cathode, and electrolyte. The anode is the negative terminal, while the cathode is the positive terminal. The electrolyte is a chemical substance that allows the flow of ions between the anode and cathode. When the battery is connected to a circuit, a chemical reaction occurs in the electrolyte, which causes a flow of electrons from the anode to the cathode. This flow of electrons creates an electrical current that can power a device.

There are many different types of batteries, including primary and secondary batteries. Primary batteries are designed to be used once and then discarded. They are typically less expensive than secondary batteries and are often used in low-power applications, such as flashlights and remote controls. Secondary batteries, also known as rechargeable batteries, can be recharged and used multiple times. They are more expensive than primary batteries, but they offer a better long-term value for high-power applications, such as laptops and electric vehicles.

The most common types of batteries include:

a) Alkaline batteries: These are primary batteries that are commonly used in household items like remote controls, flashlights, and toys.

b) Lithium-ion batteries: These are rechargeable batteries that are commonly used in mobile phones, laptops, and electric vehicles.

c) Lead-acid batteries: These are rechargeable batteries that are commonly used in automobiles, uninterruptible power supplies, and backup power systems.

d) Nickel-cadmium batteries: These are rechargeable batteries that are commonly used in cordless power tools and other high-drain applications.

e) Nickel-metal hydride batteries: These are rechargeable batteries that are commonly used in digital cameras, portable music players, and other low-drain applications.

In addition to the type of battery, there are other important factors to consider when choosing a battery, including the voltage, capacity, and size. The voltage is the electrical potential difference between the anode and cathode, and it determines the amount of electrical energy that the battery can supply. The capacity is the amount of electrical charge that the battery can store, and it determines how long the battery will last before it needs to be recharged. The size of the battery is also important, as it must be the right size and shape to fit into the device that it will be used to power.

7.2   CLASSIFICATION OF BATTERIES:

Electrochemical cells or batteries are identified as primary (non-rechargeable) or secondary (rechargeable) depending on their capability of being electrically recharged. The batteries are classified as:

1. Primary batteries (non-rechargeable).

2. Secondary batteries (rechargeable)

3. Reserve batteries (rechargeable)

1. **Primary Battery:** A primary battery, also known as a disposable battery, is designed to be used only once and then discarded. These batteries typically use a chemical reaction to produce an electric current, and once the chemicals are depleted, the battery is no longer able to produce power. Common examples of primary batteries include alkaline batteries, lithium batteries, and zinc-carbon batteries.

2. **Secondary Battery:** A secondary battery, also known as a rechargeable battery, is designed to be recharged and used multiple times. These batteries typically use a reversible chemical reaction to store and release electrical energy. Common examples of secondary batteries include lithium-ion batteries, nickel-cadmium batteries, and lead-acid batteries.

3. **Reserve Battery:** A reserve battery is a type of battery that is designed to provide backup power in the event of a power outage or other disruption. These batteries are typically used in applications where a loss of power could be dangerous or costly, such as in hospitals, data centres, and emergency lighting systems. Reserve batteries are typically designed to be used intermittently and may be rechargeable or non-rechargeable. Common examples of reserve batteries include lead-acid batteries, nickel-cadmium batteries, and lithium-ion batteries.

Primary battery/cell	Secondary battery/cell
In this cell, the redox reaction is irreversible.	In this cell, the redox reaction is reversible.
It is not rechargeable.	It is rechargeable.
It is discarded upon discharging.	It is used again (not discarded) upon discharging.
It is low cost	It is high cost
Its life is short.	Its life is longer
It is light in weight.	It is heavier in weight.
e.g. Dry cell, Daniell cell.	e.g. Lead-acid storage cell, Ni-Cd cell,

7.3   NICKEL-CADMIUM BATTERY:

Nickel-cadmium (Ni-Cd) batteries are a type of rechargeable battery that use nickel oxide hydroxide and metallic cadmium as electrodes. Ni-Cd batteries have been widely used for many applications due to their high-energy density, low self-discharge rate, and long cycle life.

1) It is an example of a secondary cell.

2) It is a rechargeable cell.

3) In this alkali, KOH is used; hence, it is known as an alkali storage battery.

4) The cell has a longer life (5 years) than Pb-acid storage cell.

5) It produces a potential of 1.4V.

6) It is more expensive than Pb-acid batteries.

7) It has a low maintenance cost.

8) The charging time is as short as 15 minutes using special chargers.

Construction:

Ni-Cd batteries are made up of several cells, each containing a positive electrode metal grid (network of metal wire) containing NiO_2 (Nickel oxide) and a negative electrode made of metallic cadmium. The plates or separators (Ebonite stick - vulcanised rubber) are placed between the electrodes to avoid a short circuit and to prevent the electrodes from touching each other while allowing the flow of ions between them. The cells are then filled with an electrolyte solution made of potassium hydroxide (KOH) or sodium hydroxide (NaOH).

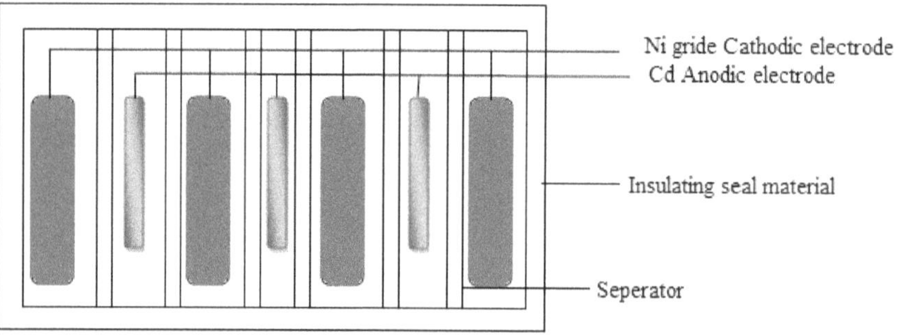

Figure 7.1: *Nickel-cadmium Battery*

Working:

During the charging process, electrons are forced onto the negative electrode, which converts the cadmium into cadmium hydroxide. At the same time, the nickel oxide hydroxide electrode releases oxygen ions that combine with the water in the electrolyte solution to form oxygen gas and hydroxide ions. The hydroxide ions then migrate through the separator to the negative electrode, where they react with the cadmium hydroxide to form cadmium and water. The reaction produces electrical energy that can be used to power devices.

During discharge, the reverse reaction takes place. The cadmium and nickel oxide hydroxide electrodes react with the hydroxide ions in the electrolyte solution to produce cadmium hydroxide, nickel hydroxide, and electrons, which flow through the external circuit to power devices.

Discharging:-

At anode -ve electrode plate:

$$Cd \longrightarrow Cd^{2+} + 2e^-$$
$$Cd^{2+} + 2OH^- \longrightarrow Cd(OH)_2$$
$$\overline{Cd + 2OH^- \longrightarrow Cd(OH)_2 + 2e^-}$$

At Cathode +ve electrode plate:

$$NiO_{2(s)} + 2H_2O_{(e)} + 2e^- \longrightarrow Ni(OH)_{2\,(s)} + 2OH^-_{(aq)}$$

Net reaction:

$$Cd_{(s)} + NiO_{2(s)} + 2H_2O_{(l)} \longrightarrow Cd(OH)_{2(s)} + Ni(OH)_2$$

Applications:

- The nickel-cadmium cell has a small size and a high rate of charge/discharge capacity, which makes it very useful.
- It also has very low internal resistance and a wide temperature range (up to 70°C).
- It produces a potential of about 1.4 V and has a longer life than lead storage cells.
- These cells are used in electronic calculators, electronic flash units, electric shavers, transistors, etc.
- Ni-Cd cells are widely used in medical instrumentation and in emergency lighting, toys, etc.
- It is also used in aircraft and space satellite power systems.

Advantages:

- Ni-Cd batteries last longer, in terms of the number of charge/discharge cycles, than other rechargeable batteries.
- Ni-Cd batteries have a much higher energy efficiency.

7.4   LI-ION BATTERY

In this type of battery, lithium ions are used instead of lithium ions; the transfer through electrolyte takes place from one electrode to another electrode. The Nobel Prize for Chemistry in 2019 was awarded to John B. Goodenough, M. Stanley Whittingham, and Akira Yoshino for their work on lithium-ion cells that have revolutionised portable electronics.

In general, the battery consists of a soluble lithium anode as an ion into carbon, and the cathode material is made up of lithium-liberating compounds.

Lithium is used because it has a very low density and a relatively high electrode potential

- They are lighter in weight.
- They produce high voltage output of about 4V compared to other batteries.
- They have improved safety, i.e. more resistance to overcharge.

The $+e°$ liberated from the oxidation process at the anode can perform useful work when they pass through the external circuit to the cathode.

Example: Lithium cobalt oxide ($LiCoO_2$) battery.

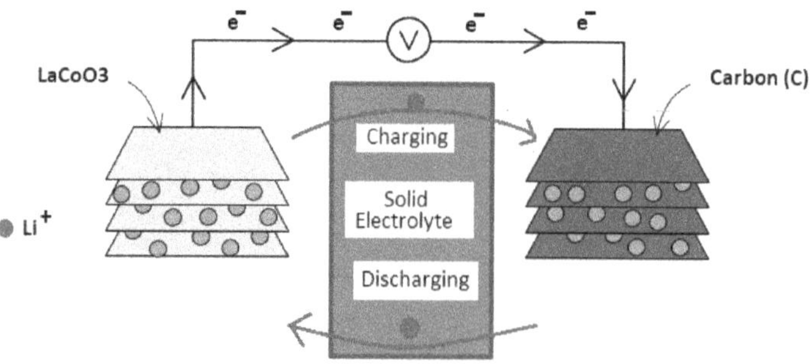

Figure 7.2: Lithium cobalt oxide (LiCoO₂) battery

Construction

1. **The Anode:** The anode is made up of a carbon electrode with a thin copper foil as the current collector.
2. **The cathode:** It is made up of lithium metal oxide compound (Li–MO_2) where M is commonly Co or Mn.
3. **Electrolyte:** A lithium salt such as LiPF6 dissolved in a binary organic solvent mixture such as ethylene carbonate – dimethyl carbonate.

Cell Representation

Li | Li+, C| $LiPF_6$ in ethylene carbonate | Li–MO_2

Working

During discharging, lithium atoms are oxidised, liberating electrons and lithium ions which migrate through the electrolyte to the cathode.

$$Li - C6 \rightarrow Li+ + 6C + e-$$

At the cathode, lithium ions are reduced to lithium atoms and inserted into the layered structure of the metal oxide.

$$Li^+ + e^- + MO_2 \rightarrow Li{-}MO_2$$

During charging, lithium atoms of the metal oxide are oxidised, liberating electrons and lithium ions. Electrons flow through the external circuit, and lithium ions flow through the electrolyte towards the graphite carbon electrode.

$$Li - MO_2 \rightarrow Li^+ + e^- + MO_2$$

At the graphite electrode, lithium ions are reduced to lithium atoms and inserted into the layered structure of graphite.

$$Li^+ + 6C + e- \rightarrow Li - C6$$

The EMF of the battery is 4.0 V.

Applications:

- Powering smartphones, laptops, tablets, digital cameras, and wearable devices.
- Providing energy storage for electric cars, scooters, bicycles, and other vehicles.
- Storing renewable energy from sources like solar and wind for later use.
- Balancing supply and demand in electrical grids and stabilising renewable energy sources.
- Powering satellites, spacecraft, and unmanned aerial vehicles (UAVs).
- Powering portable medical equipment, implantable devices, and wearable health monitors.
- Providing power for soldier equipment, unmanned vehicles, and communication systems.
- Energising cordless drills, saws, and other portable tools. **7.5.**

7.5 HYDROGEN-OXYGEN FUEL CELL

A fuel cell is an electrochemical device that converts chemical energy from a fuel and an oxidant directly into electrical energy.

Principle: The fundamental principle of a fuel cell is similar to that of an electrochemical cell, functioning like a galvanic cell. However, unlike a typical electrochemical cell, the fuel and oxidant in a fuel cell are stored externally and continuously supplied to the electrodes. At the electrodes, the fuel and oxidant undergo redox reactions, generating electricity. Fuel cells can provide a continuous supply of current as long as the reactants are consistently replenished.

$$\boxed{\text{Fuel + Oxidant} \rightarrow \text{Oxidation products + Electric Energy}}$$

Examples: 1. H_2-O_2 fuel cell
2. CH_3OH-O_2 fuel cell

Hydrogen-oxygen fuel cell: This is a widely used type of fuel cell. Like a galvanic cell, a hydrogen-oxygen fuel cell consists of two half-cells. Each half-cell contains a porous graphite electrode coated with a catalyst such as platinum, silver, or a metal oxide. These electrodes are immersed in an aqueous solution of sodium hydroxide (NaOH) or potassium hydroxide (KOH), which serves as the electrolyte.

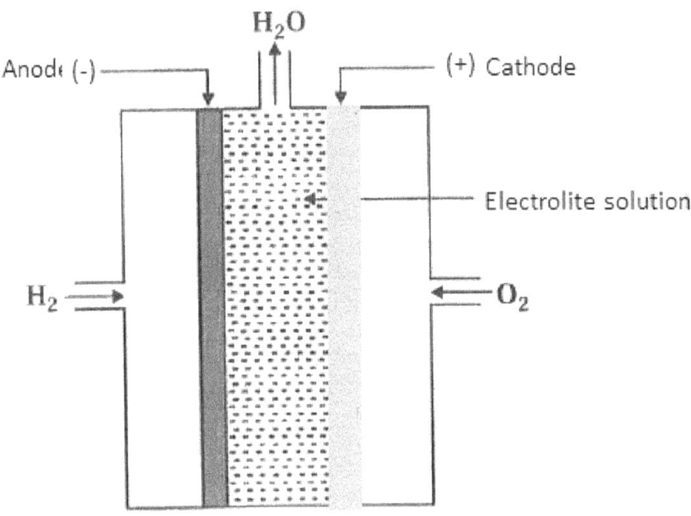

Figure 7.3: *H$_2$-O$_2$ Cell*

Working:

- **Anode**: Hydrogen gas is supplied to the anode. Under high pressure, around 50 atmospheres, hydrogen diffuses through the porous graphite electrode.
- **Cathode**: Oxygen gas is supplied to the cathode, also under similar pressure conditions, and diffuses through its respective electrode.

At the anode, hydrogen undergoes oxidation, releasing electrons and protons. The electrons travel through an external circuit, generating an electric current. At the cathode, oxygen undergoes reduction by combining with the electrons returning from the external circuit and the protons that have moved through the electrolyte. This continuous supply of hydrogen and oxygen ensures that the redox reactions persist, maintaining the generation of electrical energy as long as the reactants are replenished.

The two half-cell reactions are as follows:

$$\textbf{At anode: } 2H_2 \text{ (g)} + 4OH^- \text{ (aq)} \rightarrow 4H_2O \text{ (l)} + 4e\text{-}$$
$$\textbf{At cathode: } O_2 \text{ (g)} + 2H_2O \text{ (l)} + 4e\text{-} \rightarrow 4OH\text{-} \text{ (aq)}$$
$$\textbf{Net reaction: } 2H_2 \text{ (g)} + O_2 \text{ (g)} \rightarrow 2H_2O \text{ (l)}$$

The EMF of this cell is measured to be 1.23 V. A number of such fuel cells are stacked together in series to make a battery.

Advantages:
- It converts chemical energy directly into electrical energy with high efficiency.
- It produces water as the only byproduct, leading to zero emissions of pollutants and greenhouse gases.
- It provides a continuous supply of electricity as long as hydrogen and oxygen are supplied.
- It can use a variety of fuels, including pure hydrogen or hydrogen-rich fuels.
- It can be scaled for various applications, from small portable devices to large power plants.
- It reduces dependency on fossil fuels, contributing to energy security.
- It has a long operational life with proper maintenance.

Applications:
- It is used in powering electric vehicles, buses, trains, and even aircraft.
- It provides electricity for homes, businesses, and remote locations.
- It is used in energising laptops, smartphones, drones, and other electronics.
- It has marine applications such as propelling boats, submarines, and maritime vessels.
- It generates electricity for spacecraft and satellites.
- It supplies power for remote data collection and monitoring stations.
- It supports off-grid residences and communities with sustainable energy.
- It facilitates the growth of hydrogen infrastructure, including refuelling stations and distribution networks.

7.6 PHOTOVOLTAIC CELL:

A solar cell, also known as a photovoltaic cell (PV cell), is an electrical device that transforms light energy into electrical energy using the photovoltaic effect. Fundamentally, a solar cell is a p-n junction diode. These cells fall under the category of photoelectric cells, which are devices whose electrical properties, such as current, voltage, or resistance, change when exposed to light.

Individual solar cells can be linked together to form modules commonly known as solar panels. A typical single-junction silicon solar cell can generate a maximum open-circuit voltage of about 0.5 to 0.6 volts. Although a single cell produces a small amount of voltage, combining many of them in a large solar panel allows for the generation of substantial renewable energy.

Construction:

A solar cell is essentially a junction diode, but its construction slightly differs from traditional p-n junction diodes. A very thin layer of p-type semiconductor is deposited on a thicker n-type semiconductor layer. Fine electrodes are applied on the top of the p-type layer, allowing light to penetrate the thin p-type layer. Just beneath this layer lies the p-n junction. A current-collecting electrode is placed at the bottom of the n-type layer. The entire assembly is encapsulated with thin glass to shield the solar cell from mechanical damage.

Working:

When light hits the p-n junction, photons easily penetrate the very thin p-type layer. The energy from the photons generates numerous electron-hole pairs in the junction. This disrupts the thermal equilibrium of the junction. Free electrons in the depletion region move quickly to the n-type side, while holes move to the p-type side. The newly created electrons, once on the n-type side, cannot cross back due to the barrier potential of the junction. Similarly, the newly created holes cannot cross back once on the p-type side due to the same barrier potential. As a result, the electron concentration increases on the n-type side, and the hole concentration increases on the p-type side, making the p-n junction act like a small battery cell. This generates a voltage known as photovoltage. Connecting a small load across the junction allows a small current to flow through it.

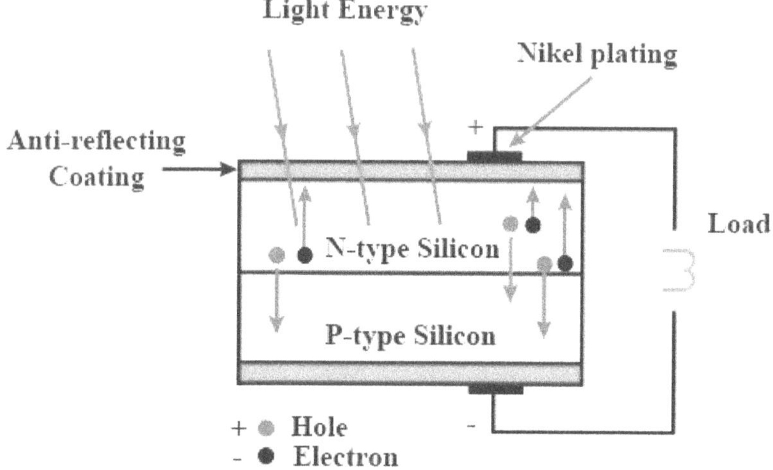

Figure 7.4: Diagram of a photovoltaic cell

Materials Used in Solar Cells: The materials used for this purpose must have a band gap close to 1.5 eV.

Commonly used materials are:

1. Silicon (Si)
2. Cadmium Telluride (CdTe)
3. Copper Indium Gallium Selenide (CIGS)
4. Perovskite Materials
5. Organic Photovoltaics (OPVs), etc.

Advantages of Solar Cells:

- Solar energy generation produces no greenhouse gases or harmful emissions, reducing the carbon footprint.
- Solar cells harness energy from the sun, an abundant and inexhaustible resource.
- Utilising solar cells reduces reliance on fossil fuels and enhances energy security.

- Once installed, solar cells have minimal maintenance and operational costs compared to traditional power plants.
- Continuous improvements in solar technology are increasing efficiency and reducing costs.
- The solar industry creates jobs in manufacturing, installation, and maintenance.

Applications of Solar Generation Systems:
- It provides electricity for homes, reducing utility bills and increasing energy independence.
- It supplies electricity to remote areas without grid access, powering homes, schools, and clinics.
- Solar energy powers irrigation systems, greenhouse lighting, and farm equipment, promoting sustainable farming.
- Solar thermal systems heat water for residential, commercial, and industrial use, reducing reliance on conventional heaters.
- Remote telecom towers and equipment are powered by solar energy, ensuring reliable operation without grid connectivity.
- Solar generation systems provide emergency power during natural disasters, supporting communication, medical care, and essential services.

7.7 HYDROGEN (H_2) AS A GREEN FUEL:

Hydrogen (H_2) is emerging as a pivotal player in the quest for sustainable and clean energy solutions. As the most abundant element in the universe, hydrogen offers immense potential for energy production with minimal environmental impact. When utilised as a fuel, hydrogen produces only water vapour as a byproduct, making it a zero-emission energy carrier. The versatility of hydrogen allows it to be integrated into various sectors, including transportation, industry, and energy storage, thus providing a multifaceted approach to reducing global greenhouse gas emissions and dependence on fossil fuels. This comprehensive exploration delves into the production, storage, and utilisation of hydrogen, emphasising its role as a green fuel in the context of a sustainable energy future.

Production:

Hydrogen can be produced through multiple methods, each varying in environmental impact and efficiency. The key to leveraging hydrogen as a green fuel lies in producing it from renewable energy sources. Here are the primary methods for hydrogen production:

1. **Electrolysis of Water**:
   - **Process**: Electrolysis involves using an electrical current to split water (H_2O) into hydrogen (H_2) and oxygen (O_2).
     The overall reaction is: $2H_2O \rightarrow 2H_2 + O_2$
   - **Renewable Energy**: When the electricity required for electrolysis is derived from renewable sources such as wind, solar, or hydropower, the hydrogen produced is termed "green hydrogen." This process is highly sustainable as it eliminates the carbon footprint associated with traditional hydrogen production methods.
   - **Efficiency and Costs**: Advances in electrolyser technology, such as proton exchange membrane (PEM) and solid oxide electrolysers, are improving efficiency and reducing costs. PEM electrolysers, for instance, offer high efficiency and rapid response times, making them suitable for integration with intermittent renewable energy sources.

1. **Biomass Gasification**:
   - **Process**: Biomass gasification converts organic materials, such as agricultural waste, into hydrogen and carbon dioxide through a high-temperature process in the presence of a controlled amount of oxygen or steam. The reaction typically involves:

$$C + H_2O \rightarrow H_2 + CO$$
$$CO + H_2O \rightarrow H_2 + CO_2$$

   - **Sustainability**: Utilising waste biomass not only provides a renewable source of hydrogen but also helps in waste management, thereby offering a dual environmental benefit. This method is particularly appealing in regions with abundant biomass resources.

2. **Photoelectrochemical Water Splitting**:
   ○ **Process**: This method uses sunlight directly to split water into hydrogen and oxygen using photoelectrochemical cells (PECs). These cells combine photovoltaic and electrochemical processes in a single device. The reaction is similar to electrolysis but driven by solar energy.
   ○ **Potential**: Still in the research and development phase, this technology promises a direct and efficient way to produce green hydrogen. Advances in materials science, particularly in developing durable and efficient photoelectrodes, are critical for the commercialisation of this technology.

Storage: Efficient and safe storage of hydrogen is crucial for its widespread adoption as a fuel. Hydrogen can be stored in various forms, each suited to different applications and scales:

1. **Compressed Gas**: Hydrogen gas is compressed and stored in high-pressure tanks, typically at pressures of 350-700 bar (5,000-10,000 psi).
2. **Liquid Hydrogen**: Hydrogen is liquefied at extremely low temperatures (-253°C or -423°F) and stored in insulated cryogenic tanks.
3. **Metal Hydrides**: Hydrogen can be absorbed and released from certain metal alloys, forming metal hydrides. The process involves reversible chemical reactions between hydrogen and metals.
4. **Chemical Storage**: Hydrogen can be stored chemically in compounds such as ammonia ($NH3$) or in liquid organic hydrogen carriers (LOHCs). Ammonia, for example, can be decomposed to release hydrogen when needed.

Applications: Hydrogen can be utilised across various sectors, providing a clean alternative to fossil fuels:

- Hydrogen fuel cells power electric vehicles (cars, buses, trucks, and trains) by converting hydrogen into electricity, emitting only water vapour.
- Hydrogen can fuel aircraft and ships, offering a zero-emission alternative to conventional aviation and marine fuels.

- Hydrogen is used in industrial processes like ammonia production for fertilisers, methanol production, and oil refining.
- Hydrogen is used in producing chemicals like methanol, which can be further processed into various industrial products.
- Hydrogen can be used in gas turbines for power generation, either in dedicated hydrogen turbines or blended with natural gas.
- Hydrogen can be produced using renewable energy sources like solar and wind, then used to generate electricity, creating a sustainable power cycle.
- Hydrogen is used as a rocket fuel because of its high-energy density and efficiency.
- Hydrogen can be utilised in high-temperature industrial processes, such as cement and glass manufacturing.

IMPORTANT QUESTIONS:

1. What is a battery and how are they classified?.
2. Explain the construction, working, and application of a lithium-ion battery.
3. Explain the construction, working, and application of Ni-Cd battery.
4. Define batteries. Write short notes on Ni-Cd Batteries.
5. Explain in detail about lithium-ion batteries?
6. Define a fuel cell. Explain the construction and uses of an H_2-O_2 fuel cell.
7. Explain construction and working for a solar cell.
8. What are fuel cells? Explain the advantages and applications.
9. Explain Hydrogen as a Green Fuel. How can it store and give its applications.
10. What are the main sources of hydrogen production for green fuel applications?

CHAPTER 8

ENVIRONMENTAL CHALLENGES

8.1 AIR POLLUTION

The Public Health Service of the United States states that Air pollution may be defined as the presence in the outdoor atmosphere of one or more contaminants or a combination thereof in such quantities and of such duration as may be, or may tend to be injurious to human, plant, or animal life, or property, or which unreasonably interfere with the comfortable enjoyment of life, or property, or the conduct of business.

The framework and make-up of the atmosphere have already been talked about in earlier parts of this chapter. The atmosphere is a living system that slowly takes in pollution from natural and man-made sources, making it a natural sink. Forest fires, volcanic eruptions, wind, and sand or dust storms released into the air. The man-made pollutants due to vehicles, industrialisation, and human activity released various CO_2, NOx, SO_2, CO_2, and hydrocarbons. Particulates are a thousand times more than natural pollutants. The pollution in the air has gotten much worse because of things like more people, factories, cities, cars, and other things people do to make themselves more comfortable. Before they reach a sink, like an ocean or a person, the toxins move through the air, spread out, and may react with other things in the air. If toxins get into the air faster than they can be taken in by natural sinks, they will slowly build up in the atmosphere. Such a change in the dynamic balance in the atmosphere caused by air pollutants released by human activities and building up in large amounts in the atmosphere could have an impact on life on earth and its surroundings. This is because the weather conditions at any given time affect how the gaseous pollution in the air is diluted and spread out.

"Air pollution may be defined as impurities present in excessive quantity to cause adverse effects on plants, animals, human beings and materials."

Causes of Air Pollution

1) **Transportation Systems:**

I. **Use of fuel in automobiles**

The use of fossil fuels generates different pollutants being released into the atmosphere. A variety of dangerous pollutants are released when fuel is burnt in automobiles. This is given as follows:

- **Carbon Monoxide (CO):** It is a colourless, poisonous gas that is harmful to the environment and human beings.
- **Nitrogen Oxides (NOx):** These are responsible for the formation of smog and acid rain. They also irritate the respiratory system.

- **Volatile Organic Matters:** Organic matter reacts with NOx to form the ozone layer of smog.
- **Particulate Matter (PM):** Fine particles penetrate into the lungs that can cause health problems.

II. Use Diesel for Trains.

The burning of coal in steam engines released smoke and soot, causing air pollution. As diesel engines replaced steam engines, they released CO, NOx, and particulate matter.

Use of Fuel for Automobiles

Automobiles are responsible for major air pollution. The internal combustion engines of cars and trucks emit pollutants such as:

- **Hydrocarbons:** These can cause respiratory issues and contribute to smog formation.
- **Sulfur Dioxide (SO_2):** Although modern fuels are typically low in sulfur, older vehicles and poor-quality fuels can still release SO_2, which leads to acid rain.
- **Lead:** Automobiles released harmful lead particles.

III. Use of Fuel for Aeroplanes

In airplanes, aviation fuels are used, which are made of petroleum such as aviation gasoline and jet fuel. The burning of aviation fuels releases the following:

- **Carbon Dioxide (CO_2):** CO_2 released into the air contributes to climate change.
- **Water Vapour:** can contribute to the development of cirrus clouds and has a net warming impact.
- **Nitrogen Oxides (NOx):** These are responsible for the formation of smog and acid rain, and also irritate the respiratory system.
- **Particulate Matter (PM):** Fine particles penetrate into the lungs that can cause health problems.

2) Industrial Emissions:

I. Emissions of Smoke

Factories are major sources of air pollution. They emit large amounts of smoke and particulate matter such as sulfur dioxide (SO_2), nitrogen oxides (NOx), carbon monoxide (CO), and particulate matter (PM).

Coke and furnace ovens are used in steel manufacturing and metallurgical industries. The process of heating coal in the absence of air releases a significant amount of particulate matter and volatile organic compounds like carbon monoxide (CO), sulfur dioxide (SO_2), nitrogen oxides (NOx), and particulate matter. These pollutants can cause hazardous issues on respiratory issues, skin irritations, and even cancer.

The steam engines are main sources of air pollution. The combustion of coal in steam engines produced smoke particles such as carbon monoxide (CO), sulfur dioxide (SO_2), nitrogen oxides (NOx), and particulate matter. These emissions are responsible for decreasing air quality, particularly in industrial regions.

II. Exhaust Released in Power Plants

The exhaust released in power plants contains various harmful pollutants as follows:

- **Sulfur Dioxide (SO_2):** The sulfur-containing fuels release SO_2. It can cause acid rain and respiratory problems.
- **Nitrogen Oxides (NOx):** These are responsible for the formation of smog and acid rain, and also irritate the respiratory system.
- **Particulate Matter (PM):** Fine particles penetrate into the lungs that can cause health problems.
- **Carbon Dioxide (CO_2):** CO_2 is a greenhouse gas responsible for global warming and climate change.
- **Mercury:** Mercury can cause neurological and developmental damage, especially in children.

III. Chemical Fumes from Oil, Zinc Refineries, and Chemical Industries

The oil refining process emits several pollutants as follows:

Hydrocarbons released in the oil refining process emit benzene, toluene, and xylene. These compounds are harmful to human health, leading to the formation of ground-level ozone gas smog. Sulfur substances released in the oil refining process emit hydrogen sulphide (H_2S) and sulfur dioxide (SO_2), causing respiratory problems and also being responsible for acid rain. In the oil refining process, during various stages of refining, these substances contribute to the formation of smog and pose health risks.

The zinc refineries process emits several pollutants as follows:

Zinc refineries produce zinc from zinc ore, which release various pollutants such as sulfur dioxide (SO_2) and particulate matter. The emissions can cause respiratory issues and environmental damage.

The chemical industry's process emits several pollutants as follows:

Volatile Organic Compounds are emitted by chemical industries during manufacturing and processing. They give rise to the formation of smog and can cause health problems.

- **Nitrogen Oxides (NOx):** Emitted during high-temperature processes, NOx contributes to smog formation and acid rain.
- **Hazardous Air Pollutants (HAPs):** Including benzene, formaldehyde, and other toxic chemicals that pose significant health risks.

IV. Emissions from Metallurgical Plants, Iron and Steel Plants, and Incineration Plants

- **Metallurgical Plants:** Metallurgical plants process metals and minerals, emitting pollutants like sulphur dioxide (SO_2), nitrogen oxides (NOx), carbon monoxide (CO), and particulate matter. The smelting process, in particular, releases large quantities of sulphur dioxide (SO_2) and particulate matter.
- **Iron and Steel Plants:** Iron and steel plants are significant sources of air pollution. The production of iron and steel involves several processes, including coke production, blast furnaces, and basic oxygen furnaces.

These processes emit pollutants such as:

- **Particulate Matter (PM):** From the handling and processing of raw materials.
- **Sulphur Dioxide (SO₂):** From the combustion of sulphur-containing fuels and raw materials.
- **Nitrogen Oxides (NOx):** From high-temperature combustion processes.
- **Carbon Monoxide (CO):** From incomplete combustion of carbon materials.
- **Heavy Metals:** Including lead, cadmium, and mercury, which can cause severe health problems.
- **Incineration Plants:** Incineration plants burn waste materials to reduce their volume and produce energy. The combustion process emits various pollutants, including:
- **Particulate Matter (PM):** Including fine and ultrafine particles that can penetrate deep into the lungs.
- **Dioxins and Furans:** Highly toxic compounds formed during the combustion of chlorine-containing materials.
- **Heavy Metals:** Including lead, mercury, and cadmium, which can cause neurological and developmental damage.
- **Acid Gases:** Such as hydrogen chloride (HCl) and sulphur dioxide (SO₂), which can cause respiratory problems and environmental damage.

3) Chemical and Radioactive Emissions:

I. Injurious Chemical Fumes from Various Industries

Industrial activities are a significant source of air pollution due to the release of various harmful chemical fumes.

- **Chemical Plants:** These plants release a variety of toxic gases and vapors, such as sulphur dioxide (SO_2), nitrogen oxides (NO_x), volatile organic compounds (VOCs), and ammonia (NH_3). These pollutants can cause respiratory problems, skin irritations, and other health issues.

- **Oil Refineries:** Refineries emit sulphur compounds, hydrocarbons, and particulate matter. The combustion of fossil fuels in these facilities leads to the release of sulphur dioxide and nitrogen oxides, contributing to acid rain and smog formation.
- **Metallurgical Plants:** These facilities emit heavy metals, including lead, mercury, and cadmium, along with sulphur dioxide and carbon monoxide. These emissions can cause neurological, developmental disorders, respiratory issues, and cardiovascular diseases.
- **Iron and Steel Plants:** These plants release large amounts of particulate matter, sulphur dioxide, nitrogen oxides, and carbon monoxide. Workers and nearby residents are at risk of respiratory diseases, heart problems, and other health issues due to prolonged exposure.
- **Incineration Plants:** Waste incineration produces harmful gases such as dioxins, furans, and heavy metals. These pollutants can have severe health effects, including cancer, reproductive and developmental problems, and damage to the immune system.
- **Coke Ovens and Furnaces:** These are significant sources of polycyclic aromatic hydrocarbons (PAHs), which are known carcinogens. Long-term exposure to PAHs can lead to various types of cancers and respiratory diseases.

II. Evolution of Radioactive Gases and Suspended Radioactive Dust from Atomic Explosions

Radioactive pollution primarily arises from atomic explosions and the release of radioactive materials into the atmosphere.

- **Atomic Explosions:** The detonation of nuclear weapons releases a vast array of radioactive isotopes, including iodine-131, caesium-137, and strontium-90. These isotopes can travel long distances in the atmosphere and deposit on the ground, contaminating soil, water, and the food chain.
- **Radioactive Gases:** Gases such as xenon-133 and krypton-85 are released during nuclear explosions. These gases can disperse widely and pose significant health risks, including an increased likelihood of cancer and genetic mutations.

- **Suspended Radioactive Dust:** Also known as radioactive fallout, this consists of fine particles that remain suspended in the air after an atomic explosion. These particles can be inhaled or ingested, leading to internal radiation exposure and increasing the risk of cancers, particularly thyroid and bone cancers.

III. Accidental Discharges from Nuclear Reactors

Accidents at nuclear reactors can lead to the uncontrolled release of radioactive materials, posing severe environmental and health risks.

- **Chernobyl Disaster (1986):** One of the most severe nuclear accidents, the Chernobyl explosion released large quantities of radioactive isotopes into the atmosphere. The immediate area was heavily contaminated, leading to long-term health effects such as thyroid cancer, leukaemia, and other radiation-induced diseases among the affected population.
- **Three Mile Island Incident (1979):** Although the release of radioactive gases was relatively low compared to Chernobyl and Fukushima, the partial meltdown at Three Mile Island highlighted the potential risks associated with nuclear reactors. It led to heightened concerns about nuclear safety and the potential for radiation exposure.

Health Impacts of Radioactive Emissions:

- **Acute Radiation Syndrome (ARS):** High doses of radiation over a short period can cause ARS, characterised by nausea, vomiting, diarrhoea, and, in severe cases, death.
- **Long-term Health Effects:** Prolonged exposure to lower levels of radiation increases the risk of cancers, genetic mutations, and other chronic health conditions.
- **Environmental Impact:** Radioactive contamination can persist in the environment for decades, affecting soil, water, and the food chain, leading to long-term ecological damage and health risks for humans and wildlife.

4) **Urbanisation and Industrial Growth in India:**

I. **Development of Industries in Various Towns and Cities**
   - **Industrialisation Wave:** Post-independence, India focused on setting up heavy industries and large-scale manufacturing units. This was essential for self-reliance and reducing dependency on foreign goods.
   - **Urban Centres:** Major cities like Mumbai, Delhi, Kolkata, Chennai, Bengaluru, and Hyderabad became industrial hubs. These cities attracted investments and skilled labour, fostering rapid urbanisation.
   - **Employment Generation:** The growth of industries created numerous job opportunities, leading to the migration of people from rural to urban areas in search of better livelihoods.

Economic Growth: Industrial activities contributed significantly to India's GDP, enhancing infrastructure, transportation and overall economic health.

II. **Increasing Number of Automobiles**
   - **Rising Demand:** With economic growth, there was an increased demand for personal and commercial vehicles. This led to the establishment of automobile manufacturing units and ancillary industries.
   - **Urban Mobility:** Automobiles became essential for urban mobility, supporting the transportation needs of a growing urban population. Cities like Delhi, Mumbai, and Bengaluru saw a surge in the number of vehicles on the road.
   - **Economic Impact:** The automobile sector contributed to job creation, technological advancements, and infrastructure development. It also played a significant role in connecting different parts of the country, facilitating trade and commerce.
   - **Pollution Concerns:** The rise in the number of vehicles led to increased emissions of pollutants such as carbon monoxide (CO), nitrogen oxides (NOx), and volatile organic compounds (VOCs). This contributed significantly to urban air pollution and related health issues.

Effects of Air Pollution

The effects of air pollution are listed below.

i.   Effect of air pollution on human health.

ii. Effect of air pollution on plants.

iii. Effect of air pollution on properties of the atmosphere

iv. Effect of air pollution on animals.

i.   Effect of Air Pollution on Human Health

Air pollution is a major factor in causing humans to get ill. Tuberculosis, bronchitis, heart and chest diseases, stomach disorders, asthma, and cancers are caused due to chemicals present in the air.

1) **Pollutant:** Carbon monoxide (CO).
   - **Characteristics:** Colourless, tasteless, odourless gas at atmospheric concentration.
   - **Source:** Incomplete combustion of coal and oil fuel.
   - **Health Effects**: At lower doses, they can impair concentration and neurobehavioral function, whereas in higher doses they can cause chest pain and even death. When inhaled, it has the ability to combine with haemoglobin of blood and reduce its ability to transfer oxygen to the brain, heart, and other important organs. But carboxyhaemoglobin contents of blood depend on the CO contents of the air inhaled, time of exposure, and the activity of the person inhaling. It is particularly dangerous for babies and people with heart disease.

2) **Pollutant:** Nitrogen Oxides (NOx)
   - **Characteristics:** Reddish-brown highly reactive gas.
   - **Sources:** Vehicle emissions, power plants, industrial activities.
   - **Health Effects:** Causes asthma, bronchitis, pneumonia. Reduces lung function, leads to respiratory illnesses and breathing difficulties. NOx may cause asthma and possibly increase susceptibility to infections. NOx irritates the lungs, causing bronchitis and pneumonia. Reduction in functioning of lungs and respiratory illness and breathing difficulty are the causes of inhalation of NOx.

3) **Pollutant:** Nuclear Waste
   - **Characteristics: Nuclear** power plants, nuclear weapon testing, war, etc.
   - **Sources:** Individual radioactive emissions and gases.
   - **Health Effects:** Causes radioactive contamination of areas; cancer, mutations, and deaths.

4) **Pollutant: Lead (Pb)**
   - **Characteristics:** Heavy metal, more harmful when inhaled.
   - **Sources:** Emissions from motor vehicles using leaded gasoline. Ingestion and inhalation occur from food, water, and dust.
   - **Health Effects:** Causes oxygen deficiency in blood, irreversible brain damage, behavioural disorders. Particularly harmful to infants and young children. Lead can be inhaled or ingested. The inhaled lead is more serious than that of ingested lead. The finer particles of lead emitted by automobiles are retained in the lungs. Lead poisoning weakens the Central Nervous System (CNS) resulting in revolution, uncontrolled mental disturbances, coma and even death.

5) **Pollutant: Suspended Particulate Matter (SPM)**
   - **Characteristics:** Health effects depend on particle size.
   - **Sources:** Combustion processes, industrial activities, road dust, burning of garbage.
   - **Health Effects:** These inhaled particulate matters may be deposited in various regions of the respiratory system. Inhalation of the smaller particles causes lung damage, breathing problems, and triggers asthma. The smaller particles deposited in the respiratory system cannot be removed by the body's natural clearance mechanisms. These smaller particulates are chemically more active and may be acidic as well, and therefore more damaging. Increased respiratory diseases, lung damage, and the possibility of premature death are the effects of long-term exposure to air pollutants.

6) **Sulfur Dioxide (SO_2)**
   - **Characteristics:** Quickly affects the respiratory system.
   - **Sources:** Combustion of fossil fuels containing sulfur, industrial processes.

  - ○ **Health Effects:** SO_2, affects people quickly, usually within the first few minutes of exposure. SO_2 exposure can lead to the kind of acute health effects typical of particulate pollution. Exposure is linked to an increase in hospitalisations and deaths from respiratory and cardiovascular causes, especially among asthmatics and those with pre-existing respiratory diseases. The severity of these effects increases with rising SO_2 levels, and exercise enhances the severity by increasing the volume of SO_2 inhaled and allowing SO_2 to penetrate deeper into the respiratory tract.

7) **Pollutants: Ozone**
  - ○ **Characteristics:** Colourless gas and powerful oxidant.
  - ○ **Sources:** Formed by photochemical reactions involving nitrogen oxides and hydrocarbons, and a large constituent of photochemical smog.
  - ○ **Health Effects:** Health Ozone is a powerful oxidant. It can react with nearly any biological tissue. Ozone damages lung tissue and causes breathing problems, including asthma, coughing, sneezing, chest pain, irritates the respiratory tract and impairs lung function, causing coughing, shortness of breath. Exercise increases these effects, and heavy exercise can bring on symptoms even at low ozone levels. Evidence also suggests ozone exposure lowers the body's defences, increasing susceptibility to respiratory infections.

8) **Pollutant:** Carbon dioxide (CO_2)
  - ○ **Characteristics:** Colourless gas found in air.
  - ○ **Source:** Combustion of coal, petrol, and diesel.
  - ○ **Health Effect:** Increasing concentration over the years causes the greenhouse effect, leading to global warming and climate change.

ii.   Effect of Air Pollution on Plants

1) **Pollutant:** SO_2
  - ○ **Effects on Vegetation:** Chlorosis (Disappearance of chlorophyll and yellowing of leaves).

2) **Pollutant:** NO_2
  - ○ **Effects on Vegetation:** Premature fall of leaves, suppressed growth of plants, and reduced yield.

3) **Pollutant:** Ozone.
   - **Effects on Vegetation:** Necrosis (dead areas on leaves), leaf damage, and reduced yield
4) **Pollutant:** PAN (Peroxyacetylnitrate)
   - **Effects on Vegetation:** Premature fall of leaves, discolouration, and Epinasty (downward curvature of leaves due to higher growth rate on the upper surface).

iii. Effect of Air Pollution on Properties of the Atmosphere

Some of the effects of air pollution on the physical properties of atmospheres.

i.   Decrease in visibility
ii. Reduction of Solar Radiation
iii. Effects on weather conditions.
iv. Effects on atmospheric constituents

iv. Effect of Air Pollution on Animals

Animals take up fluorides from the air through plants. Their milk production falls, their teeth and bones are affected. They are also prone to lead poisoning and paralysis.

Control Measurement of Air Pollution:

The two types of control measures for air pollution are
1. Dilution
2. Control at source.

1. Dilution

Tall chimneys are used to dilute the air pollutants into the atmosphere. The tall chimneys may penetrate the inversion layer of the atmosphere and disperse the contaminants by reducing the ground-level contamination.

However, the method of dilution is a short-term control measure and it is not suitable for long-term control. Because, the pollutants dispersed by the tall chimneys are carried and spread around the area of disposal. This may cause harmful effects on the surrounding area.

2. Control at Source

Control of contaminants at the source is a better option than the method of dilution. This can be achieved by the following ways.

1) Proper Use of the Existing Equipment
- Regular Maintenance and Inspection.
- Proper Installation.
- Monitoring and Reporting.
- Training and Education.
- Optimising Equipment Performance
- Upgrading and Retrofitting
- Regulatory Compliance.
- Preventive Measures.
- Feedback and Improvement.
- Regular Reviews.

2) Change in Process
I) Industry: Chemical & petroleum industries.
- **Pollutants:** Many air pollutants
- **Control measure:** The volatile substances are removed by condensation. Non-condensable gases are recycled and used for additional reactions. The hydrogen sulphide gas is recycled and used to recover the elemental sulfur.

II) Industry: Cement industry
- **Pollutants:** Dust
- **Control measure:** By reducing gas velocity within the rotary kiln, by modifying the location of the feed to the kiln, by introducing a dense curtain near the outlet.

III) Industry: Smelting & Paper industries
- **Pollutants:** Highly objectionable sulfurous material.
- **Control measure:** By hydro-metallurgical separations of ores and use of no sulphides in paper making.

IV) **Industry:** Steel & Power plants
- ○ **Pollutants:** Oxides of sulfur, Oxides of nitrogen, Fly ash particles
- ○ **Control measure:** By introducing a molten iron bath, by recirculation of flue gas and water injection, by washing the coal before pulverisation (breaking).

3) Modification or Replacement of Equipment

I) **Source:** Automobile engines.
- ○ **Type of Pollutant:** Unburnt Carbon monoxide and hydrocarbons
- ○ **Modification/Replacement:** Proper modification and maintenance of engine parts.

II) **Source:** Petroleum Refineries.
- ○ **Type of Pollutant:** hydrocarbon.
- ○ **Modification/Replacement:** Proper modification and maintenance of engine parts.

III) **Source:** Automobiles.
- ○ **Type of Pollutant:** IC engines
- ○ **Modification/Replacement:** Alternative power sources.

4) Installation of Controlling Equipment

Emission control equipment is of two types.

A. Gaseous Control Equipment

1. Wet and dry adsorption.
2. Combustion or Catalytic Incineration

B. Particulate Control Equipment

1. Gravitational settling chambers.
2. Cyclone separators
3. Fabric filters (or) Bag filters.
4. Electrostatic precipitators
5. Wet scrubbers (or) Wet collectors

8.2 WATER POLLUTION

Water is essential for the survival of any form of life. On average, a human being consumes about 2 litres of water every day. Water accounts for about 70% of the weight of a human body. About 80% of the earth's surface (i.e., 80% of the total 50,000 million hectares in area) is covered by water. Out of the estimated 1,011 million km^3 of the total water present on earth, only 33,400 m^3 of water is available for drinking, agriculture, domestic, and industrial consumption. The rest of the water is locked up in oceans as saltwater, polar ice caps and glaciers, and underground. Owing to increasing industrialisation on one hand and exploding population on the other, the demands of water supply have been increasing tremendously. Moreover, a considerable part of this limited quantity of water is polluted by sewage, industrial wastes, and a wide array of synthetic chemicals. The menace of water-borne diseases and epidemics still threatens the well-being of population, particularly in underdeveloped and developing countries. Thus, the quality as well as the quantity of clean water supply is of vital significance for the welfare of make in India receives about 1400-1800 mm of rainfall annually. It is estimated that 96% of this water is used for agriculture, 3% for domestic use, and 1% for industrial activity. An analysis conducted in 1982 revealed that about 70% of all the available water in our country is polluted. In appreciation of this situation, several steps are being taken to control water pollution.

> "Water pollution is defined as any physical, chemical, or biological change in the quality of water.
> that has a harmful effect on living organisms or makes the water unsuitable for needs."

Causes of Water Pollution

The principal causes or sources of water pollution are:

1. **Industrial Wastes:** Water gets polluted by industrial effluents containing acids, alkalis, soaps, detergents, pesticides, insecticides, fungicides, and metals like Cu, Zn, Pb, Hg, etc., which are released from chemical industries. Moreover, pollution also occurs by wastes coming from industries like sugar, textile, paper, leather, tanneries, breweries, oil refineries, distilleries, slaughterhouses, and pharmaceuticals, etc.

2. **Domestic sewage:** It includes human and household wastewater, municipal waste, etc., which directly drains into canals and rivers, causing the pollution of river water. This sewage contains human excreta, urine, kitchen waste, street waste, and organic substances that provide nutrition for bacteria and fungi. Organic sewage does not kill fish directly. It is the lack of dissolved oxygen that kills the fish.

3. **Suspended particles:** The surface water may contain a high concentration of suspended solids (organic as well as inorganic), bacteria, algae, etc. This makes water unfit for domestic as well as industrial purposes. Algae, which grow in water, and synthetic detergents which are discharged into water, together create conditions for serious water pollution.

4. **Ocean Pollution:** The pollution of oceans is also becoming very serious these days, especially due to oil spilling. About one million tonnes of oil are spilled into the ocean each year from shipping and drilling operations. This leads to various types of problems, such as a threat to the benefits of sea, shore resorts, and beach life. The greatest threat is to seabirds. Oil interferes with their flight and swimming.

5. **Soil Particles:** clays, ores, and fine particles of soil on which water flows are added to water and cause water pollution.

6. **Agricultural Runoff:** Drain from land and fields: Residual insecticides, pesticides, and fungicides are washed down into lakes, streams, rivers, etc., and pollute them.

7. **Fertiliser Plants:** Water from fertiliser plants containing nitrates, phosphates, ammonia, etc., is released into water, causing water pollution.

8. **Radioactive Materials:** Atomic explosions and the processing of radioactive materials near water sources cause water pollution.

Effects of Water Pollution

1. Presence of many infectious agents causes many diseases.

2. Change in colour of water affects the usage of water and growth of plants and organisms in water.

3. The oxygen-demanding wastes such as animal manure and plant residues deplete the dissolved oxygen content of water, which is harmful to aquatic life.

4. The inorganic substances present in water cause many damages to the water,
    a. Makes the water unfit for drinking and other purposes.
    b. Corrosion of metals exposed to such water.
    c. Causes skin cancers, damages to spinal cord, CNS, liver, and kidneys.
    d. Reduces crop yield.

5. Growth of aquatic plants and fishes is affected by the presence of acids, alkalies, and toxic substances.

6. Oil and other lubricants affect the self-purification of the stream or water body.

7. The organic chemicals such as detergents, pesticides, plastics, oil and gasoline present in the water damage the CNS and cause birth defects and genetic disorders. Also, these are harmful to the lives of aquatic ecosystems.

8. Enrichment of nutrients (Eutrophication) from the surrounding watershed affects the penetration of light through the water, causing damage to the characteristics of water and aquatic life.

9. Dumping of solid wastes results in surface water as well as groundwater pollution.

10. Disposal of coolant water used in industries increases the temperature of the surface water. This affects the solubility of oxygen in water and the aquatic ecosystem.

11. More amounts of nitrates in water due to the application of artificial fertiliser in agricultural lands can cause methaemoglobinaemia, known as blue baby. Also, it decreases the oxygen-carrying capacity of the blood in the body.

12. Oil spills or leaks from underground storage tanks on land are affecting a large area in a very short time. Oil spills at sea decrease the oxygen level in the water and cause more harm to the marine plankton and creatures living in the sea.

13. Runoff from farms, backyards, and golf courses contains pesticides such as DDT that, in turn, contaminate the water.

14. Leachate from landfill sites is another major contaminating source. It damages the ecosystem's health and reproductive capacity of wildlife. Groundwater is susceptible to contamination, as pesticides are mobile in the soil.

15. Overexploitation of groundwater results in a decline in water levels. Also, it leads to seawater intrusion into the groundwater, which deteriorates its quality.

16. Presence of radioactive materials such as iodine, radon, caesium, uranium, and thorium and their isotopes causes genetic disorders, birth defects, and certain cancers.

17. The chlorinated organic pesticides like dieldrin, aldrin and DDT are hazardous mainly due to their concentration in the food chain. They have high stability, low vapour pressure and very low solubility in water. As a result of biological magnification (accumulation of concentration from one level to another level of the food chain), these are harmful to the mammals in the longer-term effects.

18. The presence of sediments (soil and silt) causes the following damages.

    a. Fills lakes and reservoirs.
    b. Obstructs shipping channel
    c. Clogs hydroelectric turbines.
    d. Affects photosynthesis of aquatic plants.
    c. Disturbs the aquatic food chain.
    f. Carries pesticides, bacteria, and harmful substances to the receiving water body.
    g. Makes the water unsuitable for bathing, swimming, boating, and other recreational uses.

Control of Water Pollution:

Science provides many practical solutions to minimise the present level of pollution and to clear earlier problems. All of these solutions come with some cost (both social and monetary). Some of such suggestions for controlling water pollution are listed below.

1. Farmers can reduce the runoff of fertilisers from their agricultural lands to the nearby water bodies and leaching into aquifers. This can be achieved by using slow-release fertilisers and avoiding fertilisers on sloped ground. Also, this can be achieved by providing buffer zones between the surface water body and the agricultural land.

2. Overfertilisation and improper application of pesticides can be avoided.

3. By using more biological control pests, the pesticide usage may be minimized.

4. Acid/Alkali/Organic/Toxic substances in industrial or municipal wastes should be treated properly.

5. Soil erosion can be minimised by reforesting critical and important watersheds.

6. By improving manure control and planting buffer zones, the runoff and infiltration of manure from animal feedlots may be controlled.

7. Proper and complete treatment of sewage water from sewage treatment plants can decrease the amount of pollution in the receiving water body.

8. Proper treatment must be given to all the effluents from the industries.

9. By encouraging industries to reduce or eliminate the use of toxic chemicals and hazardous materials.

10. Use of recycled materials can minimise the pollution. Because the pollution during its production can be avoided by using recycled materials.

11. By preventing groundwater contamination.

12. By reusing treated wastewater for irrigation purposes.

13. By reducing poverty and birth rates.

8.3   GLOBAL WARMING

Environmental problems like air, water, and land pollution or municipal waste disposal exist in every country. The nations have identified the causes of these problems and will continue to deal with them depending on how severe they are and how serious their commitment is to their abatement. A detailed discussion of these issues follows in subsequent chapters.

Today, we have fairly good information about environmental problems. The public, being conscious of these problems, wants the governments and international agencies to become actively involved in tackling them. The citizens are willing to cooperate in the environmental clean-up process because they (especially in the developed world) have realised that the risks arising from environmental damage are real and pose a serious challenge to their lifestyle and living standards. This consciousness probably impacted us from the conservation of nature because it became clear that resources were being exploited to the extent that they may get depleted and their conservation is one of the ways out. Resource depletion or exploitation is being carried out both by individuals and business corporations, the latter doing it for profit. From a conservation attitude, a new environmentalism developed that emphasised the interrelatedness of natural systems, highlighting the human-nature relationship and the interconnectedness of everything on this planet. This led to the development of the concept of natural capital, which became the central point of attention. The use of natural capital and subsequently the concept of sustainable development became issues of global concern. While the never-ending debate continues regarding sustainable development, certain environmental problems became categorised as global and national, though there is no global environmental problem that does not have a national dimension and vice versa.

Two global environmental problems are:
(i)   Global Warming
(ii) Ozone Depletion.

In general, developing countries are more concerned with short-term problems of water resources, air pollution, land degradation, deforestation, etc. The developed countries, on the other hand, are taking more interest in global environmental issues like global warming and ozone depletion. Anil Agarwal in Global Environmental Negotiations rightly mentions that, "unless all environmental problems are addressed within an integrated perspective that takes into account the local and global, there will be little confidence within the developing world that their concerns are being taken into the global environmental agenda. For example, the convention to corintoaccoutification (CDC) could not attract much attention from the developed world, with the result that this convention became a second-class convention.

"Global warming is defined as the increase in temperature of the earth, which causes more changes in climate."

Causes of Global Warming.

- Historical Temperature Rise: A gradual increase of 4-5°C over the past 20,000 years, with a sharp rise of 0.3-0.7°C in the last century.
- Nature of Reactions: Involves nearly 150 independent reactions.

Effects of Global Warming.

Following are some of the effects of global warming:

- More heatwaves
- Expansion of desert areas
- Natural fires in forestlands
- More evaporation of water from oceans and water bodies.
- Melting of ice caps in the Arctic and Antarctic regions
- More cloud formation in the atmosphere.
- Shorter and warmer winters and longer and shorter summers
- Changes in the pattern of rainfall
- Rise in sea level.
- Flooding and submergence of low-lying coastal areas.
- Disruption in farming.
- More droughts
- More impacts on plants, animals, and humans

Control Measures of Global Warming

Some of the control and remedial measures of global warming are:

- Reduction in consumption of fossil fuels such as coal and petroleum.
- Use of biogas plants.
- Use of nuclear power plants.

- Increasing forest cover.
- Use of unleaded petrol in automobiles.
- Installation of pollution-controlling devices in automobiles and industries.

8.4 OZONE LAYER DEPLETION

Ozone is an odourless, colourless gas composed of three atoms of oxygen (O_3). The normal oxygen we breathe has 2 atoms of oxygen in it (O_2). Ozone has the same chemical structure whether it occurs miles above the earth or at ground-level.

CFC is short for Chlorofluorocarbon. These are man-made chemicals which comprise Chlorine, Fluorine, and Carbon atoms. They are used in various industrial, commercial, and household applications.

These substances are.

Non-toxic, non-flammable, and non-reactive with other chemical compounds.

The most important types of CFCs for ozone depletion are.

a.   Trichlorofluoromethane, $CFCl_3$ (called CFC-11).

b.   Dichlorodifluoromethane, CF_2Cl_2 (CFC-12)

c.   1,1,2-Trichlorotrifluoroethane, CF_2ClCFC_{12} (CFC-113)

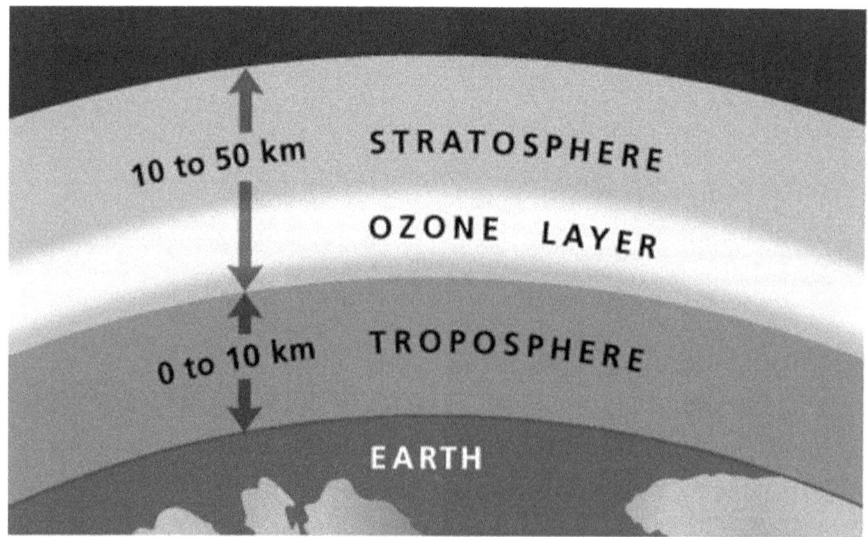

Ozone Layer Depletion Process

- **Stratosphere Region:** Located between 19 and 30 km above the Earth's surface.
- **Ozone Production and Destruction:** Ozone is constantly being produced and destroyed naturally. This dynamic process maintains the ozone layer.
- **Function of the Ozone Layer:** Absorbs ultraviolet (UV) radiation from the Sun.
- Protects life on Earth from harmful UV rays.
- **Balance of Ozone:** Normally, there is a balance between the production and loss of ozone.
- **Impact of Man-Made Chemicals:** Chlorofluorocarbons (CFCs) used as propellants and coolants are harming the ozone layer. CFCs themselves do not directly destroy ozone molecules.

Mechanism of Ozone Depletion:

CFCs decay at low temperatures, releasing chlorine atoms (Cl) and chlorine monoxide (ClO).

Chlorine atoms and ClO act as catalysts in the destruction of ozone molecules.

Catalytic Destruction:

Even small amounts of Cl and ClO can significantly accelerate the destruction of ozone.

These points summarise the key aspects of the stratosphere's ozone layer and the impact of CFCs on its balance.

The Simplest Equations Are:

$$Cl + O_3 \rightarrow ClO + O_2$$
$$ClO + O \rightarrow Cl + O_2$$
$$\text{Net effect: } O_3 + O \rightarrow 2O_2$$

Role of Chlorine Atom:

Functions as a catalyst in the destruction of ozone molecules. After breaking up one ozone molecule, the chlorine atom is freed to repeat the process and can continue to destroy ozone molecules repeatedly. Chlorine atoms remain active in the atmosphere until removed by other reactions or means. CFCs are stable compounds and can persist in the atmosphere for about 100 years.

Causes of Ozone Depletion

1) **Combustion of Fossil Fuels and Organic Matter:**
   - Pollutants: Oxides of carbon, nitrogen, sulphur, hydrocarbons, and particulate material.
   - Sources: Fossil fuel combustion, microbial decomposition.
   - Impact: Some pollutants reach the stratosphere, contributing to ozone depletion.

2) **Excessive Use of Nitrogenous Fertilisers:**
   - Pollutant: Nitrous oxide (N_2O).
   - Source: Microbial action on fertilisers.
   - Impact: N_2O accumulates in the atmosphere, where high-energy radiations convert it to nitric oxide, depleting ozone.

3) **Excessive Use of Chlorofluorocarbons (CFCs):**
   - Characteristics: Inert, stable, colourless, odourless, easily liquefied.
   - Impact: CFCs break down under high-energy radiation to release chlorine atoms, which destroy ozone molecules.
   - Scale: 16 billion kg of CFCs produced and used, significantly depleting the ozone layer.
   - Consequence: Predicted 6.5%-16% ozone depletion by 2030, with increased UV rays and higher skin cancer risk.

4) **Supersonic Transports, Rockets, and Space Shuttles:**
   - Pollutants: Oxides of carbon, nitrogen, sulphur, hydrocarbons, and particulate material.
   - Sources: Supersonic jetliners, space flights, rockets (using ammonium perchlorate as oxidant).
   - Impact: Pollutants are released directly into the stratosphere.

5) **Nuclear Tests:**
   - Pollutants: Various gases, dust, soot, and debris.
   - Impact: Surface nuclear explosions propel pollutants into the stratosphere, damaging the ozone layer.
   - Natural Sources Contributing to Stratospheric Ozone Depletion.
   - Solar Flares: Natural high-energy radiations.
   - Volcanic Eruptions: Emit pollutants like nitric oxide, chlorine atoms, and hydroxyl ions.

Effects of Ozone Layer Depletion:

a. The nature of the halogen (bromine-containing halocarbons usually have much higher ODPs than chlorocarbons because Br is a more effective ozone-destruction catalyst than Cl).

b. The number of chlorine or bromine atoms in a molecule.

c. Molecular Mass (since ODP is defined by comparing equal masses rather than equal numbers of moles).

d. Atmospheric lifetime (CH_3CCI_3 has a lower ODP than CFC-11 because much of the CH_3CCI_3 is destroyed in the troposphere)

Harmful Effects of Ozone Layer Depletion
Human Health

a. Reddening of skin in sunshine (Sunburn)

b. Skin Cancer.

c. Reduction in body's immunity to disease.

d. Eye disorders like cataracts and blindness

Other Living Things

a. The UV rays are harmful to other forms of wildlife, particularly small plants and animals living in the sea called 'Plankton'. Plankton forms the base of the ocean food chain.

b. The UV rays can damage certain crops, like rice, on which many people in the world rely for food.

c. These can damage polymers used in paint, clothing, and other materials.

Control of Ozone Depletion

Ozone depletion is primarily caused by the release of ozone-depleting substances (ODS) like chlorofluorocarbons (CFCs), halons, and other related chemicals. To address this issue, various measures and international agreements have been implemented to control and reduce the release of these harmful substances. Here are the main strategies for controlling ozone depletion:

1. **International Agreements and Protocols Montreal Protocol (1987):**
   An international treaty designed to phase-out the production and consumption of ODS. It has been amended several times to include more substances and accelerate the phase-out schedule. Widely regarded as one of the most successful environmental agreements.

2. **Regulation and Legislation and National Regulations:**
   Countries have enacted laws to control the production, use, and disposal of ODS. These regulations often include strict penalties for non-compliance, setting limits on the amount of ODS that can be released from industrial processes, vehicles, and other sources.

3. **Alternative Technologies and Substitute**
   Promoting the use of alternative substances that do not deplete the ozone layer, such as hydrofluorocarbons (HFCs), which are less harmful but still have some global warming potential. Encouraging research and development of new, more environmentally friendly technologies.
   Substitution in Industries: Transitioning from ODS to safer alternatives in refrigeration, air conditioning, foam-blowing agents, solvents, and fire extinguishing systems.

4. **Public Awareness and Education**
   Awareness Campaigns: Educating the public about the causes and effects of ozone depletion and the importance of protecting the ozone layer. Promoting responsible behaviour, such as proper disposal of products containing ODS and supporting ozone-friendly products.
   Educational Programmes: Integrating information about ozone depletion and environmental protection into school curriculum and public information resources.

5. **Technological Innovations**

   Leak Detection and Repair: Developing advanced technologies for detecting and repairing leaks in systems that use ODS, reducing emissions.

   Recycling and Recovery: Implementing systems for the recycling and recovery of ODS from old equipment, preventing their release into the atmosphere.

6. **Monitoring and Research**

   Atmospheric Monitoring: Continuous monitoring of the ozone layer and levels of ODS in the atmosphere to track progress and identify areas needing improvement.

   Scientific Research: Supporting research into the effects of ozone depletion, the recovery of the ozone layer, and the development of new technologies and strategies to protect it.

8.5   ACID RAIN

Acid rain is a type of precipitation that has a higher acidity than normal, due to the presence of elevated levels of hydrogen ions (low pH). This increased acidity is mainly caused by the emission of sulphur dioxide (SO_2) and nitrogen oxides (NO_x) into the atmosphere, which react with water, oxygen, and other chemicals to form sulphuric and nitric acids. These acidic compounds fall to the ground as rain, snow, sleet, fog, or dust, leading to environmental harm, such as damage to plants, aquatic ecosystems, buildings, and human health."

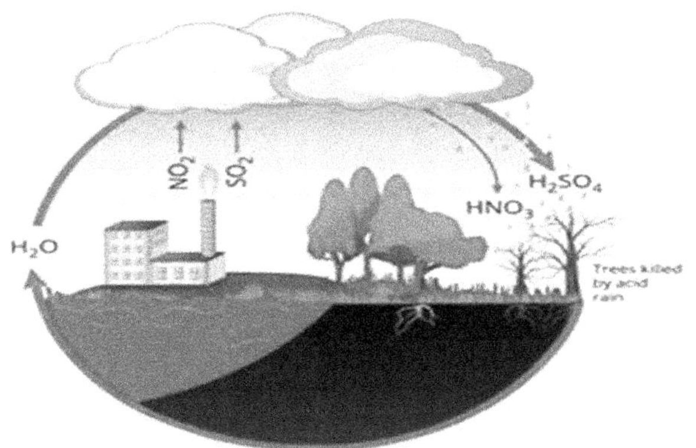

Measuring Acid Rain

Acid rain is measured using the pH scale. A lower value of pH indicates more acidity. Pure water has a pH value of 7.0. Normal rain is slightly acidic, with a pH value of 5.6, because carbon dioxide dissolves into it.

Causes of Acid Rain

Acid rain is primarily caused by the emission of sulphur dioxide (SO_2) and nitrogen oxides (NO_x) into the atmosphere. These pollutants originate from both natural and human activities and react with water vapour and other chemicals in the atmosphere to form sulphuric and nitric acids.

1) **Combustion of Fossil Fuels:**
    a. Power Plants: Burning coal and oil in power plants releases large amounts of sulfur dioxide (SO_2) and nitrogen oxides (NO_x).
    b. Vehicles: Automobiles, trucks, and buses emit nitrogen oxides (NO_x) from their exhaust systems.
    c. Industrial Processes: Factories and industries, especially those involved in refining oil and manufacturing chemicals, emit significant amounts of SO_2 and NO_x.

2) **Industrial Emissions:**
    a. Factories: Emissions from industrial plants, especially those involved in metal processing and the production of chemicals, contribute to the release of SO_2 and NO_x.
    b. Oil Refineries: Process crude oil into gasoline and other products, emitting sulfur dioxide (SO_2) during the refining process.

3) **Natural Sources:**
    a. Volcanic Eruptions: Emit sulfur dioxide (SO_2) and other gases into the atmosphere.
    b. Wildfires: Release nitrogen oxides (NO_x) and other pollutants when vegetation burns.
    c. Biological Decay: Natural processes like the decay of organic matter can release small amounts of sulphur compounds into the atmosphere.

4) **Agricultural Activities:**
   a. Fertilizers: The use of nitrogen-based fertilizers can result in the release of nitrogen oxides (NOx) into the atmosphere.
   b. Livestock: Animal waste emits ammonia, which can combine with NO_x to form nitric acid.

5) **Waste Disposal:**
   a. Incineration: Burning of waste materials in incinerators releases both SO_2 and NO_x.
   b. Landfills: Decomposition of organic waste in landfills produces methane and can release sulphur compounds.
   c. Chemical Reactions Leading to Acid Rain.

Formation of Sulphuric Acid (H_2SO_4):

$$SO_2 + OH \rightarrow HOSO_2$$
$$HOSO_2 + O_2 \rightarrow HO_2 + SO_3$$
$$SO_3 + H_2O \rightarrow H_2SO_4$$

Formation of Nitric Acid (HNO_3):

$$NO_2 + OH \rightarrow HNO_3$$

These acids are then carried by wind and atmospheric currents and fall to the ground as acid rain, causing environmental harm.

Effects of Acid Rain

Acid rain can cause serious problems for many different animals and plants.

1. Both dry and wet deposition of sulphur dioxide significantly increase the rate of corrosion of limestone, sandstone, and marble.
2. Forest tree population is affected and decreased by acid rain.
3. Acid rain, in combination with ozone, may damage the waxy coating on leaves and needles. This may weaken or damage them and provide opportunities for disease to enter the tree.

4. Acid rain may change the characteristics of soil and eventually pollute the streams and lakes.

5. Acid rain adds hydrogen ions to the soil. These hydrogen ions leach the important nutrients such as Calcium, Magnesium and Potassium and affect availability to the roots of the plant.

6. It may reduce the number of zooplankton, phytoplankton, molluscs, and seal crustaceans.

7. It reduces the decomposition of dead plants and animals.

8. Calcium deficiency in fishes can lead to bone malformation.

9. The health effects that people have to worry about are not caused by acid rain, but are caused when people breathe in these tiny particles or ozone, which can lead to bronchitis and can even cause permanent lung damage.

10. The chemicals found in acid rain can cause paint to peel and stone statues to begin to appear old and worn down, which reduces their value and beauty.

Control of Acid Rain

The formation of acid rain can be minimised by using the following methods.

1. By reducing pollution from industries,

2. By using other sources of energy,

3. By using cleaner automobiles.

1. **Reducing Pollution from Industries:** The release of sulfur dioxide is reduced from the coal-burning power plants in the following ways.

   o By using less sulfur coal.

   o By washing the coal to remove some of the sulfur.

   o By installing pollution-controlling devices like scrubbers to remove the sulfur dioxide.

2. **By using other sources of energy:** By producing energy without using fossil fuels, the possibility of acid rain can be minimised. The use of fossil fuel can be reduced by using renewable energy sources, such as solar and wind power. Renewable energy sources help in reducing acid

rain because they produce much less pollution. These energy sources can be used to power machinery and produce electricity.

3. **By using cleaner automobiles:** Automobiles are the major sources of the acid rain pollutants. By using pollution control devices like catalytic converters or by using natural gas in the automobiles, the possibility of the formation of pollutants that are responsible for the formation of acid rain can be minimised.

8.6 SOIL POLLUTION

Soil pollution is defined as the addition of substances, biological organisms into the soil, resulting in a change of the soil quality, which affects the normal use of the soil or endangers public health and the living environment.

8.6.1 Sources of Soil Pollution

1. **Urban Waste**

   Both domestic and commercial wastes are classified as urban wastes. All solid wastes of urban wastes are commonly termed as 'refuse', which contains garbage and rubbish materials like papers, fibres, plastics, glass, bottles, street sweepings, leaves, abandoned vehicles, and other discarded products.

2. **Industrial Waste**

    More quantity of solid as well as liquid wastes is discharged by most industries onto the soil. The industrial wastes are the major source of soil pollution. Industrial wastes mainly consist of organic and inorganic compounds along with non-biodegradable materials. Due to the filtering capacity of the soil, most of the chemicals present in the liquid wastes accumulate in the soil and cause soil pollution. These chemicals alter and deteriorate the characteristics of the soil and its fertility.

8.6.2   Causes of Soil Pollution

Solid waste management involves the systematic control of the generation, collection, storage, transport, treatment, and disposal of solid waste. Effective waste management is crucial for maintaining environmental quality, public health, and sustainability.

Causes of Urban and Industrial Waste

Urban Waste:

a. Population Growth: Rapid urbanization leads to increased waste generation.

b. Consumption Patterns: Higher living standards and consumerism result in more waste.

c. Lack of Awareness: Public ignorance about waste management practices needed in waste issues.

d. Inadequate Infrastructure: Poor waste collection and disposal systems are prevalent in many urban areas.

e. Packaging Materials: Extensive use of non-biodegradable packaging materials adds to urban waste.

Industrial Waste:

a. Manufacturing Processes: Various industrial activities produce waste as by-products.

b. Outdated Technologies: Inefficient technologies lead to higher waste production.

c. Resource Extraction: Activities like mining generate large quantities of waste.
d. Regulatory Gaps: Lack of stringent regulations and enforcement results in improper waste management.
e. Process Residues: Chemical, thermal, and mechanical processes often produce solid waste residues.

Control Measures for Urban Waste

a. Segregation at Source: Encourage households to separate biodegradable and non-biodegradable waste. Implement colour-coded bins for easy segregation.
b. Recycling Programs: Promote recycling of paper, plastics, glass, and metals. Establish recycling centres and encourage community participation.
c. Composting: Encourage composting of organic waste. Provide community composting facilities and training.
d. Public Awareness Campaigns: Educate the public on the importance of waste reduction, recycling, and proper disposal. Use media, workshops, and school programmes to spread awareness.
e. Improved Infrastructure: Invest in better waste collection, transportation, and disposal systems. Ensure regular maintenance and monitoring of waste management facilities.

Control Measures for Industrial Waste

a. Cleaner Production Techniques: Adopt technologies that minimise waste production at the source. Implement process optimisation to reduce waste generation.
b. Waste Audits: Conduct regular waste audits to identify waste sources and potential reduction measures. Use audit results to improve waste management practices.
c. Reuse and Recycling: Encourage industries to reuse materials and recycle waste within the production process. Develop industrial symbiosis where waste from one industry is used as a resource by another.

d. Regulatory Compliance: Enforce stringent regulations on industrial waste management. Ensure industries comply with environmental standards and regulations.

e. Waste-to-Energy Technologies: Implement technologies that convert industrial waste into energy. Use incineration, pyrolysis, and gasification to produce energy from waste.

f. Hazardous Waste Management: Ensure proper handling, storage, and disposal of hazardous waste. Use specialised facilities for the treatment and disposal of hazardous materials.

Effective solid waste management requires a combination of technical solutions, regulatory measures, and public participation. By implementing these control measures, urban and industrial waste can be managed efficiently, leading to a cleaner and healthier environment.

For more comprehensive strategies on solid waste management, visit Create More Customers Agency.

Effects of Soil Pollution

1. Removal of the topsoil of land causes low fertility for crop production.

2. Disposal of industrial effluents and domestic wastes on land causes the accumulation of chemicals and loss of fertility.

3. Presence of arsenic (As) in the soil causes chronic poisoning which leads to loss of appetite and weight, diarrhoea, gastrointestinal problems, and sometimes skin cancer.

4. Soil flora and fauna may be adversely affected.

5. The crop produced in a polluted land will be of inferior quality.

6. Deforestation is threatening not only the existence of many species and the livelihood of many more people, but can also influence the climate.

7. Toxic chemicals leached from landfilling areas into the soil underneath causing an unusually large number of birth defects, cancers, and respiratory, nervous, and kidney diseases.

8. The disposal of cadmium from mining, metallurgy, chemical, and electroplating industries causes chronic poisoning, formation of kidney stones, and sometimes kidney failure.

9. Accumulations of methylmercury compounds are much more toxic than other forms of mercury. It causes neurological problems and damages renal glomeruli and tubules.

IMPORTANT QUESTIONS:

1. Define air pollution. List three major causes of air pollution related to transportation.
2. How does carbon monoxide affect human health?
3. Describe the health effects of nitrogen oxides (NOx).
4. What are the health effects of inhaling lead (Pb)?
5. List three methods of controlling air pollution at the source.
6. What are the effects of sulfur dioxide (SO_2) on vegetation?
7. Define water pollution. List three principal causes of water pollution.
8. What type of industrial wastes contribute to water pollution?
9. How does domestic sewage pollute water bodies?
10. What impact does agricultural runoff have on water pollution?
11. How do fertilizers contribute to water pollution?
12. What are the effects of radioactive materials on water quality?
13. What is acid rain? What pollutants primarily cause acid rain?
14. Name three human activities that contribute to acid rain.
15. List two natural sources of sulfur dioxide (SO_2).
16. How does the use of nitrogen-based fertilizers contribute to acid rain?
17. Explain the formation of sulfuric acid (H_2SO_4) in the atmosphere.
18. What is ozone, and where is it found in the atmosphere?
19. What are Chlorofluorocarbons (CFCs)? How do CFCs contribute to ozone layer depletion?
20. Describe the role of chlorine atoms in the destruction of ozone.
21. What are the harmful effects of increased UV radiation due to ozone depletion?
22. Define soil pollution.
23. List three sources of soil pollution.
24. How does industrial waste contribute to soil pollution?
25. What are the effects of soil pollution on crop production?

26. Explain how urban waste management can help control soil pollution.

27. Explain the primary sources of industrial emissions that contribute to air pollution and their impacts on the environment and human health.

28. Discuss the health effects of air pollution on human health, focusing on specific pollutants such as carbon monoxide, nitrogen oxides, lead, and suspended particulate matter.

29. Describe the control measures of air pollution at the source, providing examples from different industries such as chemical, cement, and petroleum industries.

30. Explain the effects of air pollution on plants and animals, detailing how specific pollutants impact vegetation and animal health.

31. Discuss the major causes of water pollution, including industrial wastes, domestic sewage, and agricultural runoff.

32. Explain the various effects of water pollution on human health, aquatic life, and the environment.

33. Describe the effects of inorganic substances present in water on human health. Give details on skin cancers, CNS damage, and corrosion of metals.

34. Explain the effectiveness of various control measures for water pollution.

35. Discuss the impact of chlorinated organic pesticides on the environment and human health.

36. How overexploitation of groundwater leads to water pollution, including the process of seawater intrusion and its consequences on water quality.

37. Describe the process of acid rain formation, including the chemical reactions involved.

38. Discuss the environmental impacts of acid rain on soil, plants, and aquatic life.

39. Explain the role of industrial emissions in the formation of acid rain.

40. Evaluate the effectiveness of various methods to control acid rain.

41. Explain the long-term effects of acid rain on human health and infrastructure.

42. Explain the process of ozone layer depletion, including the chemical reactions involved.
43. Discuss the environmental and health impacts of ozone layer depletion.
44. Explain the effectiveness of the Montreal Protocol in controlling ozone depletion.
45. Describe the various human activities that contribute to ozone layer depletion.
46. Describe the causes and sources of soil pollution in urban and industrial areas.
47. Discuss the effects of soil pollution on human health and the environment.
48. Explain the effectiveness of various control measures for urban and industrial waste.
49. Explain how hazardous waste management can prevent soil pollution.

CHAPTER 9

BIOCHEMICAL TECHNOLOGY AND BIOINFORMATICS

9.1 INTRODUCTION

Biochemical technology encompasses commercial techniques that utilise living organisms or their derivatives to produce or modify products. These techniques aim to improve economically important plants and animals and develop microorganisms for environmental applications. Historically, biotechnology isn't a novel concept, as ancient practices such as fermentation and crossbreeding utilised biological processes without understanding the underlying mechanisms. Modern biotechnology, however, focuses on advanced techniques like recombinant DNA and cell fusion.

" Biochemical engineering is concerned with conducting biological processes on an industrial scale. This area links biological sciences with chemical engineering. The role of biochemical engineers has become more important in recent years due to the dramatic developments of biotechnology."

Recombinant DNA Technology: This technique involves directly manipulating the genetic material of cells. Genetic engineering, a key aspect of recombinant DNA technology, involves splicing foreign genes into plasmids and inserting them into organisms. The objective is for these foreign genes to be expressed, leading to the production of new products by the host organism. Cell Fusion involves combining two different types of cells to form a hybrid cell. The fusion aims to combine desirable characteristics from both parent cells, such as producing monoclonal antibodies (MAbs) using specialised immune system cells fused with tumour cells to achieve both rapid growth and the ability to produce antibodies. Applications of biotechnology include producing pharmaceuticals like insulin, growth hormones, and vaccines, developing disease-resistant crops, and creating genetically modified microorganisms for higher yield production of chemical compounds.

9.2   DNA AND RNA

DNA (Deoxyribonucleic Acid):

Structure: DNA is a macromolecule composed of linear polymers built from nucleotide subunits. Each nucleotide contains:

1) A five-carbon sugar (deoxyribose), namely.
2) A nitrogenous base (purine: adenine (A), guanine (G); pyrimidine: cytosine (C), thymine (T)).
3) A phosphate group.

Double Helix: DNA consists of two complementary strands forming a double helix, with a diameter of about 20 Å and a complete turn every 34 Å. Each strand is connected by hydrogen bonds between specific base pairs (A-T and G-C), ensuring the transmission of genetic information during cell replication.

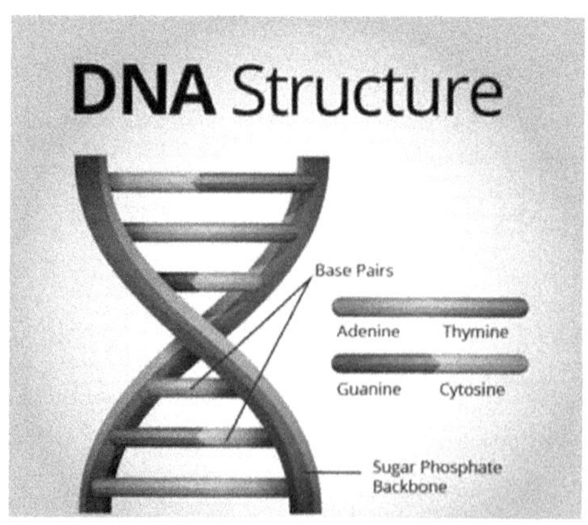

Genetic Information: The sequence of bases (A, G, T, C) in DNA dictates the order of amino acids in proteins. The genetic code, comprising codons (sequences of three bases), specifies which amino acids will be assembled to form proteins. This specificity allows for the accurate transmission of genetic information from one generation to the next.

Function of DNA:

Function	Description
Storage of Genetic Information	Encodes genetic instructions in genes.
Transmission of Genetic Information	Inherited through replication and heredity.
Protein Synthesis	Template for mRNA during transcription guides protein assembly in translation.
Regulation of Cellular Activities	Controls gene expression and cellular functions.
Evolution	Provides genetic variation and enables adaptation through mutations and recombination.

DNA's ability to store, transmit, and regulate genetic information makes it fundamental to all biological processes and the continuity of life.

RNA (Ribonucleic Acid):

Structure: RNA is similar to DNA but contains ribose sugar instead of deoxyribose and uses uracil (U) instead of thymine (T). RNA nucleotides are joined by phosphodiester bonds to form a linear polynucleotide chain.

Function of RNA:

RNA plays a crucial role in protein synthesis. There are various types of RNA, including messenger RNA (mRNA), transfer RNA (tRNA), and ribosomal RNA (rRNA), each serving distinct functions in translating genetic information from DNA into proteins.

Biochemical technology leverages advanced techniques to modify organisms for various applications, while the structure and function of DNA and RNA are fundamental to understanding genetic manipulation and protein synthesis.

RNA (RIBONUCLEIC ACID)

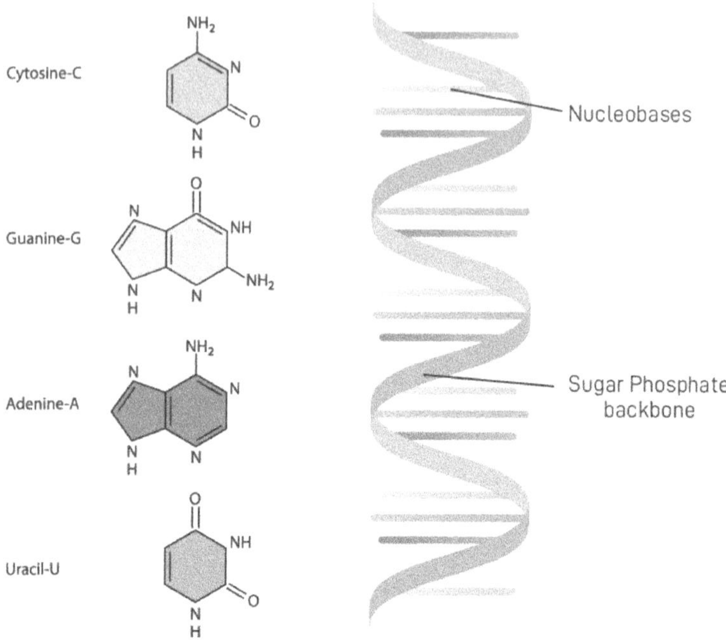

RNA Type	Function
mRNA (Messenger RNA)	Carries genetic information from DNA to ribosomes for protein synthesis.
tRNA (Transfer RNA)	Transports specific amino acids to the ribosome during protein synthesis.
rRNA (Ribosomal RNA)	Structural and functional components of ribosomes catalyse peptide bond formation.
snRNA (Small Nuclear RNA)	Involved in RNA splicing, removing introns from pre-mRNA.
miRNA (MicroRNA)	Regulates gene expression by binding to complementary mRNA sequences.
siRNA (Small Interfering RNA)	Similar to miRNA, involved in gene silencing and regulation.
lncRNA (Long Non-Coding RNA).	Regulates gene expression at multiple levels, including chromatin modification and transcription.

Difference between DNA and RNA

Feature	DNA	RNA
Sugar	Deoxyribose	Ribose
Nitrogenous Bases	Adenine, Thymine, Guanine, Cytosine.	Adenine, Uracil, Guanine, Cytosine.
Strand Structure	Double-stranded (double helix).	Single-stranded
Function	Genetic information storage.	Protein synthesis, gene regulation.
Types	One primary form	mRNA, tRNA, rRNA, snRNA
Stability	More stable	Less stable
Location	Nucleus (eukaryotes), mitochondria.	Nucleus, cytoplasm, ribosomes.

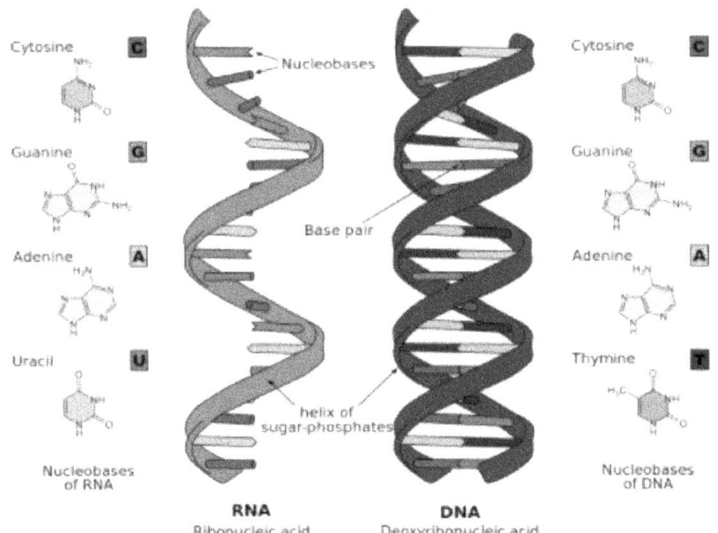

9.3   GENETIC ENGINEERING

Genetic engineering is the directed manipulation of the hereditary material. It is based on a set of molecular techniques collectively called recombinant DNA (DNA) technology. In essence, rDNA technology consists of the splicing of a piece of DNA to a suitable carrier, which is then introduced into a convenient cell that allows the 'passenger' or 'foreign' DNA to express itself in the new surroundings.

The introduced foreign DNA is amplified into several thousand copies together with the carrier DNA. This has been, until recently, the only way of acquiring a measurable quantity of DNA in the purest of forms. The latest strategy of amplifying a length of DNA is the one that uses the Polymerase Chain Reaction or the PCR technique. This technique, unlike conventional gene cloning methods, requires no cloning in host cells. Why does one need to 'clone a piece of DNA? Where does one begin to answer such a question? Recombinant DNA technology has become a tool that is so fine-honed and the sphere of its influence so staggeringly large that perhaps it would be easier to tick off areas of research where it cannot be utilised profitably. Indeed, there is hardly a question in the enigma of the living system that will not profit by being phrased in terms of cloned DNA.

The many phenomena of molecular biology burst on the scene almost a century after the birth of the concept of a gene. The double helix model of the genetic material provided the insight into Mendel's factors and the molecular antics of the genetic material began to be comprehensible. New facts were requisitioned into applications and became the basis for more incisive tools; recombinant DNA technology had emerged.

- **Definition:** Genetic engineering involves the deliberate modification of an organism's genetic material.
- **Recombinant DNA (rDNA) Technology:** A set of molecular techniques enabling the splicing of a DNA fragment to a suitable carrier, which is then introduced into a host cell for expression and amplification.

Purpose of DNA Cloning:

- Amplification of DNA: Initially, rDNA technology was the primary method to obtain pure DNA in large quantities.
- Polymerase Chain Reaction (PCR): A modern technique that amplifies DNA without the need for cloning in host cells.

Recombinant DNA Technology:

1) **Foundational Discoveries:**
   - Watson and Crick DNA Model: Provided insight into genetic material structure.
   - Key Enzymes: Enzymes like ligases (joining DNA backbones) and restriction enzymes (cleaving DNA at specific sites) are crucial for rDNA technology.

2) **Gene Cloning Process:**
   - Vector Selection: Choose a vector DNA that can replicate independently and is suitable for carrying the foreign DNA.
   - DNA Fragmentation: The donor DNA and vector DNA are cleaved into pieces, mixed, and hybrid molecules are formed.
   - Transformation: Hybrid DNA molecules are introduced into host cells (commonly E. coli). Transformed cells containing hybrid DNA are identified and cultured.
   - Selection and Culturing: Identify colonies with the desired DNA fragment and culture them for sufficient hybrid DNA extraction.

3) **Historical Milestones:**
   - First Gene Cloning (1973): By Herbert Boyer and Stanley Cohen.

4) **Enzymes in rDNA Technology:**
   - Restriction Enzymes: Create staggered cuts, producing 'sticky ends' that facilitate the joining of donor and vector DNA.
   - Ligase: Seals DNA backbones.
   - Other Enzymes: DNA and RNA polymerases, exonucleases, nucleases, and reverse transcriptase (synthesises DNA from an RNA template).

5) **Key Experimental Techniques:**
   ○ Gel Electrophoresis: Separates DNA fragments by size.
   ○ Southern Blotting: Transfers DNA from gels to membranes for specific region identification.
   ○ DNA Sequencing: Determines the nucleotide sequence of DNA.
   ○ Site-Directed Mutagenesis: Introduces specific mutations to study DNA functions.

6) **Polymerase Chain Reaction (PCR):**
   ○ Mechanism: Amplifies specific DNA sequences using heat-stable DNA polymerase, primers, and thermal cycling.
   ○ Significance: Enables exponential DNA amplification in vitro.

7) **Monoclonal Antibodies and Hybridomas:**
   ○ Hybridomas: Cells that proliferate and produce specific antibodies.
   ○ Applications: Used for identifying proteins and nucleic acids, purifying proteins, and targeted drug delivery.

Future Prospects:

Molecular Biology and rDNA: Expected to continue being a dynamic and impactful field, driving advancements in genetics and biotechnology. Recombinant DNA technology, through its foundational principles and diverse applications, has revolutionised molecular biology, enabling precise genetic manipulation for research and practical applications.

9.4   WASTE TREATMENT AND MANAGEMENT USING BIOTECHNOLOGY

Biotechnology offers innovative solutions for waste treatment and management by leveraging the capabilities of microorganisms and biological processes. These techniques are environmentally friendly and can be more efficient and sustainable compared to traditional methods. Here are key approaches and examples of how biotechnology is applied in waste treatment and management:

1. **Bioremediation:**

    The use of microorganisms to degrade or detoxify pollutants from the environment, including soil, water, and air.

    o **Application:** Microbes such as bacteria, fungi, and algae are employed to break down hazardous substances into less toxic or non-toxic compounds.

    o **Example:** Pseudomonas bacteria are used to clean up oil spills by breaking down hydrocarbons.

    o **Phytoremediation:** Using plants to absorb, concentrate, and detoxify contaminants in soil and water. Plants like sunflowers and *Populus trichocarpa* can extract heavy metals from contaminated sites.

2. **Wastewater Treatment:**

    o **Activated Sludge Process:** Utilises a diverse community of microorganisms to decompose organic matter in sewage and industrial wastewater.

    o **Aerobic Treatment:** Oxygen is supplied to support the growth of aerobic bacteria that degrade organic pollutants.

    o **Anaerobic Treatment:** In the absence of oxygen, anaerobic microorganisms break down organic matter, producing biogas (methane) that can be used as an energy source.

    o **Biofilms and Membrane Bioreactors (MBRs):** These systems use microbial communities attached to surfaces or within membranes to enhance the degradation of contaminants.

3. **Solid Waste Management:**

    o **Composting:** A natural process where organic waste (e.g. food scraps, yard waste) is broken down by microorganisms into nutrient-rich compost that can be used as fertiliser.

    o **Aerobic Composting:** Involves the decomposition of organic material in the presence of oxygen, producing carbon dioxide, water, and heat.

    o **Vermicomposting:** Uses earthworms and microorganisms to convert organic waste into high-quality compost.

- ○ **Biogas Production:** Anaerobic digestion of organic waste (e.g., agricultural waste, manure, food waste) by microorganisms produces biogas, which can be used for energy, and digestate, which can be used as a fertiliser.

4. **Bioplastic Production:**
   - ○ **Biodegradable Plastics:** Microorganisms can produce bioplastics such as polyhydroxyalkanoates (PHAs) from renewable resources. These bioplastics are biodegradable and can reduce plastic waste.
   - ○ **Example:** Polyhydroxybutyrate (PHB) is produced by bacteria such as Ralstonia eutropha and is used to make biodegradable plastic products.

5. **Industrial Waste Management:**
   - ○ **Bioaugmentation:** Adding specific strains of microorganisms to contaminated sites to enhance the degradation of pollutants.
   - ○ **Biosorption:** Using biological materials (e.g., algae, bacteria, fungi) to adsorb heavy metals and other pollutants from industrial effluents.

Biotechnological Approaches in Waste Treatment and Management

Approach	Description and Application	Example
Bioremediation	Use of microbes to degrade pollutants in soil, water, and air	Pseudomonas for oil spill clean-up
Phytoremediation	Use of plants to absorb and detoxify contaminants	Sunflowers Extracting Heavy Metals
Wastewater Treatment	Microbial degradation of organic matter in wastewater	Activated sludge process.
Aerobic Treatment	Oxygen-supported microbial decomposition.	Aeration tanks in sewage treatment
Anaerobic Treatment	Microbial breakdown of waste in the absence of oxygen produces biogas	Anaerobic digesters
Biofilms and MBRs	Microbial communities on surfaces/membranes for enhanced treatment.	Membrane bioreactor systems
Composting	Microbial breakdown of organic waste into compost	Aerobic composting, vermicomposting.

Approach	Description and Application	Example
Biogas Production	Anaerobic digestion of organic waste produces energy	Biogas plants
Bioplastic Production	Microbial production of biodegradable plastics	PHB production by Ralstonia eutropha
Bioaugmentation	Adding specific microbes to enhance pollutant degradation.	Enhanced bioremediation.
Biosorption	Use of biological materials to adsorb pollutants	Algae adsorbing heavy metals.

9.5   INDUSTRIAL BIOCHEMICAL TECHNOLOGY

Biochemical technology applies biological processes for industrial purposes, leading to the production of various valuable products such as fermented goods, biofuels, and bioplastics. These applications are not only vital for modern industry but also contribute to sustainable development by reducing reliance on fossil fuels and minimising environmental impact.

1. **Fermentation**

    Fermentation is a metabolic process that converts carbohydrates into alcohols, acids, gases, or other organic compounds using microorganisms like bacteria, yeast, or fungi. This process is used in food production, pharmaceuticals, and bio-industrial applications.

    Applications:

    Food and Beverage Industry: Fermentation is used to produce a variety of food and beverages such as bread, yogurt, cheese, beer, wine, and vinegar.

    o **Ethanol Production:** Yeast ferments sugars to produce ethanol and carbon dioxide, crucial in beer and wine production.

    o **Lactic Acid Fermentation:** Bacteria such as Lactobacillus convert sugars into lactic acid, essential in yogurt and cheese production.

    o **Pharmaceuticals:** Production of antibiotics, vitamins, amino acids, and hormones.

- ○ **Penicillin:** Produced by the fungus Penicillium through submerged fermentation.
- ○ **Industrial Enzymes:** Fermentation is used to produce enzymes used in detergents, textiles, and food processing.
- ○ **Amylase:** Enzyme used in the breakdown of starch into sugars in food and beverage industries.

Process:
- ○ **Batch Fermentation:** Microorganisms are cultured in a closed system until the substrate is exhausted.
- ○ **Continuous Fermentation:** Fresh substrate is continuously added, and products are continuously removed, maintaining steady-state conditions.

2. **Biofuels**

Biofuels are renewable fuels derived from biological materials such as plants, algae, or waste. They offer an alternative to fossil fuels, helping to reduce greenhouse gas emissions and dependence on non-renewable resources.

Types of Biofuels:
- ○ **Bioethanol:** Produced from the fermentation of sugars found in crops like corn, sugarcane, and cellulosic biomass (e.g. agricultural residues).
- ○ **Process:** Saccharification (breaking down complex carbohydrates), followed by fermentation using yeast or bacteria.
- ○ **Biodiesel:** Made from vegetable oils, animal fats, or recycled cooking oils through a process called transesterification.
- ○ **Process:** Oils are reacted with an alcohol (usually methanol) in the presence of a catalyst to produce biodiesel and glycerin.
- ○ **Biogas:** Generated from anaerobic digestion of organic waste materials like manure, food waste, and sewage sludge.
- ○ **Process:** Microorganisms break down organic matter in the absence of oxygen, producing methane-rich biogas.

Applications:
- ○ **Transportation:** Bioethanol and biodiesel can be used as direct substitutes for gasoline and diesel, respectively, or blended with them.
- ○ **Power Generation:** Biogas can be used to generate electricity and heat in combined heat and power (CHP) systems.

3. **Bioplastics**

Bioplastics are a type of plastic derived from renewable biomass sources, such as vegetable fats and oils, corn starch, or microorganisms, as opposed to traditional plastics which are derived from petroleum.

Types of Bioplastics:
- ○ **Polylactic Acid (PLA):** Made from fermented plant starch (usually corn). PLA is biodegradable and used in packaging, disposable tableware, and medical implants.
- ○ **Production Process:** Fermentation of sugars to lactic acid, followed by polymerisation.
- ○ **Polyhydroxyalkanoates (PHAs):** Produced by microorganisms through the fermentation of sugars or lipids. PHAs are biodegradable and used in packaging, agricultural films, and medical applications.
- ○ **Production Process:** Microbes like Ralstonia eutropha convert carbon sources into PHA granules stored inside the cell, which are later extracted and processed.
- ○ **Starch Blends:** Blended with conventional plastics to improve biodegradability. Used in packaging, agriculture, and consumer goods.

Applications:
- Packaging: Biodegradable packaging materials reduce environmental impact and waste.
- Agriculture: Biodegradable films and plant pots reduce plastic waste and improve sustainability.
- Medical: Biocompatible materials for sutures, implants, and drug delivery systems.

Application	Description	Example Products
Fermentation	Metabolic process converting carbohydrates into alcohols, acids, or gases using microbes.	Bread, yogurt, beer, antibiotics, enzymes.
Biofuels	Renewable fuels derived from biological materials.	Bioethanol, biodiesel, and biogas
Bioplastics	Plastics made from renewable biomass sources.	PLA, PHAs, starch blends.

9.6 BIOINFORMATICS AND ITS RELATION WITH MOLECULAR BIOLOGY

Bioinformatics is an interdisciplinary field that combines computer science, mathematics, and biology to analyse and interpret biological data. It involves the development and application of computational tools and techniques to manage, analyse, and visualise biological data. This field plays a crucial role in understanding the complexities of biological systems and has become essential in modern molecular biology research.

Areas of Bioinformatics:

- **Sequence Analysis:**
  - ○ DNA/RNA Sequencing: Bioinformatics tools are used to assemble, align, and annotate DNA and RNA sequences. This helps in identifying genes, regulatory elements, and mutations.
  - ○ Protein Sequencing: Tools analyse protein sequences to predict their structure, function, and interactions.
- **Genomics:**
  - ○ Genome Annotation: Identifying coding regions (genes), non-coding regions, and other functional elements in a genome.
  - ○ Comparative Genomics: Comparing genomes of different species to understand evolutionary relationships and functional conservation.

- **Proteomics:**
  - Protein Structure Prediction: Using computational models to predict the 3D structure of proteins from their amino acid sequences.
  - Protein-Protein Interactions: Analysing interactions between proteins to understand cellular pathways and functions.
- **Transcriptomics:**
  - Gene Expression Analysis: Analysing RNA-seq data to study gene expression patterns under different conditions.
  - Alternative Splicing: Identifying different splicing variants of genes and their functional implications.
- **Systems Biology:**
  - Pathway Analysis: Mapping and analysing biological pathways to understand cellular processes..
  - Network Analysis: Studying biological networks (e.g., protein interaction networks, gene regulatory networks) to identify key regulators and modules.
- **Structural Biology:**
  - Molecular Modelling: Creating 3D models of biomolecules to study their structure and interactions.
  - Docking Simulations: Predicting how small molecules (e.g., drugs) bind to proteins, aiding in drug discovery.

Relation of Bioinformatics with Molecular Biology

1. **Gene and Genome Analysis:**
   - Gene Identification and Annotation: Molecular biologists use bioinformatics tools to identify and annotate genes within a genome. This involves predicting coding sequences, introns, exons, and regulatory regions.
   - Mutation and Variant Analysis: Bioinformatics aids in identifying genetic mutations and variations, which are crucial for understanding genetic diseases and traits.

2. **Protein Analysis:**
   - Protein Structure Prediction: Bioinformatics tools help molecular biologists predict the 3D structure of proteins from their amino acid sequences, providing insights into protein function and interaction.
   - Functional Annotation: Analysing protein sequences to predict functional domains and active sites.

3. **Expression Studies:**
   - Transcriptome Analysis: Bioinformatics enables the analysis of RNA-seq data to study gene expression patterns, helping molecular biologists understand gene regulation and identify differentially expressed genes.
   - Microarray Data Analysis: Analysing microarray data to study expression levels of thousands of genes simultaneously.

4. **Evolutionary Biology:**
   - Phylogenetic Analysis: Bioinformatics tools construct phylogenetic trees to study evolutionary relationships between species or genes.
   - Comparative Genomics: Comparing genomes of different organisms to identify conserved and divergent elements.

5. **Systems Biology:**
   - Pathway Reconstruction: Molecular biologists use bioinformatics to reconstruct and analyse metabolic and signalling pathways, helping to understand complex biological processes.
   - Network Analysis: Studying the interactions and regulatory networks within a cell to identify key players and potential therapeutic targets.

Bioinformatics and molecular biology are deeply intertwined, with bioinformatics providing the computational tools and methodologies essential for analysing and interpreting the vast amounts of data generated in molecular biology. This synergy accelerates our understanding of biological systems and contributes to advancements in genomics, proteomics, systems biology, and beyond, ultimately leading to new discoveries and applications in medicine, agriculture, and biotechnology.

Important Questions

1. Define biochemical engineering. What is recombinant DNA technology?
2. Describe the process of genetic engineering.
3. What are genetically modified microorganisms used for in biotechnology?
4. What is the significance of the structure and function of DNA in genetic manipulation?
5. What is the shape of the DNA molecule? Which nitrogenous bases pair together in DNA?
6. How does RNA differ from DNA in terms of the sugar it contains?
7. What is recombinant DNA (rDNA) technology?
8. Name the technique that amplifies DNA without cloning in host cells.
9. Who discovered the DNA double helix model?
10. What is the activated sludge process in wastewater treatment?
11. Describe the difference between aerobic and anaerobic treatment in wastewater management.
12. How is biosorption applied in industrial waste management?
13. Give an example of a biodegradable plastic and its microbial producer.
14. What is fermentation? Name two applications of fermentation in the food industry.
15. What is continuous fermentation?
16. What is bioinformatics?
17. Describe the role of bioinformatics in protein structure prediction.
18. What is the role of bioinformatics in gene expression analysis?
19. Explain the role of biochemical engineers in the context of recent developments in biotechnology.
20. Describe the structure of DNA, including the components of a nucleotide.
21. Explain the significance of the double helix structure of DNA.
22. Discuss the role of DNA in storing and transmitting genetic information.

23. Explain how RNA differs from DNA in structure and function.
24. Describe the function of different types of RNA in protein synthesis.
25. Explain the process of cell fusion and its applications in biotechnology.
26. Discuss the process by which genetic information is transmitted from DNA to proteins.
27. Explain the various functions of DNA in the cell.
28. Describe the structural differences between DNA and RNA.
29. Describe the steps involved in the transcription and translation of genetic information.
30. Explain the differences in stability and function between DNA and RNA.
31. Describe the gene cloning process, including vector selection and transformation.
32. Describe the process and significance of polymerase chain reaction (PCR).
33. Explain the future prospects of molecular biology and recombinant DNA technology.
34. Discuss the key experimental techniques used in recombinant DNA technology.
35. Describe the mechanism and applications of polymerase chain reaction (PCR).
36. Explain the role of microorganisms in bioremediation and give an example.
37. Discuss the methods and importance of wastewater treatment using biotechnology.
38. Explain the process and benefits of composting in solid waste management.
39. Discuss the various approaches of industrial waste management using biotechnology.
40. Discuss the environmental benefits of using biotechnology in waste treatment and management.
41. Explain the process of fermentation and its applications in food and pharmaceuticals.

42. Describe the process and benefits of continuous fermentation in industrial applications.
43. Explain the environmental impact of using biofuels and bioplastics.
44. Discuss the future prospects of biochemical technology in sustainable development.
45. Explain the role of bioinformatics in DNA/RNA sequencing.
46. Describe the process and importance of protein structure prediction using bioinformatics.
47. Explain the role of bioinformatics in studying gene expression patterns.
48. Describe the relationship between bioinformatics and molecular biology in gene and genome analysis.

CHAPTER 10

CEMENT

10.1 INTRODUCTION

The term cement is used for materials possessing adhesive and cohesive properties, which make them capable of binding minerals like bricks, stones, tiles, etc. into a compact, coherent structure. It is mixed with water, forms a rigid, continuous structure with a good compressive strength. That hardened mass can have varying degrees of strength.

There are various types of cement used in construction works for various purposes. Thus, it is important to understand the properties of each type of cement and their uses.

Types of Cement:

The following are the types of cement that are in practice:

- **Rapid-Hardening Cement**

  It has a high amount of lime content. It attains high strength in the early days and is used in concrete where formwork is removed at an early stage.

- **Quick-setting Cement**

  It has a small percentage of aluminium sulphate as an accelerator and a reducing percentage of gypsum with fine grinding. It is used in works to be completed in a very short period and concreting in static and running water.

- **Low Heat Cement**

  It is manufactured by reducing tricalcium aluminate. It is used in massive concrete construction like gravity dams.

- **Sulphate-resistant Cement**

  It is prepared by maintaining the percentage of tricalcium aluminate below 6%, which increases power against sulphates. It is used in construction exposed to severe sulphate action by water and soil in places like canals linings, culverts, retaining walls, siphons, etc.

- **Blast Furnace Slag Cement**

  It is obtained by grinding the clinkers with about 60% slag and resembles more or less the properties of Portland cement. It can be used for works where economic considerations are predominant.

- **High Alumina Cement**

  It is obtained by melting a mixture of bauxite and lime and grinding with the clinker. It is rapid-hardening cement with initial and final setting times of about 3.5 and 5 hours, respectively. It is used in works where concrete is subjected to high temperatures, frost, and acidic action.

- **White Cement**

  It is prepared from raw materials free from iron oxide. It is more costly and is used for architectural purposes such as precast curtain wall and facing panels, terrazzo surfaces, etc.

- **Coloured Cement**

  It is produced by mixing mineral pigments with ordinary cement. They are widely used for decorative works on floors.

- **Pozzolanic Cement**

  It is prepared by grinding pozzolanic clinker with Portland cement. It is used in marine structures, sewage works, and for laying concrete underwater such as bridges, piers, dams, etc.,

- **Air-Entraining Cement**

  It is produced by adding indigenous air-entraining agents such as resins, glues, sodium salts of sulphates, etc., during the grinding of clinker. This type of cement is especially suited to improve the workability with a smaller water-cement ratio and to enhance the frost resistance of concrete.

- **Hydrographic Cement**

  It is prepared by mixing water-repelling chemicals. This cement has high workability and strength.

- **Portland Cement**

  It is the basic ingredient of concrete. Concrete is formed when Portland cement creates a paste with water that binds with sand and rock to harden. Cement is manufactured through a closely controlled chemical combination of calcium, silicon, aluminium, iron and other ingredients. The credit for the discovery of Portland cement is given by William Aspdin (1824). It gets its name from its resemblance (upon hardening) to the famous Portland limestone (obtained from quarries on the Isle of Portland), the traditionally preferred choice for building churches, mansions, and palaces.

10.2   RAW MATERIALS FOR CEMENT

The primary raw materials used in the manufacture of cement are:

1. **Calcareous Materials:**
   - **Limestone:** Contains 65 to 80% calcium carbonate ($CaCO_3$) and is the main source of lime.
   - **Chalk**
   - **Marl**
   - **Alkali Waste:** Contains precipitated $CaCO_3$, obtained during the manufacture of caustic soda.

2. **Argillaceous Materials:**
   - **Clay:** Supplies silica, alumina and iron oxides.
   - **Shale**
   - **Slate**
   - **Blast Furnace Slag:** A byproduct of the steel manufacturing process, providing additional silica and alumina.

3. **Additives (Retarders):**
   - **Gypsum ($CaSO_4 \cdot 2H_2O$):** Prevents the cement from hardening too quickly.
   - **Plaster of Paris ($CaSO_4 \cdot 1/2\ H_2O$):** Used occasionally for the same purpose.

These materials are combined in precise proportions, ground to a fine powder, and then heated in a kiln to produce cement clinker. The clinker is then ground with gypsum to produce the final cement product.

Chemical Composition of Cement:

The main composition of cement and its influence on the properties of cement are given below.

Component	Chemical Formula	Percentage by Weight (%)
Lime	CaO	60-67
Silica	SiO_2	17-25
Alumina	Al_2O_3	0.5-6
Iron Oxide	Fe_2O4	0.5-6
Magnesia	MgO	0.1-4
Sulphur Trioxide	SO_3	45352
Alkalis (Sodium Oxide)	Na_2O	0.2-1.3
Alkalis (Potassium Oxide)	K_2O	0.2-1.3
Gypsum (Calcium Sulphate)	$CaSO_4 \cdot 2H_2O$	3-5
Loss on Ignition	-	0.5-3

Significance of the Chemical Constituents:

1. **Lime (CaO):**
   - **Role:** Major constituent of cement.
   - **Effect:** Increases setting time.
   - **Optimal Amount:** Insufficient lime reduces strength, while excess lime results in unsound cement prone to disintegration.

2. **Silica (SiO_2):**
   - ○ **Role:** Second major and active component.
   - ○ **Effect:** Higher percentages enhance strength but extend setting time.
   - ○ **Optimal Amount:** High-silica cement takes longer to reach full strength.
3. **Alumina (Al_2O_3):**
   - ○ **Role:** Active constituent.
   - ○ **Effect:** Higher percentages boost strength and decrease setting time.
4. **Iron Oxides (Fe_2O_3):**
   - ○ **Role:** Provides the characteristic grey colour.
   - ○ **Effect:** Contributes to the strength and hardness of the cement.
5. **Gypsum ($CaSO_4 \cdot 2H_2O$):**
   - ○ **Role:** Prevents rapid-hardening of cement slurry.
6. **Magnesium Oxide (MgO):**
   - ○ **Role:** Imparts strength when used in small amounts.
   - ○ **Effect:** Excessive amounts make the cement unsound.
7. **Sulfur Trioxide (SO_3):**
   - ○ **Role:** Ensures the soundness of cement in small quantities.
8. **Alkali Oxides ($Na_2O + K_2O$):**
   - ○ **Effect:** Excess amounts cause the cement to become efflorescent (surface salt deposits).

10.3 CHEMICAL COMPOSITION OF MANUFACTURED CEMENTS

The properties of cement depend upon the relative proportions of the components present. The properties of the particular cement can be modified by varying the amounts of various components. The properties of a particular cement can be modified by varying the amounts of various components.

The main constituents of Portland cement are
i.   Tricalcium silicates
ii. Dicalcium Silicates
iii. Tricalcium Aluminate.

iv. Tetracalcium alumino ferrite

v. Gypsum

vi. Some amount of free CaO and MgO.

Average composition of these Portland cement is as follows;

Sr.No.	Name of compounds	Chemicals formulas	Abbreviation	%
1	Tricalcium Silicates	$3CaO.SiO_2$	C_3S	45
2	Dicalcium Silicates	$2CaO.SiO_2$	C_2S	25
3	Tricalcium Aluminate	$3CaO.Al_2O_3$	C_3A	10
4	Tetra-calcium aluminoferrite	$4CaO.Al_2O_3.Fe_2O_3$	C_4AF	10
5	Pentacalcium trialuminate	$5CaO.3Al_2O_3$	C_5A_3	03
6	Gypsum	$CaSO_4.2H_2O$	——	02
7	Magnesium Oxides	MgO	——	03
8	Free Calcium Oxides	CaO	——-	02

Where

$$C = CaO, A = Al_2O_3, s = SiO_2 \text{ and } F = Fe_2O_3$$

Significance of the Constituents:

1. **Tricalcium Silicates [$3CaO.SiO_2$]**

    It is a major and most important component.

    o It undergoes hydration quickly and liberated considerable heat (500 kJ/kg)

    o It develops considerable strength (first strength).

    o It provides quick-setting. (final setting within 7 to 8 days).

    o It provides high resistance towards chemical attacks.

2. **Dicalcium Silicates [$2CaO.SiO_2$]**

    It is the second major and most important component.

    o It undergoes hydration slowly with evolution of little quantity of heat (250 kJ/kg)

- ○ It provides progressive increase in strength (Final strength).
- ○ It provides slow setting, which requires months and years for completion (however most of the strength is gained with in first 28 days)

3. **Tricalcium Aluminate [3CaO.Al$_2$O$_3$]**
   - ○ It is hydrated very much rapidly with the evaluation of a large amount of heat (880 kJ/kg)
   - ○ It provides instantaneous setting (flash setting or initial setting) in presence of water.
   - ○ It provides little strength during flash setting.

1. **Tetra-calcium alumino-ferrite [4CaO.Al$_2$O$_3$. Fe$_2$O$_3$]**
   This component is practically inactive, because it undergoes a slow hydration (420 kJ/kg).

2. **Others:** Free CaO, Fe$_2$O$_3$, MgO, etc., have no discernible effect on the properties of cement.

10.4   MANUFACTURING OF CEMENT

Manufacture of cement lies in mixing calcareous and argillaceous materials together very thoroughly in a ratio that the required composition is obtained. The mixture is heated at a temperature of 1500-1700^0. The clinker obtained is cooled and mixed with 2-3% gypsum and then finely pulverised.

Depending on the conditions maintained during the manufacturing process, it can be classified into two types,

1. **Dry Process**
   In this process, the mixture of raw materials is subjected to calcination in a dry state. The raw materials are crushed and ground separately to form a fine powder. Then these are mixed in the required proportion to form a raw mixture. This process is generally used when the raw materials are very hard, such as cement rock or blast furnace slag. Thus, it has limited scope.

2. **Wet Process**

In this process, the raw materials (Calcareous materials and Argillaceous materials) are crushed and ground to particles and then mixed with 30 to 40% water, and a cement slurry is obtained. This slurry paste is then subjected to calcination. This process is universal and applicable to any type of raw materials.

Wet Process of Cement:

The wet process for manufacturing of Portland cement is used to a very large extent than the dry process. It is considered a better and convenient process for the manufacture of cement, especially where limestone of soft variety is available in abundance. It involves the following steps.

1. **Crushing and Grinding**

The raw materials like calcareous materials i.e. limestone, etc., and argillaceous i.e., clay, etc., are crushed by a gyratory crusher and stored in a storage tank. The grinding of raw materials is carried out in a ball mill and tube mill. Before grinding, the materials are mixed with 30-40% water. This gives the mud-like mixture called cement slurry. The cement slurry is collected in a tank where it is analysed for proper composition and can be corrected by adding the required amount of the deficient raw material. The slurry is fed at the upper end of a long rotary kiln as shown in the following figure.

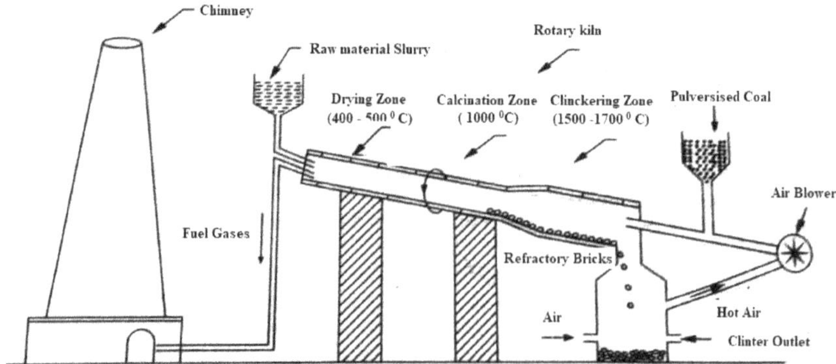

Figure 10.1: Rotary kiln for cement manufacturing

2. **Rotary Kiln:**

   This raw materials slurry is then calcined in the rotary kiln. The modern rotary kiln is a long cylinder made up of steel, lined with refractory bricks. The length of the kiln ranges from 50-350 feet and the diameter from 6-12 feet. Generally, the rotary kiln is slightly inclined 0.5 to 0.75 inches in one foot to the horizontal. It is based on heavily friction rollers. The kiln generally rotates at a speed of 0.5 to one revolution.

The slurry is fed from the upper end of the rotary kiln, while the burning fuel (powdered coal or oil or natural gas) and air are introduced from the lower end of the kiln. A long flame is produced which is forced into the interior part of the kiln by an air blower. The temperature in the lower part is about 1500-1700°C and it decreases in the upper part of the kiln. The temperature at the top is about 400°C. The hot gases from the flame heat the elements of the slurry and convert them into water vapour, CO_2, and other gases that escape from the chimney into the atmosphere. Due to the slope and slow rotation of the kiln, the slurry continuously moves towards the hottest end. Thus, the slurry moves in the kiln into different zones of increasing temperature.

(a) **Drying Zone:** The upper part of the rotary kiln is known as the drying zone where the temperature is about 400°C. In this zone, most of the water evaporates and escapes with some gases through the chimney. The dry materials pass down the kiln.

(b) **Calcination Zone:** The central part of the kiln is known as the calcination zone where the temperature is about 1000°C. Here, limestone is decomposed to give CaO and CO_2.

$$CaCO_3 \longrightarrow CaO + CO_2$$
$$\text{Lime stone} \qquad\qquad \text{Quick lime}$$

(c) **Clinkering zone or burning zone:** The material lastly enters the hottest zone (1500-1700°C), known as the burning or clinkering zone, where lime and clay react with each other forming silicates and aluminates.

$$2\ CaO + SiO_2 \longrightarrow 2\ CaO.SiO_2$$
$$3\ CaO + SiO_2 \longrightarrow 3\ CaO.SiO_2$$
$$3\ CaO + Al_2O_3 \longrightarrow 3\ CaO.Al_2O_3$$
$$4CaO + Al_2O_3 + Fe_2O_3 \longrightarrow 4\ CaO.Al_2O_3.Fe_2O_3$$

These calcium silicates and calcium aluminates are combined together to form small, hard, greyish stones called cement clinkers. The formation of clinkers in the rotary kiln is an exothermic reaction.

The hot clinkers are cooled by the steam of air either by rotary cooler or by air quench type cooler. The rate of cooling should be moderate, which gives high strength to the clinkers. The hot air produced is economically used for drying the coal before pulverisation. The cooling is an important process that has to be controlled properly to produce a definite degree of crystallisation of the melted clinkers.

(d) **Grinding of clinkers:** The cooled clinkers are then ground with 2-4% gypsum into a fine powder in steel ball mills. It is found that the finer the cement, the greater the strength of the concrete made from it. The gypsum is added to retard the setting time of cement when it comes in contact with water. The storage and packaging of cement need special care. The cement retains its properties until it comes in contact with moisture. The cement coming out of the grinding ball mill is stored in concrete storage 'silos'. Then it is fed to automatic packing machines where it gets packed in bags and then sent for marketing.

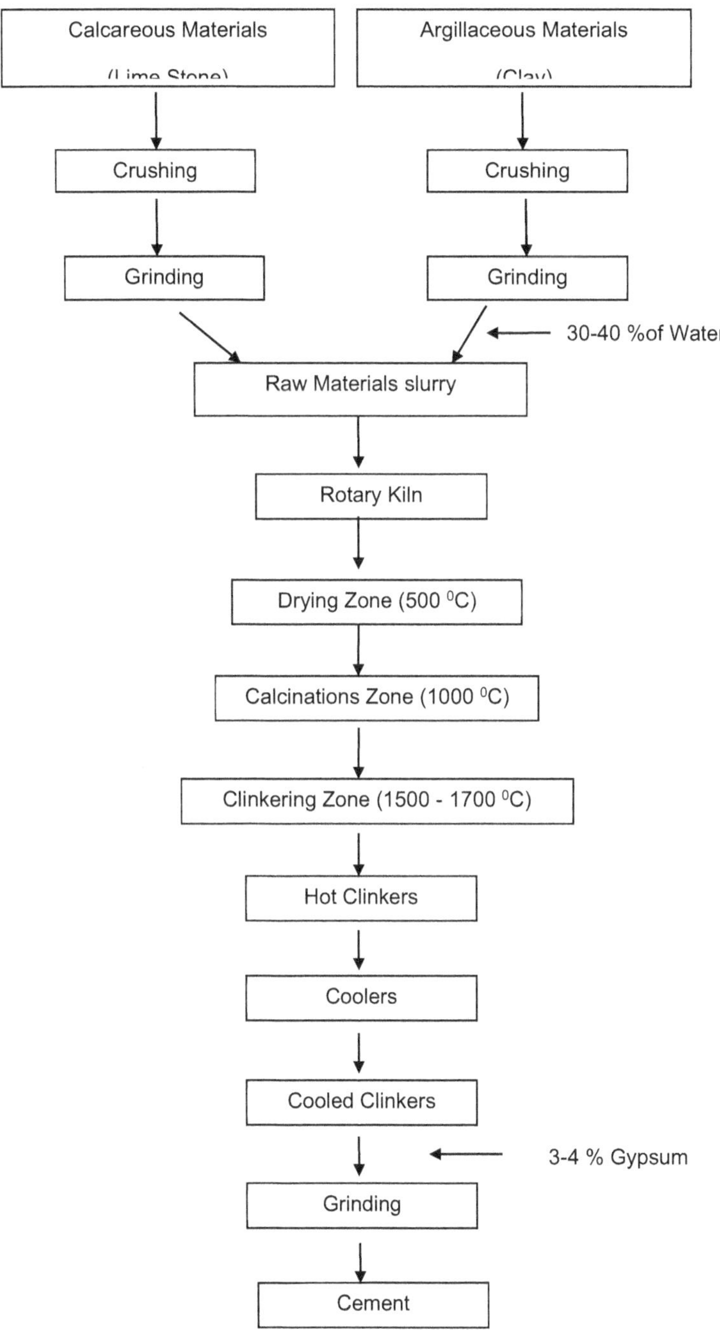

Calcareous Materials
(Lime Stone)
Argillaceous Materials
(Clay)
Crushing
Crushing
Grinding
Grinding
30-40 %of Water
Raw Materials slurry
Rotary Kiln
Drying Zone (500 ^{0}C)
Calcinations Zone (1000 ^{0}C)
Clinkering Zone (1500 - 1700 ^{0}C)
Hot Clinkers
Coolers
Cooled Clinkers
3-4 % Gypsum
Grinding
Cement

10.5 SETTING AND HARDENING OF CEMENT

When cement is mixed with water and allowed to stand, it gets hard rigid materials. This is known as setting. Thus, the setting is defined as stiffening of the original mass due to initial gel formation and chemical reaction. Finally, solidification of the stiffened mass takes place to form compact rock-like material, known as hardening. Hardening is due to the formation of strength in concrete due to crystallisation. Setting and Hardening occur in three stages.

(1) Initial Setting or Flash Setting:

The early strength achieved by the mixture during the first 24 hours is known as initial set or flash set. When water is mixed with cement, a plastic mixture is formed, which can be modulated as desired. But with the lapse of time, the mixture gradually loses its plasticity due to the beginning of the initial setting. Generally, the initial setting starts after 30 minutes; therefore, the moulding can be done within one hour only.

Initial setting is mainly due to the hydration of tricalcium aluminates and gel formation of tetracalcium aluminoferrite. It is hydrated quite rapidly to form the crystalline hydrates with the evolution of a very high amount of heat (880 kJ/kg). These hydrates are soluble and hence provide stiffness.

$$3\ CaO.Al_2O_3 + 6H_2O \longrightarrow 3\ CaO.Al_2O_3.\ 6H_2O + 880\ kJ/kg$$

tricalicum aluminate hydrared tricalicum aluminate

$$4\ CaO.Al_2O_3.\ Fe_2O_3 + 7\ H_2O \rightarrow 3\ CaO.Al_2O_3.\ 6H_2O + CaO.Fe_2O_3.H_2O + 420\ kJ/kg$$

Tetra-calcium Alumino Ferrite Crystals Gel

2. Final Setting

The strength gained by the mixture during 24 hours to 7 days is called final setting. Final setting begins after some hours of mixing. After its beginning, the concrete mixture can neither be moulded into shape nor can it be remixed. Final setting is mainly due to the beginning of simultaneous hydrolysis and hydration reactions of tricalcium silicate.

$$3\ CaO.\ SiO_2 + H_2O \xrightarrow{\text{Hydrolysis}} 3\ CaO.\ SiO_2 + Ca(OH)_2\ Crystal$$

$$2\ CaO.\ SiO_2 + 4\ H_2O \xrightarrow{\text{Hydration}} 2\ CaO.\ SiO_2.\ 4\ H_2O\ Gel$$

$$3\ CaO.\ SiO_2 + 5\ H_2O \longrightarrow 2\ CaO.\ SiO_2.\ 5\ H_2O + Ca(OH)_2$$

The reactions are slow and evolve less heat (500 kJ/kg). These are completed within 7 days and are responsible for strength and early hardness.

3. Hardening

After final setting, the concrete begins to gain strength continuously. This process is called hardening. The strength develops from 7 days to 28 days. The extent of hardening depends on the chemical combination of cement and the quantity of water. If water is not supplied continuously, then the concrete dries up and the hardening stops. While if the concrete is kept moist, the hardening continues for years together. However, with the lapse of time, the rate of hardening decreases. Hardening is mostly due to the hydration and hydrolysis of dicalcium silicate to form tobermorite gel.

$$2[2CaO.\ SiO_2] + H_2O \xrightarrow{\text{Hydrolysis}} 3\ CaO.\ 2SiO_2.\ + Ca(OH)_2\ Crystal$$

$$3\ CaO.\ 2SiO_2.\ + 3\ H_2O \xrightarrow{\text{Hydration}} 3CaO.\ 2SiO_2.\ 3H_2O$$

tobermorite gel

$$3\ CaO.\ 2SiO_2.\ + 4\ H_2O \xrightarrow{\text{Hydration}} 3\ CaO.\ 2SiO_2.\ 3\ H_2O + Ca(OH)_2$$
$$\text{tobermorite gel.} \qquad\qquad\qquad\qquad \text{Crystal}$$

These reactions are very slow and evolve the least heat (250 kJ/kg). They require more than one year for completion and hence their effect on the strength and hardness of the concrete continues for a longer time. However, the tobermorite gel undergoes gradual stiffness and provides the final strength to the concrete within 28 days.

10.6 HEAT OF HYDRATION

The heat produced during setting and hardening of cement is known as the heat of hydration of cement. When water is mixed with the cement, its molecular constituents undergo hydration and hydrolysis reactions. These are exothermic, and hence heat is liberated. On average, 500 kJ/kg of heat is evolved during the complete hydration of cement. This heat is also known as the heat of setting and hardening.

Sr.No.	Molecular constituents	Chemical formula	Heat of hydration
1	Tricalcium Aluminate	$3\ CaO.Al_2O_3\ (C_3A)$	880 kJ/kg
2	Tricalcium Silicates	$3\ CaO.\ SiO_2\ (C_3S)$	500 kJ/kg
3	Dicalcium Silicates	$2\ CaO.\ SiO_2\ (C_2S)$	250 kJ/kg
4	Tetra-calcium aluminoferrite	$4\ CaO.Al_2O_3.\ Fe_2O_3\ (C_4AF)$	420 kJ/kg

It is essential that the heat generated during the hydrolysis should be dissipated rapidly; otherwise, shrinkage cracks may occur in large concrete constructions. Thus, curing plays an important role in the proper hardening.

10.7 SOUNDNESS OF CEMENT

Cement that is allowed to dry out and continuously stored underwater undergoes some shrinkage and expansion. These movements are quite minute, however, and are considered to be a soundness of cement. The cement is said to be sound if the volume changes are well within the tolerance limit laid down by ISI specifications. If they are beyond the limit, the cement is said to be unsound. Unsoundness of cement is due to an excess proportion of MgO, CaO, and sulphates in cement.

The cement is said to be defective if the proportions of the above-mentioned constituents are in excess. Due to them, the cement undergoes slow hydration. Therefore, the ill effects on the soundness are observed after a considerable period of time. As such, it is very essential to detect the unsoundness before making use of cement by an accelerated test such as the Le Chatelier test.

Le Chatelier Test of Cement:

Cement of good quality does not contain the impurities like free lime, magnesia, and sulphates, so this should be checked before use. If it contains impurities, it can expand after reacting with the water, which will result in unwanted outcomes such as cracking, undesired expansion of the dimensions, and lower strength. Le Chatelier's Apparatus is the standard apparatus prescribed to check the presence of impurities in cement. Cement is said to be sound when the expansion is below 10 mm.

Prepare a cement paste of 78% of standard consistency of the cement and fill it into the split brass cylinder. Cover the top and bottom of the cylinder and put it in water at 27 °C for 24 hours. After 24 hours, measure the separation between the two indicators at their pointed ends. Then heat the whole water and immersed cylinder with paste up to a boiling temperature in 30-35 minutes and then boil for 3 hours. After cooling it down, measure the separation between the two pointers again. The difference between the two measurements represents the unsoundness of the cement.

IMPORTANT QUESTIONS:

1. Explain the wet process used for manufacturing the cement.
2. Explain the following terms, 1.Setting and Hardening of cement 2. Heat of hydration
3. Draw flow diagram of rotary kiln used to manufacture of Portland cement by wet process and state it working.
4. What are raw materials of cement? Give its significance.
5. Describe the manufactured of Portland cement by rotatory kiln technology.
6. Describe the Setting and Hardening of cement.
7. Explain briefly setting and hardening of cement.
8. Explain Heat of hydration
9. What is gypsum? Why is it added to cement.
10. Name the raw materials necessary for preparation of Portland cement.
11. Write the chemical reactions involved in the manufactured of Portland cement

12. Discuss the various reactions of water with cement constituents which takes places during setting and hardening of cement.

13. Explain the role of gypsum in setting and hardening of cement.

14. What are the raw materials required for cement manufacture? Explain role and significance of every constituent.

15. What are molecular compositions of manufactured cement? Give its significance.

CHAPTER 11

PHASE RULE

11.1 GIBBS PHASE RULE:

The phase rule is a fundamental principle of physical chemistry that describes the relationship between the number of phases, components, and degrees of freedom in a system at equilibrium. The phase rule was developed by American chemist J. Willard Gibbs in the late 19th century and is also known as the Gibbs phase rule.

The Gibbs phase rule is a fundamental concept in thermodynamics that describes the number of degrees of freedom or variables that can be independently varied in a system at equilibrium. It relates the number of phases, components, and the degrees of freedom in a system.

The Gibbs phase rule states that for a system at equilibrium, the number of degrees of freedom (F) is given by:

$$F = C - P + 2$$

where C is the number of components (i.e., chemical species) in the system, P is the number of phases (i.e., physically distinct and homogeneous regions), and 2 is a constant representing the degrees of freedom associated with pressure and temperature.

The degree of freedom represents the number of variables that can be independently varied while keeping the system at equilibrium. For example, in a two-component system with one phase, the degree of freedom is one, meaning that we can vary either temperature or pressure while keeping the system at equilibrium. In a three-component system with two phases, the degree of freedom is zero, meaning that neither temperature nor pressure can be varied without disturbing the system's equilibrium.

The Gibbs phase rule is a powerful tool in understanding the behaviour of multi-component systems and is widely used in chemistry, materials science, and engineering.

11.2 PHASE, COMPONENTS & DEGREES OF FREEDOM:

1. **Phase**: A phase is a portion of a heterogeneous system that is chemically uniform, physically distinct, and mechanically separable from other parts of the system by a clear boundary surface. It is denoted by P.

For Example:

a. A gaseous mixture, being thoroughly miscible in all proportion, will constitute one phase only. Thus, a mixture of N2 and H2 forms phase only. **P=1**

b. If two liquids are miscible (i.e., alcohol and water), they will form one liquid phase only. **P=1**

c. A solution of a substance in a solvent consists of phase only, e. g, glucose solution in water. **P=1**

d. If two liquids are immiscible (i.e., benzene and water), they will form two separate phase only. **P=2**

e. At freezing point, water consists of three phase: **P = 3**

$$\text{Ice}_{(s)} \rightleftharpoons \text{Water}_{(l)} \rightleftharpoons \text{Water vapour}_{(g)}$$

2. **Component**: Component refers to the smallest number of independent variables that are involved in the equilibrium state of a heterogeneous system, and which can be used to express the composition of each phase through chemical equations. The symbol C is used to represent

components, and the total number of components may not necessarily match the number of chemical species.

For example:

a.   In the water system,

$$\text{Ice}_{(s)} \rightleftharpoons \text{Water}_{(l)} \rightleftharpoons \text{vapour}_{(g)}$$

The chemical composition of all three phases is H_2O. Hence, it is **a one-component system.**

b.   The sulfur system consists of four phases, rhombic, monoclinic, liquid and vapour, the chemical composition of all phases is S. hence, **it is one-component system.**

c.   In the dissociation of NH_4CI in a closed vessel,

i. $NH_4CI_{(g)} \rightleftharpoons NH_4CI_{(g)} \rightleftharpoons NH_{3(g)} + HCI_{(g)}$

The proportions of NH_3 and HCl are equivalent and hence, the composition of both phases (solid and gaseous) can be expressed in terms of NH_4Cl alone. Hence, the number of components is one. However, if NH_3 or HCl is in excess, the system becomes a two-component system.

d.   In the thermal decomposition of $CaCO_3$

$$CaCO_{3(s)} \rightleftharpoons CaO_{(s)} + CO_{2(g)}$$

The composition of each of the three phases can be expressed in terms of at least any two of the independently variable constituents, $CaCO_3$, CaO and CO_2. Suppose $CaCO_3$ and CaO are chosen as the two components, the composition of different phases is represented as follows:

$$\text{Phase: } CaCO_3 = CaCO_3 + 0 \text{ CaO}$$
$$\text{Phase: } CaO = 0 \text{ } CaCO_3 + CaO$$
$$\text{Phase: } CO_2 = CaCO_3 - CaO$$

Thus, it is a two-component system.

3. **Degree of freedom or variance**: The term degree of freedom, or variance, represents the minimum number of independent variables such as temperature, pressure, and phase composition that must be arbitrarily specified to completely describe the system. The degree of freedom is denoted by F, with F=0 indicating fixed variables, F=1 indicating two fixed variables, and so on.

   For example

   a.   In case of water system,

   b.   Ice(s) $\rightleftharpoons$ Water$_{(l)}$ $\rightleftharpoons$ Vapour$_{(g)}$,

   If all three phases are present in equilibrium, then no condition needs to be specified, as the three phases can be in equilibrium only at a particular temperature and pressure. If a condition (e.g. temperature or pressure) is altered, the three phases will not remain in equilibrium and one of the phases disappears.

   b.   For a system consisting of water in contact with its vapour,

$$\text{Water}_{(l)} \rightleftharpoons \text{Vapour}_{(g)}$$

   We must state either the temperature or pressure to define it completely. Hence, the degree of freedom is one, or the system **is univariant.**

   c.   For a system consisting of water vapour phase only, we must the values of both the temperature and pressure in order to describe the system completely. Hence, the system is bivariant or has **two degrees of freedom.**

   d.   For a system consisting of

$$\text{NaCl}_{(s)} \rightleftharpoons \text{NaCl}_{(aq)} \rightleftharpoons \text{water vapour}_{(g)}.$$

   We must state either the temperature or pressure because the saturation solubility is fixed at a particular temperature or pressure. Hence, the system is univariant.

11.3   MERITS AND DEMERITS OF PHASE RULE:

Merits of Phase Rule:

- It is applicable to both physical and chemical equilibria.
- It require no information regarding molecular/ micro-structure, since it is applicable to macroscopic system.
- It is a convenient method of classifying equilibrium states in terms of phases, components and degrees of freedom.
- It helps us to predict the behaviour of a system, under different sets of variables.
- It indicates that different systems with same degree of freedom behave similarly.
- It does not take into cognizance of either the nature or quantities of component present in the system.
- It helps in deciding whether under a given set of condition:

Demerits of the phase rule:

- It can be applied only for system in equilibrium. Consequently, it is of little value in case of very slow equilibrium state attaining system.
- It applies only to a single equilibrium system: and provided no information regarding any other possible equilibria in the system.
- It requires utmost care in deciding the number of phases existing in an equilibrium sate, since it considers only the number of phases, rather than their amounts. Thus, even if a trace of the phase is present, it accounts towards the total number of phases.
- It conditions that all phases of the system must be present simultaneously, under the identical conditions of temperature and pressure.
- It conditions that solid and liquid phases must not be in finely –divided state; otherwise deviations occurs.

11.4   DERIVATION OF PHASE RULE

Consider a heterogeneous system having P phases and C components. Now, according to the definition, the degree of freedom (F) of the system is the minimum of independent variables that must be fixed arbitrarily to define the system completely. But the number of these variables is equal to the total number of variables minus the number of relations between them at equilibrium, since each relation diminishes the number of independent variables by one.

Now let us calculate the total number of independent variables:

i. Temperature: At equilibrium, the temperature of every phase is the same, so there is only one temperature variable for the entire system.

ii. Pressure: At equilibrium, each phase has the same pressure, so there is only one pressure variable for the entire system.

iii. Concentration: Concentration of each component is generally expressed in terms of mole fractions. As a rule, the number of composition variables required for each phase is (C-1), since the composition of all components may be expressed by stating the mole fraction of all except one of the components. For example, if there are two components A and B in one phase and if we know the concentration (or mole fraction) of one (say A), the concentration of the other (i.e., B) can be automatically found, because the sum is always unity. Thus, if the mole fraction of A is 0.4, that of B is known to be 1-0.4 or 0.6. Similarly, if we have three components and if the composition of two is known, that of the third can be found out. Thus, if we have C components, we must know the concentration of C-1 component. So for P phases, the total composition variables are P(C – 1).

Hence, total number of variables.

= 1 (for temperature) + 1 (for pressure) + P (C – 1) (for composition)

= P (C – 1) + 2

Now let us calculate the number of relations at equilibrium. We know that for a system in thermodynamic equilibrium, the chemical potential (μ), which is related to the concentration of a component in all the particular component I, we have at equilibrium:

$$[\mu i]\alpha = [\mu i]\beta = [\mu i]\gamma$$

Consequently, there are two equilibrium relationships for each component if there are 3 phases. Hence, for P phases, the number of such relationships for each component is (P-1),

Consequently, for C components, such relationships will be C (P – 1),

iv. Degree of freedom, F = Total number of independent variables.

Number of relationships between these variables

$$= [P(C-1) + 2] - [C(P-1)]$$
$$= C - P + 2.$$

This is nothing but a mathematical statement of the phase rule.

11.5   APPLICATION OF THE PHASE RULE TO WATER SYSTEM.

It is a one-component system. The water system consists of three phases, namely, ice, water, and water vapour.

$$\text{Ice}_{(s)} \rightleftharpoons \text{Water}_{(l)} \rightleftharpoons \text{Water vapour}_{(g)}$$

Since H_2O is the only chemical compound involved, it is a single or one-component system. From the phase rule, when C = 1,

$$F = C - P + 2 = 1 - P + 2 = 3 - P$$

i.e., the degree of freedom depends on the number of phases present at equilibrium. Three different cases are possible:

(i)   P = 1; F = 2   (bivariate system)

(ii) P = 2; F = 1   (univariate system)

(iii) P = 3; F = 0   (invariant system)

From the above, it is clear that for any one-component system, the maximum number of degrees of freedom is two. Therefore, such a system can be represented completely by a two-dimensional Diagram. The most convenient variables are the pressure and the temperature. The water system is shown in Fig.11. 1. The diagram consists of:

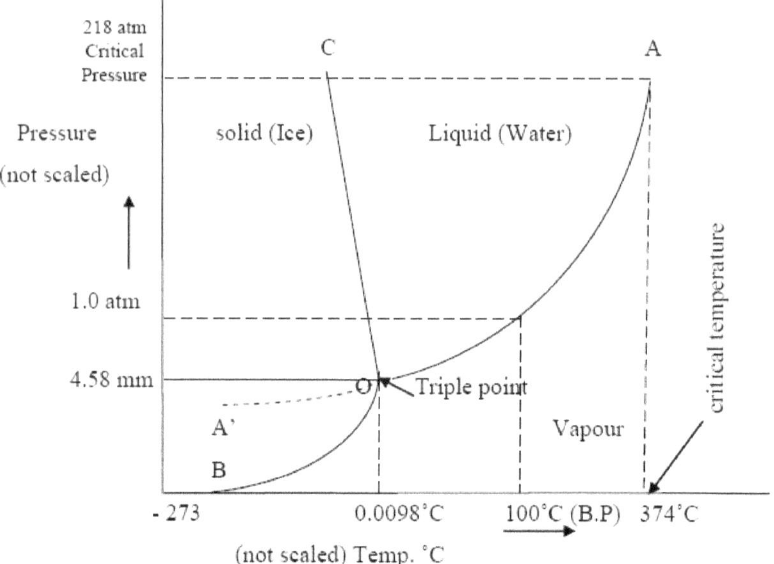

Figure 11.1: Phase diagram of the water system

1. **Areas**: AOB, AOC, and BOC are the fields of existence of vapour, liquid, and ice phase, respectively. Within these single-phase areas, the system is bivariant because to locate any point in an area, temperature as well as pressure coordinates need to be known. This also follows from the phase rule equation:

$$F + P = C + 2$$
$$F + 1 = 1 + 2$$
$$F = 2$$

Hence areas represent a bivariate system.

2. **Curve (Boundary lines):** Separating the areas are lines OA, OB, and OC, connecting the point at which two phases can co-exist in equilibrium. In order to locate any point on a particular line, either temperature or pressure coordinate should be known, because for a fixed value of one

coordinate, the second is automatically fixed. In other words, any point on boundary lines has one degree of freedom or is univariant. This also follows from the phase rule equation:

$$F = 3 - P = 3 - 2 = 1.$$

a. **Curve OA:** The curve OA, dividing the liquid from the vapour region, is called vapour pressure curve of liquid-water or vaporization curve. At any given temperature, there is one and only one pressure at which water vapour is in equilibrium with liquid-water. Similarly, at any given pressure, there is one temperature at which water vapour is in equilibrium with liquid-water. In other words, the system is univariant, i.e., has one degree of freedom. The curve OA has a natural upper limit at +374°C, which is the critical point, beyond which the phase merges into vapour phase and they are no longer distinguishable from each other.

a. **Curve OB:** The curve OB is the sublimation curve of ice. It gives the conditions under which water vapour is in equilibrium with solid ice. The point B has a natural limit at -273oC, beyond which the two phases merge into each other.

c. **Curve OC:** The curve OC, which divides the solid-ice region from the liquid-water region, is called **melting curve** because it indicates how the melting temperature of ice or the freezing temperature of water varies with pressure. The slope of OC towards the pressure axis shows that the melting point of ice is decreased by increasing pressure.

3. **Triple point**: The three curves OA, OB, and OC meet at O, at which solid, liquid and vapour are simultaneously at equilibrium. This point at 273.16 K is called a triple point. Since three phases coexist, the system is invariant (F=3-3=0). In other words, there is no degree of freedom at O, i.e., neither pressure nor temperature can be altered, even slightly, without causing the disappearance of one of the phases.

4. **Metastable curve OA'**: As water does not always freeze at 0°C, so if the vessel containing water and vapour is perfectly clean and free from dust, it is possible to supercool water several degrees below its freezing point 0. The dotted curve OA', a continuation of the vapourization curve AO, represents the pressure curve of supercooled water. This curve represents a metastable system. On slight disturbance, the supercooled water at once changes to solid ice. It may be noted that the metastable vapour pressure of supercooled water is higher than the vapour pressure of ice.

11.6   REDUCED PHASE RULE (OR) CONDENSED SYSTEM:

The maximum number of degrees of freedom for a two-component system will be three when the system exists as a single phase.

$$F = C - P + 2;$$
$$F = 2 - 1 + 2;$$
$$F = 3$$

In order to represent the conditions of equilibrium graphically, it requires three coordinates, namely P, T, and C. This requires a three-dimensional graph, which cannot be conveniently represented on paper. Therefore, any two of the three variables must be chosen for graphical representation.

A solid-liquid equilibrium of an alloy has practically no gaseous phase, and the effect of pressure is negligible. Therefore, experiments are conducted under atmospheric pressure.

Thus, the system in which only the solid and liquid phases are considered, and the gas phase is ignored, is called a condensed system.

Since the pressure is kept constant, the phase rule becomes.

$$F' = C - P + 1$$

This equation is called the reduced phase rule (or) condensed phase rule.

Eutectic System:

A two-component (binary) system consisting of two substances, which are miscible in all proportions in the liquid phase, but which do not react chemically, is known as the eutectic (easy to melt) system, e.g. a mixture of lead and silver comprises such a system.

- **Eutectic Mixture** is a solid solution of two or more substances having the lowest freezing point of all the possible mixtures of the components. This is taken advantage of in alloys of low melting point, which are generally eutectic mixtures.

- **Eutectic point:** Two or more solid substances capable of forming solid solutions with each other by the property of lowering each other's freezing point; and the minimum freezing point attainable corresponding to the eutectic mixture is termed the eutectic point (means lowest melting point).

11.7 APPLICATION OF THE PHASE RULE TO A TWO-COMPONENT SYSTEM (BI-CD SYSTEM):

Cadmium-bismuth is a two-component system such as Bi (m.p. 271 °C) and Cd (m.p. 321 °C). Molten Cd and Bi mix together in all proportions to form a homogeneous system. Bi and Cd do not react with each other to form an intercomponent system. This system consists of the following four phases taking part in equilibrium.

- Solid Bi
- Solid Cd
- Solution of Cd and Bi
- Vapours of Cd and Bi

However, if the system is studied at constant atmosphere, then the vapour phase can be ignored for a condensed system. Then the reduced phase rule equation can be applied.

$$F' = C-P+1$$
$$P + F' = 3 \text{ for a two-component system.}$$

The system can be represented by a temperature-composition (T-C) phase diagram as given below.

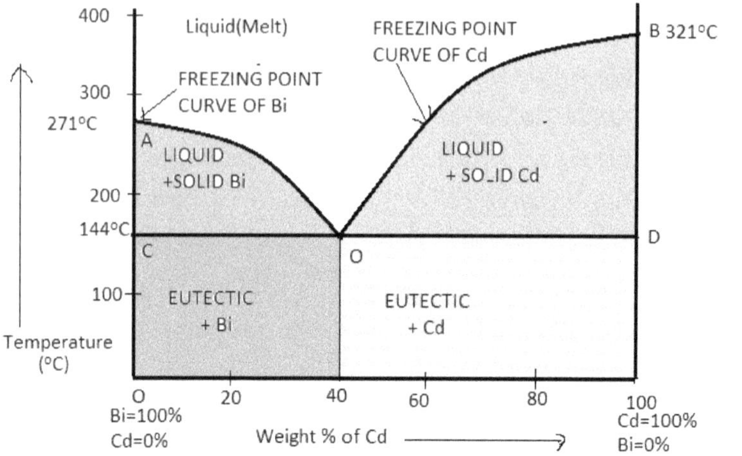

Figure 11.2: Phase diagram of Bi-Cd System

A] Curves:

a. Curve AO

The point A represents the melting point of 100% Bi, which is 271°C. The addition of Cd to pure Bi lowers its melting point to the point O, which is 144°C. The curves represent the melting point or freezing point curves of Bi. All along the curve AO, the solid Bi is in equilibrium with the liquid alloy.

The equilibrium along the curve is.

$$Bi(s) \rightleftharpoons liquid\ alloy.$$

The curve or system is univariant (F=1). It is proved by the following condensed phase rule.

$$F' = C-P+1$$
$$=2-2+1 =1$$

b. **Curve BO:**

The point B represents the melting point of 100% Cd, which is 321°C. Addition of Bi to pure Cd lowers its melting point up to the point O, which is 144°C. The curve represents the melting point or freezing point curve of Cd. All along the curve AO, the solid Bi is in equilibrium with the liquid alloy.

The equilibrium along the curve is.

$$Cd\ (s) \Leftrightarrow liquid\ alloy$$

The curve or system is univariant (F=1). It is proved by the following condensed phase rule.

$$F' = C-P+1$$
$$=2-2+1 =1$$

c. **Curve COD.**

It is known as the solidus line because all along this line, a mixture of solid metals and solid alloys is in equilibrium with the mixture of solid + liquid.

$$F' = C-P+1$$
$$=2-2+1 =1$$

B] Area:

a. **Area AOB:** It represents the liquid phase. The liquid is a homogeneous solution of Bi and Cd. The liquid is said to be unsaturated as it is not in contact with any solid. However, when it is cooled, a solid phase may separate out from the liquid phase. Now the liquid phase can be said to be saturated as it is in contact with a solid phase.

This area is bivariant. It is proved from the condensed phase rule.

$$F' = C-P+1$$
$$=2-1+1 =2$$

b. **Area AOC:** It represents the presence of crystalline Bi in the liquid alloy.

i.e. Bi(s) + Liquid alloy.

The area is univariate. It is proved from the condensed phase rule.

$$F' = C-P+1$$
$$=2-2+1 =1$$

c. **Area BOD:** It represents the presence of crystalline Cd in the liquid alloy.

i.e. Cd(s) + Liquid alloy.

The area is univariate. It is proved from the condensed phase rule.

$$F' = C-P+1$$
$$=2-2+1 =1$$

C] Point O (Eutectic Point):

It is the point of interception of the curves AO and BO. It corresponds to the lowest temperature (144°C) at which the solution melts. The composition at this point is fixed, which is 60% Bi and 40% Cd. It is called the eutectic composition.

The following are the phases existing at equilibrium.

$$Bi(s) \Leftrightarrow liquid\ alloy \Leftrightarrow Cd\ (s)$$

Thus, it has zero degrees of freedom. This is proved by the condensed phase rule.

$$F' = C-P+1$$
$$=2-3+1 =0$$

IMPORTANT QUESTIONS:

1. Discuss the application of the phase rule to the water system.
2. Explain the Cadmium-Bismuth (Cd-Bi) System.
3. State the Phase Rule and Explain the term involved with the help of a suitable example.
4. Applications and limitations of the Phase Rule.
5. State the Gibbs Phase Rule. Discuss its application to the water system.
6. Explain the term "Phase," components, and degrees of freedom with a suitable example.
7. Explain the basic principle and instrumentation of IR spectroscopy.
8. State the Gibbs Phase Rule. Discuss its application to the Bi - Cd system.
9. What is Gibbs' Phase rule? Explain the terms: Phase, Components, and Degrees of Freedom.
10. Explain the Phase Rule of a One-Component System (Water System).
11. What is the condensed phase rule and explain its application to a two-component system (Bi-Cd).
12. Explain the application of the condensed phase rule to the two-component system Cadmium Bismuth.

References

1. S. S. Dara, A Text book of Engineering Chemistry, S.Chand & Co New Delhi. Eleventh Edition.
2. P.C. Jain and Monica Jain, Engineering Chemistry, Dhanpat Rai & sons New Delhi, Sixteenth Edition.
3. Dr. Sunita Rattan, A Textbook of Engineering Chemistry, S.K. Kataria & Sons
4. M Afshar Alam, Sapna Jain, Hena Parveen, Green Computing Approach Towards Sustainable Developent, Wiley Interscience Publications
5. A. K. Das and M. Das, An Introduction to Nanomaterials and Nanoscience, CBS Publishers and Distributors.
6. Voet, D.J., Voet, J.G., Pratt, C.W., Principles of Biochemistry, John Wiley, Fouth Edition
7. Masters, G. M., Introduction to Environmental Engineering and Science, Prentice-Hall of India Pvt. Ltd.
8. Rajaram & Kuriacose, Text book of Engineering &Technology, Vol I & II
9. Manasi Karkare, Nanotechnology Fundamentals and Applications, I. K International Publishers.
10. William C. O'Mara, Robert B. Herring, Handbook of Semiconductor Silicon Technology, Noyes Publications Park Ridge, NJ, USA.1st Edition.